GUTTERSNIPES AT PLAY

—

BEYOND
RIVERSIDE DRIVE

- A COMPANION COOKBOOK -

INSPIRED BY
THE PENDERGAST NOVELS
OF
DOUGLAS PRESTON &
LINCOLN CHILD

COMPILED – WRITTEN
ILLUSTRATED
BY
CHRIS ROYAL

- DEDICATIONS -

To: all my Friends and Family, who believed in me a whole lot more than I believed in myself.

To: Douglas Preston and Lincoln Child for their amazing novels and also for their support and encouragement.

To all the fans of Agent A.X.L. Pendergast out there.

And most of all, to my Mom & Dad: my Teachers and my Best Friends.

FOR MADELYN & ROYCE

—

Introduction

Back in 2004, I was wandering around the local CVS, trying to decide on some "happies" for my girlfriend at the time, to go along with the Nyquil she had sent me to procure. A couple magazines: check. Honey roasted peanuts: check. How about the customary Whitman's Sampler? Why of course. Oh, and a paperback, can't forget a good paperback. Hm-mm, this looks interesting - "Cabinet of Curiosities." Creepy cover art and 666 pages, even creepier, this should work.

That was the beginning of my love affair with the writings of Douglas Preston and Lincoln Child, my one true guilty pleasure. "Cabinet" was, I think, my Goldilocks moment in literature. Sorry Stephen King, too long. Sorry Mr. Conrad, too deep. This Pendergast character is, well, just right.

So, I did what most folks do. I worked backwards. Starting with "Relic" and then on to "Reliquary" I discovered this new world where the unusual becomes explainable, a place where "monsters" are only unfortunate mutations, to be pitied somewhat.

Fast forward a couple of years. Now there are all these recurring characters. People so well fleshed out that I became emotionally involved with them. These are personalities we all know, in our own lives. I had become hooked - truly invested in the stories.

And now, here's the "epiphany." My job takes me to some, shall we say, austere locations. The days can be extremely long and emotionally draining. The landscapes are rather drab and the meals even drabber. One evening I noticed something very strange. I was re-reading "Cabinet of Curiosities" and my stomach started growling. Broiled Lamb with Capers - Roast Beef – Roast Goose – Roast Mutton – Boiled Ham & Cabbage – Roasted Vegetables.

I was actually salivating. I had read this book three times; I had read ALL these books at least three times and never noticed it: THE FOOD. From wonderful descriptions of meals served in fancy New York restaurants to good old home cooking in a small town Kansas diner. The food sounded marvellous. I dreamed of rare roast beef that night, I think. So I started dog-earring my paperbacks while on my last deployment and kept a notebook by my bunk. Slowly, a list developed - a reference guide of sorts, a vast collection of classic recipes. Here is where one can find all manner of delectable goodies from the world of Agent A.X.L. Pendergast, from 891 Riverside Drive and beyond. Enjoy.

—

RELIC

DRIED BEEF

CAFETERIA LASAGNA

HAM & CHEESE EGGS

HARE PATE

THE BONES GUINNESS MEAT LOAF

CORNED BEEF HASH

SMOKED PORK

CATFISH SANDWICH

CHILIES & PEPPERONI PIZZA

GULF PRAWNS

TUNA & STURGEON CAVIAR BLINI

SCOTTISH COD ROE CEVICHE

ASSORTED HORS D'OEUVRES

SLICED KOBE BEEF

AHI TUNA

CRACKERS & CAMEMBERT

PATE

GOING AWAY WHITE CAKE

CRAYFISH GUMBO

WHITTLESEY'S DRIED BEEF - This is just the thing to tide you over while you search for the missing Professor Crocker.

- 1 lb. chuck steak
- 1/3 cup light soy sauce
- 1/3 cup honey
- 1/4 cup lemon juice
- 4 cloves fresh garlic, crushed
- 2 tsp. Worcestershire sauce
- 1 tsp. onion powder
- 1/2 tsp. salt
- 1/2 tsp. black pepper

Prepare a large baking sheet fitted with some sort of wire rack. Be sure to put some tin foil down on the bake sheet to make clean-up easier.

Put the steak in the freezer for 30 minutes, or until firm, but pliable.

Slice the steak about 1/8 inches thick across the grain.

In a bowl, combine the marinade ingredients and mix well. Mix and coat the beef strips with the sauce mixture. Refrigerate for at least 2 hours.

Preheat the oven to 180° F.

Place the strips on a wire rack on a baking sheet. Bake the beef for about 10 to 12 hours, or until meat has completely dried. - Serves 4

CAFETERIA LASAGNA - The Natural History Museum is famous for many things, including this savory dish.

- 2 lbs. lean ground beef
- 5 cups prepared tomato sauce
- 1 (15 oz.) container ricotta or cottage cheese
- 2 eggs, beaten
- 1 cup fresh grated Parmesan
- 4 cups grated Mozzarella
- 2 tsp. chopped fresh parsley
- 1 tsp. dried basil
- 1/4 tsp. ground black pepper
- 1/2 tsp. salt
- 1 (9 oz.) box Barilla no-boil lasagna noodles

Preheat the oven to 375° F.

In a large skillet, add the ground beef and brown it over medium heat. Season with salt and pepper to taste. Now add the tomato sauce and turn heat to low. Simmer uncovered for 20 minutes.

In a large bowl fold together the ricotta or cottage cheese, eggs, 1/3 cup grated Parmesan, about 1/2 cup grated mozzarella, salt, parsley, basil, and black pepper.

Spread 1 cup of the tomato sauce in the bottom of a 13 x 9 casserole dish, then lay 3 lasagna noodles lengthwise down in the sauce. Spoon 3/4 cup of the ricotta mixture over the noodles, and spread it evenly with the back of a spoon. Sprinkle 1 cup of the mozzarella evenly over the whole thing. Repeat with the steps, for a total of 4 layers of noodles. Sprinkle the remaining mozzarella over the top layer of tomato sauce, and top with the rest of the Parmesan cheese.

Cover the lasagna tightly with tin foil, and bake for 1 hour.

Remove the lasagna from the oven, and remove the tin foil. Return to the oven and bake, uncovered, for about 10 minutes or until nicely browned.

Remove from the oven and let rest for 10 minutes before serving. - Serves 4 to 6

VINNIE'S HAM & CHEESE SCRAMBLED EGGS - This hearty breakfast may or may not be the best thing to eat right before investigating a gruesome crime scene, but you be the judge.

- 4 eggs, room temperature
- 1/2 tsp. Worcestershire sauce
- 3 Tbs. milk
- Salt and pepper
- 1 thick slice of ham, chopped
- 1/3 cup sharp Cheddar cheese, shredded
- Heinz ketchup
- 2 Tbs. green onion, chopped

Spray a frying pan with cooking spray. Heat the pan over medium heat.

Whisk together the eggs, Worcestershire sauce, milk, salt, and pepper with a fork.

Pour egg mixture into pan and stir continually for about 2 to 3 minutes, until eggs are cooked. Turn off heat, but don't take the pan off the burner.

Add the diced ham and cheese to the pan and fold until everything is well mixed and cheese is all melty.

Top with a generous squeeze of ketchup and garnish with green onions. - Serves 1

HARE (RABBIT) PATE - You won't find this on the Blarney Stone's menu or any five flavors of mineral water for that matter.

- 1 thick slice of bread
- 2 cups milk (more or less)
- 1 farm raised rabbit, cut into pieces
- 1 stick butter
- 1 parsley sprig
- 1 thyme sprig
- 3 bay leaves
- 4 peppercorns

- Salt
- Water
- 1/4 cup mushrooms, sliced
- 3 egg yolks
- 6 Tbs. brandy
- Salt and pepper to taste

Place bread in a shallow bowl and pour about 2 cups of milk over it.

Add 3 Tbs. butter to an iron skillet, over medium to medium-high heat and cook rabbit pieces until lightly browned on all sides.

Transfer rabbit to a medium saucepan and add parsley, thyme, 2 bay leaves, peppercorns and salt. Add just enough water to cover the rabbit meat. Bring the water to the boil and then lower heat to a simmer, cover and cook for 2 to 3 hours or until very tender.

Drain the rabbit, reserving the broth and pull the meat from the bones. Mince the meat and then place it in a food processor. Strain the broth into a separate bowl or large measuring cup.

Add 1 Tbs. butter in the skillet and sauté mushrooms over medium heat about 5 minutes. Add the mushrooms to the rabbit meat.

Squeeze the slice of bread to remove the excess milk and add to the rabbit mixture. Pulse the rabbit mixture to form a smooth puree. Moisten the puree with a little of the rabbit broth, then pulse in the remaining butter, egg yolks, brandy, salt and pepper.

Place the remaining bay leaf in the bottom of a pate dish and spoon in the rabbit mixture.

Smooth the top, wrap completely with tin foil and steam for 3 hours.

Allow to cool for 2 hours and then refrigerate at least 4 hours before serving. - Serves 4 to 6

THE BONES GUINNESS MEATLOAF - One taste of Mr. Boylan's family recipe will transport you right back to 72nd Street. All that's missing are some scapula and femurs nailed to the wall.

- 2 Tbs. olive oil
- 1 medium yellow onion, chopped
- 1/2 cup carrots, finely diced
- 1/2 cup celery, finely diced
- 4 large cloves garlic, finely minced
- 3/4 cup Guinness stout
- 2-1/2 cups stale bread - crumbled
- 1 cup milk
- 2 lb. ground beef
- 2 eggs, beaten
- 1/2 cup grated sharp Cheddar cheese
- 1/4 cup chopped fresh parsley
- 1 Tbs. Worcestershire sauce
- 2 tsp. salt
- 1/2 tsp. black pepper
- 10 strips thick cut bacon, uncooked

Heat 2 Tbs. of the oil in a 12 inch iron skillet over medium-low heat. Cook the onion, carrots, celery, and garlic until softened and just beginning to brown, about 10 minutes.

Add the Guinness, and simmer for 5 minutes. Transfer to a large bowl and let cool.

In a small dish soak the bread in the milk; lightly squeeze bread to remove some of the excess milk. Finely chop bread in crumbles and add to the bowl with the vegetable mixture.

Preheat oven to 375° F.

Add ground beef and eggs to the vegetable mixture. Sprinkle cheddar cheese and parsley over the meat, and then add Worcestershire, salt, and pepper. Use your hands to gently mix all the ingredients until just combined.

Line a 9 x13 inch baking pan with parchment paper. Transfer the meatloaf mixture to the baking pan and form into a loaf about 5 x 9. Finish off the meatloaf by laying the strips of bacon over it and then tucking the ends of the bacon under the meatloaf.

Bake for 45 minutes; then remove pan from oven and carefully pour off most of the drippings. Return to oven for 15 minutes or until meat thermometer reads 160 in the center of the meatloaf. Remove from oven and let rest for 10 minutes. - Serves 4 to 6

CORNED BEEF HASH - Let your mind drift back, while you enjoy this flavorful dish. Back to that morning in the rain forest near the tepui of Cerro Gordo.

- 3 (1/2 lb.) red potatoes
- Olive oil
- 1 lb. cooked corned beef

- 1/2 cup onion, chopped
- 1 clove garlic
- 1/4 tsp smoked paprika
- Salt and pepper to taste

Preheat oven to 400° F.

Cut the potatoes into quarters and place them in a roasting pan. Toss them with olive oil and salt. Roast the potatoes for about 15 minutes.

While you're waiting for the potatoes to roast, chop up the corned beef, onion and garlic and combine them in a medium bowl.

Take the potatoes out of the oven and allow them to cool. Chop up the cooked potatoes and combine them with the corned beef mixture in the bowl. Season the mixture with some freshly ground black pepper to taste. Remove the hash from the bowl into a lightly oiled iron skillet and press the down with the back of a large metal spoon. Cook over medium-low heat for about 15 minutes until the bottom is nice and crispy.

Using a metal spatula cut the hash into 4 wedges. Flip each wedge and cook for another 15 minutes or until the bottom is nice and brown. Re-season with salt, pepper and smoked paprika. - Serves 4

OVEN "SMOKED" PORK ROAST - It's not Xingu dried peccary but it will just have to do.

- 1 (4 lb.) bone in pork roast
- Salt and pepper
- 2 Tbs. bacon fat or vegetable oil
- 10 to 12 garlic cloves, peeled
- 2 onions, sliced
- 2 cups apple cider
- 1 Tbs. Liquid Smoke

Move oven rack to its lowest position. Preheat oven to 350.

On a stove top, heat bacon fat or oil in a Dutch oven over medium high heat.

Salt and pepper all sides of the pork roast.

Once the grease is hot, place the roast in Dutch oven.

Allow the pork roast to brown for 3 minutes, then rotate and continue the 3-minute cooking until all sides are browned.

Arrange garlic cloves and onion slices around the roast and allow them to brown for 5 minutes or so, stirring occasionally. Add apple cider and then Liquid Smoke, stir and bring to a boil.

Cover Dutch oven with its lid and place in the oven and roast for 1 hour. Remove Dutch oven and flip roast over. Replace lid and cook and additional 1 hour.

Transfer roast from Dutch oven to a roasting pan, cover with tin foil and allow to rest 20 minutes. Using two large forks pull the pork into shreds.

Serve on rolls with or without sauce. - Serves 6 to 8

CATFISH SANDWICH - A welcome surprise to any lunchbox, even if Agent Coffey did suggest it.

- 1-1/2 lbs. catfish fillets
- 1 box (8.5-ounce) Jiffy corn bread mix
- 2 Tbs. Tony Chachere's Creole Seasoning
- 1 egg
- 1/2 cup all purpose flour
- Canola oil, for frying

Sauce:

- 1 scallion, finely chopped
- 1-1/4 cups Hellmann's mayonnaise
- 1 Tbs. capers, finely chopped
- 1 tsp. Creole seasoning
- 1/2 tsp. crushed garlic
- 2-1/2 tsp. lemon juice

Assemble:

- 1 loaf frozen garlic bread, baked per instructions
- 1/4 head shredded lettuce
- 2 large tomatoes, sliced

Cut catfish fillets in half; set aside.

In a pie dish or plate, combine corn bread mix and Creole seasoning; set aside. In a second pie dish, lightly beat egg with 1 Tbs. water to make an egg wash; set aside.

Dredge each catfish fillet in third dish of flour; dip into egg wash and then dredge in the corn bread mixture. Set aside on a plate.

In a deep fat fryer or Dutch oven, heat oil over medium to medium-high heat to 375. Fry catfish until golden brown, about 5 minutes or so. Remove the fish onto plate lined with paper towels.

In a small bowl, stir scallions, mayonnaise, capers, Creole seasoning, crushed garlic, lemon juice together. Set aside.

Spread warm garlic bread with remoulade sauce. Build sandwiches with fried catfish, lettuce and tomato. - Serves 4

ANTONIO'S PIZZA PEPPERONI & GREEN CHILIES - No need for Greg's computer to fax this order in to Antonio's.

Sauce:

- 1 (28 oz.) can whole peeled tomatoes
- 1 Tbs. extra-virgin olive oil
- 1 Tbs. butter
- 2 cloves garlic, finely diced
- 1 Tsp. dried oregano
- 1 Tsp. red pepper flakes
- Salt to taste
- 1 Tbs. dried basil
- 1 yellow onion, finely diced
- 1 Tsp. sugar

Put all the ingredients in a food processor and purée. Place sauce in a medium size pot and simmer, uncovered, over medium-low heat. Stir sauce occasionally until it reduces by half, about 1 hour. Remove from heat and allow sauce to cool to room temperature.

Dough:

- 4-1/2 cups bread flour, plus more for dusting

- 1-1/2 Tbs. sugar
- 1-1/2 Tsp. salt
- 2 Tbs. instant yeast
- 3 Tbs. extra-virgin olive oil
- 1-3/4 cups lukewarm water
- 1/4 cup corn meal for dusting your baker's peel

Combine flour, sugar, salt, and yeast in food processor using the dough blade. Pulse 3 times to combine. Add olive oil and water. Run food processor until mixture forms ball that dances around the bowl above the blade. Continue processing 15 seconds longer.

Transfer dough ball to lightly floured surface and knead for 10 minutes until a smooth. Divide dough into three equal parts and place each one in a separate, lightly oiled container. Cover tightly with plastic wrap and let the dough rise in a warm place, until it doubles in volume (about 45 minutes).

Adjust oven rack, with the pizza stone on it, to middle position and preheat oven to 500° F. Allow about 1 hour before you start baking. Turn out a single dough ball onto lightly flour surface. Gently press dough into an 8 inch circle, leaving outer edge about 1 inch thicker than the rest. Gently stretch the dough by draping it over your knuckles, into a 14 inch circle about 1/4 inches thick. Transfer dough to your baker's peel or a cookie sheet turned upside down that is lightly dusted with corn meal.

- 1 batch Antonio's famous pizza sauce
- 1 lb. sliced pepperoni
- 1 (12 oz.) can green chilies, drained
- 1 lb. grated full-fat mozzarella cheese

Spread 1/3 of the sauce evenly over the crust, leaving a 1/2 inch border along edge. Evenly spread 1/3 of your cheese over sauce. Add 1/3 of your pepperoni and sprinkle on the green chilies. Carefully slide the pizza onto pizza stone and bake until cheese is melted and brown spots appear on the surface, about 12 to 15 minutes.

Remove from the oven with baker's peel or, using a fork, slide the pizza onto the back of cookie sheet. Place on a large cutting board and cut into 6 slices. Repeat with remaining two dough balls, remaining sauce, and remaining cheese.

Serve immediately and remember, real New York pizza is eaten folded in half. - Makes 3 (14 inch) pizzas

GULF PRAWNS - A mainstay at many a hoity-toity Museum function to be sure. Well, this and Wright's droning on and on behind a microphone.

- 1 Tbs. butter, melted
- 2 Tbs. minced garlic
- 2 lb. large shrimp, peeled
- 2 Tbs. lemon juice
- 2 Tbs. Worcestershire sauce
- 1/4 cup good amber beer, warm
- 3 Tbs. cold butter cut into pieces

Seasoning:

- 1 tsp. ground cayenne pepper
- 2 tsp. ground black pepper
- 1 tsp. salt
- 1 tsp. dried leaf thyme

- 1 tsp. dried rosemary, crumbled
- 1/4 tsp. basil
- 1/4 tsp. paprika

Combine seasoning ingredients in a small bowl. Using an iron skillet over medium heat, heat the butter until hot and foamy. Add garlic and sauté for about 30 seconds. Stir in shrimp, lemon juice, Worcestershire sauce, and 2 Tbs. of your seasoning mix.

Fold everything together to coat and sauté for about 1 minute.

Add the warm beer and simmer until the shrimp are cooked, about 2 minutes longer. Remove from heat and add cold butter. Stir until butter has melted.

Place shrimp and liquid into a large bowl and serve with slices of crusty bread for dipping. - Serves 2 to 4

TUNA & STURGEON CAVIAR BILINI - Oh, go ahead, eat five. It's what an investigative reporter does.

Blini:

- 3/4 cup all purpose flour
- 1 Tbs. sugar
- 1 (1/4 oz.) pack active dry yeast
- 1/4 tsp. salt
- 1 cup milk
- 1/4 cup butter, cut into pieces
- 2 eggs, beaten
- Melted butter

Whisk together first 4 ingredients in a large bowl.

Warm up the milk and butter in a saucepan over low heat; stir just until butter melts. Pour warm milk mixture into flour mixture and whisk until its silky smooth. Cover bowl with plastic wrap and let batter rise in a warm place, until the batter doubles in volume.

Whisk the batter to deflate and then whisk in eggs.

Heat a large nonstick pan over medium heat brushed lightly with melted butter with a balled up paper towel. Working in batches, spoon 1 Tbs. batter onto griddle, spaced 2 inches apart. Cook until bubbles form on top, about 1 to 2 minutes. Flip the blini and cook 1 minute or until golden brown on bottom.

- 1 (12-ounce) sushi-grade yellow fin tuna steak, diced
- 2 Tbs. red onion, minced
- 2 Tbs. fresh chives, minced
- 2 Tbs. olive oil
- 1 Tbs. fresh lime juice
- 2 tsp. capers, minced
- 1/4 tsp. salt
- 1/8 tsp. freshly ground black pepper

- Blini
- Crème fraîche or sour cream
- Sturgeon caviar

Combine tuna and the rest of the above ingredients in medium bowl and fold. Spoon mixture onto blini; top with crème fraîche or sour cream and caviar.

SCOTTISH COD ROE CEVICHE WITH CAPERS AND LEMON - Bet you can't eat just one, laddie.

- 1 lb. (5 tins) Scottish cod roe*
- 1/4 cup capers, chopped
- 1/4 red onion, diced very small
- 3 lemons, juiced
- 1 green apple, peeled and diced very small
- 1 Tbs. freshly chopped cilantro
- 1/8 cup olive oil
- Salt and freshly ground black pepper
- 4 English cucumbers
- Fresh dill
- Lemon zest

In a large mixing bowl, combine onion, lemon juice, apple, cilantro and extra virgin olive oil. Season mixture with salt and pepper, and then gently fold the cod roe into the marinade. Cover with plastic wrap and refrigerate overnight.

Peel cucumbers and cut them into 1/4 inch thick slices. Strain cod roe mixture and spoon onto cucumber disks. Top with a sprig of fresh dill and lemon zest.

*http://recipesforcaviar.appspot.com/For-Sale-Online-John-West-Soft-Cod-Roes-100g.html

ASSORTED HORS D' OEUVRES - With six choices you might just have to balance some plates.

Prosciutto Wrapped Asparagus:

- 1 lb. prosciutto
- 1 bundle (30 stalks) asparagus

Grill asparagus until tender and wrap prosciutto around 3 asparagus pieces.

Crab Rolls:

- 1 lb. cooked lump crab meat
- 1/4 cup onion, finely diced
- Old Bay seasoning
- 2 (8 oz. each) packages cream cheese, room temperature
- 2 packages crescent rolls

Mix crabmeat, cream cheese, diced onions and season with Old Bay to taste. Place mixture on crescent roll dough and roll. Bake as directed until golden brown.

Chipped Beef Pin Wheels:

- 1 (8 oz.) package dried beef
- 1 (8 oz.) container pimento cheese spread, room temperature
- 1 (8 oz.) package cream cheese, room temperature

Lay a slice of dried beef out flat and cover it with a thin layer of room temperature pimento cheese. Add another slice of dried beef; cover it with cream cheese, and then one more sheet of dried beef. Roll them up and cut into 1/2 inch thick pieces.

Potato Cheese Puffs:

- 2 lbs. baking potatoes, peeled and cut into chunks
- 2 tsp. salt
- 1 egg, beaten
- 1 Tbs. butter
- 2 Tbs. powdered milk
- 1/4 cup blue cheese
- 1/2 cup all-purpose flour
- Salt
- Vegetable oil, for frying
- Lawry's season salt

Place the potatoes in a large stock pot and cover with cold water. Add the salt and bring to a boil. Reduce to a simmer and cook until tender, about 20 minutes. Drain the potatoes in a colander and then return them to the pot. Continue cooking until all the excess water has evaporated, about 2 minutes.

Mash the potatoes in a large mixing bowl. Stir in the beating egg, butter, powdered milk, blue cheese and flour; season with some additional salt to taste. Roll the potato mixture into 1 inch balls and place them on a baking sheet. Cover with plastic wrap and refrigerate for 30 minutes.

Heat the vegetable oil to 360° F.

Deep fry the potato balls (in batches) for about 3 to 5 minutes or until they have browned. Drain them on several layers of paper towels, season with Lawry's season salt and transfer the potato balls back to the baking sheet.

Preheat oven to 350° F and bake the potato balls for about 10 minutes right before serving. – makes 50 puffs

---

Ham and Swiss Pin Wheels:

1 lb. honey baked ham, sliced

- 1 (8 oz.) container spreadable Swiss cheese
- Green onions

Take one piece of ham and spread Swiss cheese. Place 1 stick of green onion in center and roll. Continue until all ham is used.

Place in refrigerator until Swiss cheese firms up. Slice in small pin wheel shapes.

Brie and Salmon Rounds:

- 1 (12 oz.) package smoked salmon
- 1 (8 oz.) package of brie cheese, softened
- 1 French baguette
- 1 tsp. olive oil
- 1 tsp. black pepper
- 1 Tbs. Grey Poupon mustard

Preheat oven to 375° F.

Slice French baguette in 1/2-inch thick slices and arrange on a cookie sheet. Drizzle baguette with olive oil. Place a dab of brie onto each piece of bread. Cut salmon into equal portions and place on top of brie. Cook for 8 minutes. Brush the salmon lightly with the Grey Poupon mustard and sprinkle with pepper to taste.

"Hold on, hold on a minute, it's coming this way….."

SLICED KOBE BEEF - It's not Steak Tartare, but it's the next best thing.

- 1 lb. Kobe beef steak or beef tenderloin, sirloin
- 1/2 lb. shiitake mushrooms thinly sliced,
- 2 onions, thinly sliced
- 3 stalks celery, sliced on the diagonal
- 1 bunch green onions, cut to 1 inch lengths
- 3 cups of fresh spinach
- 5 oz. can of bamboo shoots
- 2 Tbs. vegetable oil
- 1/2 cup Campbell's beef consommé
- 2 Tbs. sugar
- 2 Tbs. sake
- 1/3 cup soy sauce

Place beef in a freezer for 30 minutes for ease of slicing. Slice the beef into thin strips (1/4 inch thick and 2 inches long).

Heat oil in a large iron skillet or wok and barely brown the meat.*

Scoot the meat to one side of skillet and mix with beef broth, soy sauce, sake and sugar.

Dump the onions, celery, mushrooms and bamboo in different sections of the skillet and cover.

Let simmer for about 7 minutes then add spinach and cook for 5 more minutes.

*Beef may be sliced and served raw and dipped quickly in simmering sauce liquid.

AHI TUNA WITH HONEY-ORANGE GLAZE - You'll have the crowd rushing toward this one quicker than you can say "dead body."

- 4 (6 oz.) Ahi tuna fillets
- 2 oranges, juiced
- 1/4 cup olive oil
- 2 Tbs. rice vinegar
- 2 cloves garlic, crushed and minced
- 1 Tbs. grated fresh ginger
- Salt and black pepper to taste
- 1/4 cup honey
- Vegetable oil

In a glass bowl, whisk together orange juice, olive oil, rice vinegar, garlic, and ginger. Lay the tuna fillets on a platter, season with salt and pepper to taste. Coat the tuna evenly with half of the orange glaze. Cover and let tuna marinate for 30 minutes in the refrigerator. Add the honey to the remaining glaze and mix well with a whisk.

Heat a large iron skillet on high heat. When skillet is very hot, lightly oil, and place tuna fillets on the skillet. Cook for about 2 minutes, and flip over, brushing more glaze over the cooked side. Grill 2 minutes more. When the tuna is cooked, transfer to a plate and pour the honey orange glaze over the fillets. - Serves 4

AHI TUNA SASHIMI

- 1 lb. very fresh Ahi tuna
- 1 carrot
- 1 Daikon radish
- Soy sauce
- Wasabi

Use a very sharp knife to remove any skin from the fish.

Place the fish in the freezer and chill for 20 minutes or until it is just firm enough to be cut thinly and evenly into slices, about 1/8 inch thick.

Try to make each cut in a single motion, in one direction.

Use a micro-plane to scrape the carrot and daikon into long fine strips or cut them into fine julienne strips. Arrange the fish pieces on a platter. Garnish with the carrot and daikon radish. Serve with the soy sauce and wasabi. - Serves 2

BAKED CAMEMBERT AND HOMEMADE CRACKERS - Go ahead, eat yourself under the table.

- 1-1/4 cups white flour
- 1 Tbs. sugar
- 1/2 tsp. salt
- 1/2 stick unsalted butter cut into small pieces
- 1/3 cup water

Preheat oven to 400° F.

Line a baking sheet with parchment paper. Put flour, sugar and salt in a food processor and pulse 5 times. Add butter and blend until butter is completely incorporated.

With the blade turning, add water and blend until a smooth dough forms.

Lightly flour your work surface and roll the dough into a large rectangle. Make the dough just as thin as possible. Use a pizza cutter to cut the dough into 2 inch squares.

Bake the crackers on the prepared baking sheet until crisp and lightly browned, about 10 minutes.

- 1 wheel Camembert cheese
- 1 large sprig fresh thyme
- 1/4 cup honey
- 1/2 cup toasted walnuts

Preheat oven to 350° F.

Place the thyme sprigs on the top of the Camembert wheel. Place the Camembert on a paper lined baking sheet.

Bake for 12 minutes and then transfer to a serving platter. Drizzle with honey and scatter toasted walnuts over the top. Serve immediately with your homemade crackers.

HOUSE PATE

- 1/2 lb. chicken liver
- 1/2 lb. pork liver (if pork liver can't be found use another 1/2 chicken liver)
- 1 mild onion, minced
- 1/2 cup good red wine, cognac or brandy
- 6 cloves crushed garlic
- 1 tsp. Dijon mustard
- 1 Tbs. lemon juice
- 1 stick butter
- 2 Tbs. olive oil
- Salt
- 2 Tbs. black pepper
- 2 Tbs. dried thyme
- 1 Tbs. dried rosemary

Sauté the livers and onions in olive oil over medium heat. Cook until the livers are just browned and the onions are tender. Add wine (be careful of flame up if you are using cognac or brandy), garlic, mustard, herbs and lemon juice and cook uncovered until most of the liquid has gone.

Transfer the mixture into a food processor and blend to a smooth paste. Add 1 Tbs. butter at a time until smooth. Add salt to taste. Place the pate in a terrine and refrigerate until firm. Garnish with fresh herbs and serve with crusty bread.

GOING AWAY WHITE CAKE - Served with a magnum of vintage champagne, this is the perfect way to say Bon Voyage.

- 2-1/4 cups cake flour
- 1 cup milk, room temperature
- 6 eggs, room temperature
- 1-3/4 cups granulated sugar
- 4 tsp. baking powder
- 1 tsp. salt
- 1-1/2 sticks butter, room temperature
- 2 tsp. almond extract
- 1 tsp. pure vanilla extract

Preheat oven to 350° F.

Spray two 8 inch cake pans with cooking spray and dust well with flour.

Separate egg whites and save the yokes for another dish. Pour milk, egg whites, almond and vanilla into medium bowl and mix until blended.

Mix flour, sugar, baking powder, and salt in a separate bowl with a whisk. Add butter and beat on low, with an electric hand mixer, for 2 minutes. Add half of milk mixture to flour and beat at medium speed for another 2 minutes. Add remaining milk mixture and beat for 2 minutes more.

Divide batter into the two cake pans. Bake for 30 minutes or until toothpick inserted in the center of cakes comes out clean. Allow cake to cool completely. While cake is cooling you can make the icing.

- 2 cups butter, room temperature
- 1/2 cup Coffee Mate powdered creamer
- 1 tsp. pure vanilla extract
- 1 bag (16 oz.) powdered sugar
- Between 1/2 to 3/4 cup ice cold water

In a large bowl, beat the butter, creamer and vanilla extract together until smooth. Gradually beat in powdered sugar. Add just enough water for the frosting to reach your desired thickness. Add food coloring to small batches of the icing and pipe flowers or designs if desired.

CRAYFISH GUMBO - If the Professor were here, he'd tell you this gumbo is "truly magnificent."

- 1 cup flour
- 3/4 cup oil
- 2 cups onion, chopped
- 2 cup celery, chopped
- 2 cup green pepper, chopped
- 6 cloves garlic minced
- 3 bay leaves
- 1 (10 oz.) can stewed tomatoes
- 2 cups diced smoked sausage
- 8 cups chicken stock
- 1 tsp. salt
- 1 tsp. black pepper
- 1/2 to 1 tsp. cayenne pepper
- 2 Tbs. parsley, chopped
- 3 lbs. crawfish tails, peeled
- 1 cup green onions, chopped
- File' spice

Place the oil and flour in a heavy stock pot over medium-low heat and make a paste or roux. Whisking constantly, slowly cook roux to a nutty brown color.

Add onions, celery, green pepper and garlic and cook 10 minutes. Add broth, tomatoes, sausage, seasonings and bay leaves. Turn heat to low and simmer for 1 hour, stirring occasionally. Add crawfish tails and parsley then simmer for 20 more minutes.

Cook about 2 cups of white rice in a separate pot while the gumbo is finishing.

Serve with mound of rice over the gumbo. Shake a bit of file spice over rice and sprinkle with chopped green onions. - Serves 6 to 8

"...the low, pale head, horribly elongated, the crease of Pendergast's bullet a white stripe above the eyes..."

RELIQUARY

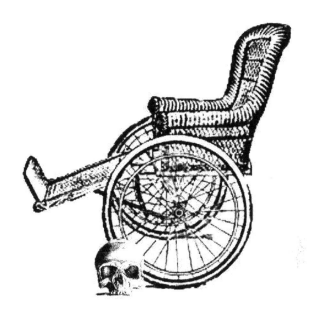

POPEYE'S FRIED CHICKEN

SCONES W/ HONEY BUTTER

QUICHES

SPICED FILBERT NUTS

RED FLANNEL HASH

TRACK RABBIT

COLD WATER SCALLOPS IN LEMON PHYLLO

TUNA SANDWICH

PEMMICAN

CROISSANTS ROLLS

LAP SANG SOUCHONG TEA BISCUITS

LUNCHBOX CHICKEN

2 LB SWORDFISH STEAK

FRUTTI DEL MARE

POPEYE'S FRIED CHICKEN - Set aside the Slim-Curve shakes and reward yourself with this oh-so-spicy treat.

- 1 fryer or broiler chicken, cut up
- 2 Tbs. white pepper
- 1 tsp. cayenne pepper
- 2/3 cup all purpose flour
- 2 tsp. paprika
- 1 Tbs. salt
- 3 eggs, beaten
- Oil for frying (about 3 cups)

Heat oil over medium heat in a wide,

deep skillet – on the stove (or electric skillet) to 325° F.

Add flour, salt, peppers, and paprika to a large bowl and stir to combine. Beat the eggs in a separate bowl.

Dip each piece of chicken into the egg, and then dredge in flour mixture.

Once chicken is coated, it should be placed on a rack, allowed to air dry for about 5 minutes.

Place the chicken pieces in the hot oil, skin side down, one piece at a time – in small batches. Be sure to leave enough space between pieces so they are not crowded. They need space to become crispy. Turn chicken until all sides are nice and golden brown and meat is thoroughly cooked, about 10 to 12 minutes per side, if cooking in a skillet.

Once the chicken finishes cooking, remove from oil and place on a paper towel to allow grease to drain. - Serves 4

HERB SCONES WITH MARMALADE, HONEY, BUTTER AND CLOTTED CREAM - That was quite a spread at the Wisher's place. A shame it was for the "real" 11 o'clock appointment.

- 2 cups flour
- 1 tsp. cream of tartar
- 1/2 tsp. baking soda
- 1/2 tsp. salt
- 1/2 stick butter, cold and cut into small cubes
- 1/2 cup milk
- 1/2 Tbs. lemon juice
- 3 Tbs. honey
- 1 Tbs. fresh thyme leaves, finely chopped
- 1 egg

Preheat oven to 425° F.

Lightly spray a 13 x 9 cake pan with cooking spray.

Place the flour, cream of tartar, baking soda and salt in a large mixing bowl and then add in the butter cubes. Using a fork, work in the butter until the mixture sort of looks like course cornmeal.

Put milk, lemon juice, honey, thyme and egg in a small bowl and whisk together until well combined. Fold the wet ingredients into the dry until well incorporated.

Roll the dough out to about 1 inch thick and, using a 3-inch round drinking glass or cookie cutter, cut out circles of dough. Place scones in cake pan. Bake for 12 to 14 minutes or until golden brown. Remove from oven and serve with orange marmalade, honey, butter and clotted cream*. - serves 2 to 4

*http://www.igourmet.com/shoppe/Clotted-Cream.asp?src=froogle&gclid=CILW78neubcCFVMV7Aod2jQA_Q

ASSORTED QUICHES - The quiche trolley at the Café des Artistes has nothing on these jewels.

- 1 cup flour
- 1/4 tsp. salt
- 1/4 cup (1/2 stick) cold butter
- 1/4 cup shortening
- 1/4 cup ice water
- 1 to 2 cup desired precooked filling*
- 1 to 2 cup desired shredded cheese*
- 3 eggs
- 1 to 1-1/2 cups milk or half & half

Preheat oven to 425° F.

Mix flour and salt in medium bowl. Cut in butter and shortening with a fork until mixture makes coarse crumbs. Add ice water slowly, a bit at a time and mix until dough clings together. Press dough into ball and place in a 1 gallon Ziploc bag. Flatten dough to 1/2 inch thick disc and refrigerate 20 minutes.

Keeping the dough in the bag, undo the Ziploc and cut the three seams of the bag with a sharp knife or scissors. Roll the dough out to a 12-inch round between the plastic sheets. Remove top plastic sheet and flip dough onto a 9 inch pie plate. Adjust dough to center, remove the plastic. Fold under and flute edge on dough. Sprinkle toppings and cheese into bottom of pan. Whisk together eggs and milk or half & half until well blended; pour into crust.

Bake for 15 minutes at 425° F and then reduce temperature to 350° F. Bake 30 more minutes or until a toothpick inserted in center comes out clean. Let stand 15 minutes before serving.

- Quiche Lorraine: 8 slices chopped bacon, 1 diced yellow onion, 1 cup Gruyere cheese
- Onion & Mushroom Quiche: 16 oz. mushrooms, 1/2 diced yellow onion, 2 minced garlic, 1-1/2 tsp. thyme, 2 cups Gruyere cheese
- Asparagus & Ham Quiche: 1/2 a diced yellow onion, 1 cup chopped asparagus, 1/2 cup diced ham, 2 cups Swiss cheese.

SPICED FILBERT NUTS - The perfect thing to nibble on while contemplating your favorite Howard Chandler Christy model.

- 4 cups Filbert nuts
- 3 Tbs. butter
- 3 Tbs. light corn syrup
- 1/2 cup brown sugar
- 1/4 cup chopped fresh rosemary
- 2 tsp. salt
- 1/8 tsp. cayenne
- 1/2 tsp. chili powder
- 1/2 tsp cinnamon
- 1/2 tsp. ground clove

Preheat oven to 350° F.

Place the butter and corn syrup in a rimmed baking pan and heat in oven until the butter has completely melted.

In a medium-size bowl, mix together the filberts, brown sugar, rosemary, salt, cayenne, chili powder, cinnamon and clove.

Pour the nut mixture on to the baking pan; fold the mixture with a metal spatula to incorporate it with the butter/syrup mixture. Return the pan to the oven and bake until the sugar caramelizes around the nuts, stirring every few minutes for about 20 minutes total. While the nuts are roasting prepare a second baking pan with a light coating of cooking spray. When the nuts finish roasting, remove them from the oven and scrape them out onto the prepared pan. Move the nuts around to keep them from clumping together until the nuts have cooled off.

RED FLANNEL HASH - Be your own griddle man and create your favorite Greek coffee shop breakfast.

- 1/4 cup vegetable oil
- 4 medium red potatoes, diced
- 1 white onion, diced
- 4 small red beets, peeled and diced
- 8 slices of bacon or 1/2 lb. ham diced
- 2 cloves garlic, finely chopped
- salt and pepper
- 1/2 cup parsley, finely chopped
- 4 eggs cracked and carefully placed raw in 4 small cups
- 4 Tbs. butter

Preheat oven to 475° F.

Place the vegetable oil in a large iron skillet and place the pan in the oven until the oil starts to smoke, about 5 minutes.

While the oil heats combine the potatoes, onion, beets and garlic in a large mixing bowl. Sprinkle generously with salt and pepper and toss to coat thoroughly.

Remove the pan from the oven, place vegetables in the pan and spread evenly. Top with the diced bacon and roast in the oven until vegetables begin to crisp, about 20 minutes.

Carefully remove the pan from the oven, fold, (if using ham, add it at this point) and return to the oven to roast until the potatoes and beets are fork tender and browned, about another 25 to 30 minutes.

Carefully remove the pan from the oven. Make 4 divots in the hash with the back of a large spoon and gently pour 1 egg into each of the divots.

Season the eggs with salt and pepper and place pats of butter on top of the hash. Return the pan to the oven and allow the eggs to cook until whites are firm. Sprinkle with the parsley and serve the hash from the pan. - Serves 4

TRACK RABBIT - "Le Grand Souris en Brochette" translates into a remarkable delicacy.

- 1 medium onion, sliced
- 1 cup flavored fortified wine (Ripple, Night Train or Thunderbird)
- 1 Tbs. olive oil

- 3 cloves garlic, crushed
- 2 rosemary sprigs, coarsely chopped
- 2 thyme sprigs
- Kosher salt and freshly ground black pepper

Combine all ingredients in a gallon Ziploc bag along with meat. Seal and shake. Refrigerate for about 3 hours.

- 1 (3 lb.) whole rat, rabbit or chicken (marinated 12 hours)
- 1 pinch salt
- 1/4 cup butter, melted
- 1 Tbs. salt
- 1 Tbs. paprika
- 1/4 Tbs. ground black pepper

Season the inside of the animal with salt. Place onto a spit, set grill heat to high and cook for 10 minutes.

Mix together butter, salt, paprika and pepper. Turn the grill down to medium and baste the animal with the butter mixture. Close the grill lid and cook 30 minutes for rat, 45 for rabbit or 1 to 1 and 1/2 hours for chicken.

The animal should be cooked until the internal temperature reaches 180° F with a meat thermometer stuck in its thickest part. Remember to baste occasionally. Remove from the spit and let the meat rest for 10 minutes before serving.
- Serves 2

COLD WATER SCALLOPS IN LEMON PHYLLO WITH CAVIAR - You have got yourself a deal.

- 4 sheets phyllo dough
- 6 Tbs. butter, melted with the juice of 1/2 lemon

Preheat oven to 400° F.

To make the lemon phyllo pockets: Brush each sheet of phyllo dough with the lemon butter while layering one on top of each other. Cut the lemon phyllo dough into 8 squares and gently press each square into the cup of a standard muffin tin.

Bake for about 5 minutes or until a light golden brown. Remove the pockets from the oven and allow them to cool in the muffin tin.

- 2 lb. cold water scallops
- 1/2 tsp. salt
- 1/2 tsp. black pepper
- 4 Tbs. butter
- 4 Tbs. white wine
- 2 tsp. lemon zest
- 1 Tbs. fresh lemon juice
- 1/4 cup sour cream
- 6 oz. red caviar
- 1 Tbs. lemon zest

Season the scallops with the salt and pepper.

In an iron skillet over medium-high heat, melt the 4 Tbs. of butter and sear the scallops for 3 minutes, flip a sear the others sides 3 minutes more. Scallops should be firm but still slightly under-cooked. Transfer scallops to a dish and set aside.

Add white wine, lemon zest and lemon juice to the skillet and bring it to a simmer.

Place the scallops back into the skillet, spoon the liquid over to coat and heat through.

Carefully remove the phyllo pockets from the muffin tin and divide the scallops among the pockets. Top with sour cream, caviar and lemon zest. Serve immediately. - Serves 2

TUNA SANDWICH - Don't let Waxie interrupt your enjoyment of this quick chow-time classic.

- 2 carrots cut into chunks
- 2 celery stalks, stalks cut into thirds
- 3 (6 oz.) cans fancy tuna, drained and rinsed well
- 1/2 cup Hellmann's mayonnaise
- 1/4 cup cream cheese
- 2 Tbs. lemon juice
- 1 Tbs. spicy brown mustard
- 1/2 cup bread and butter pickles
- 1 to 2 Tbs. pickle juice
- 1 Tbs. celery seed
- Salt and pepper to taste

Open tuna cans and empty them in a colander. Rinse tuna under cold water for about 1 minute. Take the tuna in both hands and squeeze as much water out as you can and set dry tuna back in colander.

Place the pickles in the food processor and pulse until finely diced. Add the carrots and celery and pulse 8 times, or until they are just coarsely chopped. Add mayonnaise, cream cheese, and lemon juice. Pulse 3 or 4 times or until the mixture is smooth but not a paste.

Transfer the carrot mixture to a bowl.

Fold in the tuna, pickle juice (just enough to moisten) and then salt and pepper. Adjust seasoning to taste. Spread on lightly toasted bread and top with lettuce and tomato. - Serves 6

PEMMICAN - Shoe leather never tasted so good.

- 1-1/2 lbs. lean beef (filet mignon, top round, London broil)
- 1/2 lb. beef suet, cut into 1 inch cubes
- 1/2 cup frozen blueberries
- 1/2 cup raisins
- 1 Tbs. salt
- 1/2 Tbs. black pepper
- 1/2 Tbs. allspice

Allow meat to firm up in the freezer for 30 minutes, and then slice it into very thin strips. Spread the sliced meat strips on tin foiled cookie sheet, being careful no edges touch. Dry the sliced meat inside an oven (with the oven door cracked 1 inch) set at 175° F for 8 to 12 hours, turning the meat strips every few hours. Meat should be brittle when it's done drying.

Place the berries and raisins in a shallow pan and dry them in the oven at the same time you dry the meat.

Meanwhile, put the beef suet into an iron skillet and cooked it over a low heat. Stir the fat occasionally, being sure not to allow it to burn. Once the suet has stop bubbling, strain the pure fat into a heat proof container and set aside.

Once meat and berries are completely dry, put them in a food processor, add salt, pepper and allspice and grind them to a fine powder. Transfer mixture to a medium mixing bowl. Reheat rendered fat in microwave until piping hot. Carefully add hot fat to the powdered mixture a bit at a time, stirring so the fat soaks into the powder. Only add enough fat to create thick "dough" like paste. Allow the pemmican to cool and firm up, and then roll into small walnut sized balls.

CROISSANT ROLLS – Take a deep breath, take a seat and take your time with these treats.

- 3 -1/2 cups flour
- 2 -1/4 tsp. active dry yeast
- 1/3 cup water, warm
- 3/4 cup milk, warm
- 1-1/2 Tbs. sugar
- 2 eggs beaten
- 1 tsp. salt
- 4 Tbs. butter, softened
- 6 Tbs. butter, softened (filling)

In a large bowl, add the yeast, sugar and salt in the warm water and stir to combine. Add the flour to the wet ingredients and blend. Add in the eggs and milk, and mix to make the dough.

Add the butter and knead by hand until the dough is smooth (about 10 minutes). Cover with plastic wrap and let it rise for 1 hour in a warm spot, until dough doubles.

Cut into 2 equal parts and form them into balls. On a floured surface roll each ball into a 16 inch disc (like a pizza crust). Spread about 3 Tbs. of soft butter onto each of the dough rounds.

Use a pizza cutter to cut the dough into 12 equal slices. Starting from the wide edge of the slice, roll the dough up toward its point. Once rolled, curl the edges into a croissant and place on a greased cookie sheet. Repeat rolling with the rest of the slices. Spray the croissants lightly with cooking spray and let them rise covered, for about 20 minutes.

Preheat the oven to 400° F. Bake for 14 to 18 minutes until puffed and golden brown. - Serves 8

LAP SANG SOUCHONG TEA BISCUITS - No need to head down to Route 666 for a cuppa and a chin-wag, it's safer at home.

- 2 cup all purpose flour
- 1/2 cup sugar
- 1/2 cup powdered sugar
- 2 Tbs. Lap Sang Souchong tea
- 1/2 tsp. salt
- 1 tsp. pure vanilla extract
- 1 tsp. water
- 2 sticks butter

Preheat oven to 375° F.

In a food processor pulse all the dry ingredients together until the lap sang leaves become finely ground.

Add vanilla, water and butter to the dry ingredients. Pulse the food processor again until a smooth dough forms. Scoop the dough out onto a large piece of wax paper. Wrap the paper around the dough and roll into a 2 inch log. Place the log in the freezer for 30 minutes to firm the dough up.

Unwrap the dough and score along the length with the tines of a fork all the way down and around the log. Slice the log into 1/3 inch thick pieces. Place a batch on a cookie sheet, about 2 inches apart.

Bake until the edges are lightly browned, about 10 minutes. Let biscuits cool on sheets for 5 minutes.

LUNCHBOX CHICKEN - Just the thing to indulge in while touring the Astor Tunnels and beyond.

- 1 (3 lb.) chicken
- 1/2 onion, quartered
- 1 apple, cut in chunks
- 4 sprigs fresh rosemary
- 2 tsp. salt
- 2 tsp. pepper
- 1 tsp. ground oregano
- 1 tsp. chili powder
- 1 tsp. ground sage
- 1 tsp. dried basil
- 1 tsp. dried marjoram
- 2 tsp. paprika

- 1 tsp. ground allspice
- 1 tsp. garlic powder

Move oven rack to the lower third level and preheat oven to 400° F.

Rinse chicken, pat dry, and trim off any excess fat. Mix all spices together in a small bowl and generously rub chicken inside and out with spice blend. Place onion, apple and rosemary inside cavity.

Lay a standard-size brown paper grocery bag on its side (if preferred, a roaster bag can be used). Place the chicken inside bag and fold to close.

Place bagged chicken in a rimmed baking pan. Transfer chicken to the oven. Roast chicken for 1-1/2 hours. Remove chicken from oven and carefully cut open bag to release steam. Let the meat rest for 10 minutes before carving. - Serves 4

2 LB SWORDFISH STEAK - A specialty at Mercer's on South Street. If you don't catch a buzz, you can breathe easy.

- 2 Tbs. Sesame oil
- 2 Tbs. light soy sauce
- 1 Tbs. of grated ginger
- 1 clove garlic, minced
- 1 green onion, thinly sliced
- 1 tsp. lemon juice
- 2 lb. swordfish steak

Mix the first 6 ingredients together, coat the swordfish steak with the marinade and refrigerate in a Ziploc bag for 1 hour.

Heat a non-stick pan over medium high heat. When the pan is hot, remove the swordfish steak from the bag and sear for 5 minutes on the first side and 2 to 3 minutes on the other.

Remove from pan and slice into 1/4-inch thick slices (fish will be rare). Sprinkle with more green onion slices. - Serves 1 to 2

FRUTTI DI MARE SALAD - You don't have to avoid this for the foreseeable future, just fix it at home.

- 1/2 lb. fresh clams, cleaned
- 1/2 lb. fresh mussels, cleaned
- 1/2 lb. frozen baby octopus, thawed and cut into pieces
- 1/2 lb. frozen calamari, thawed and cut into pieces
- 1/2 lb. large, shelled shrimp, tails on
- 1/4 cup extra-virgin olive oil
- 3 Tbs. fresh lemon juice
- 3 cloves garlic, minced
- 1 Tbs. finely chopped parsley
- 1/2 cup sliced celery with leaves
- 1/2 tsp. salt
- Freshly ground black pepper
- 3 cups mixed greens
- Parsley, finely chopped

Using a 4 quart Dutch oven, over medium-high heat, add octopus and cover with about 4 inches of water. Bring water to a boil, reduce heat and simmer 30 minutes until meat is tender. Remove octopus with a slotted spoon and set aside in an ice bath.

Add calamari to the same simmering water for 1 minute until the rings just become white. Remove calamari from water and set aside in the ice bath.

Empty all but about 2 inches of water from pot and bring it back to a boil.

Steam shrimp in water, with lid on the pot, for 3 to 5 minutes or until they are pink. Remove shrimp and place in the ice bath.

Steam mussels in water, with lid on the pot, for 3 to 5 minutes until mussels open. Be sure to throw away any mussels that don't open. Remove mussels and set aside.

Steam clams in the same water, with lid on pot for 3 to 5 minutes or until clams open. Again, throw away any of the clams that refuse to open (they make you sick).

Whisk together olive oil, lemon juice, garlic, parsley, celery, salt and pepper. Combine all the cooled, cooked seafood in a large serving bowl. Pour the dressing over seafood and toss. Cover and refrigerate for 2 hours.

Divide the mixed greens between 2 large plates; top with the seafood mixture and some more chopped parsley. - Serves 2

"Minutes passed in silence as the rat sizzled."

CABINET OF CURIOSITIES

MOREL AND BLACK TRUFFLE MOUSSE

STEAK AU POIVRE

REALTOR BREAKFAST

ALMOND CROISSANTS W/ BUTTER

PIGS IN A BLANKET

HAM AND BRIE SANDWICHES

BLT

CHINESE PRESSED DUCK

COOKED SQUID

COLD WATER LOBSTER TAILS

BROILED LAMB W/ CAPERS

ROAST BEEF

ROAST GOOSE

ROAST MUTTON & POTATOES

BOILED HAM & CABBAGE

NEW YORK STEAMED OYSTERS

GRILLED CORN W/ BUTTER RAG

BREADCRUMBS

FRENCH CHOCOLATE

POTATOES & CABBAGE

DOUBLE CORNED BEEF ON RYE

DOUGHNUTS

MOREL AND BLACK TRUFFLE MOUSSE - The aroma of the deep woods and musk is just, heavenly.

- 12-16 dried morel mushrooms, sliced
- 1/2 cup white wine
- 3 stalks of green onion chopped
- 1/2 cup chopped parsley
- 1-1/2 sticks butter
- 2 Tbs. black truffle butter*
- 1/2 cup Parmesan cheese, grated
- 1 tsp. salt
- 3/4 cup heavy cream

Soak the dried morels in white wine until they are fully reconstituted. (Reserve 2 of the best looking soaked mushrooms as garnish).

Sauté the morels, onions and parsley in butter and truffle butter until soft. Add the white wine that the mushrooms were soaked in and reduce until dry. Let mixture cool completely in the refrigerator.

In food processor, add mixture, Parmesan cheese and salt; pulse until finely chopped. With a mixer, whip the cream to stiff peaks then fold in the cold mushroom mixture. Spread mousse on crackers and decorate with parsley and slices of the reserved sautéed morel mushrooms.

*http://www.igourmet.com/shoppe/Black-Truffle-Butter-by-Aux-Delices-des-Bois.asp

STEAK AU POIVRE - This entrée would make anyone forget that the dinner conversation is strictly off the record.

- 2 (10 oz.) rib-eye steaks
- 4 Tbs. olive oil
- 4 Tbs. course ground peppercorns
- 1 stick butter
- 4 Tbs. Cognac
- 1/2 cup beef stock
- Salt and pepper

Preheat oven to 450° F.

Rub the steaks well with olive oil, and coat them in the crushed peppercorns.

Heat the rest of the olive oil in an iron skillet over high heat. Add 3 oz. of the butter and put the 2 steaks in the pan, but don't crowd them. Sear on both sides for 4 minutes per side.

Transfer the skillet to the preheated oven and cook 5 to 7 minutes. Remove the skillet from the oven and remove the steaks to plates. Cover the steaks with tin foil while they rest.

Move the pan away from any flame and carefully add the Cognac to the still hot pan, stirring and scraping with a wooden spoon to deglaze and get all the goodie.

Place the skillet back on the stove and reduce the liquid by about half. Stir in the beef stock and reduce again, over medium heat, until thickened. Stir in the rest of the butter, salt and pepper to taste, and pour the sauce over the steaks. - Serves 2

REALTOR BREAKFAST - Served on damask with a freshly ironed copy of the Times – this might be the perfect meal for the heartless.

- 1 cup PG Tipp's tea
- 2 Wellington Traditional Water Crackers
- 2 tsp. Stakich's Royal jelly *

* Royal jelly may cause allergic reactions, such as hives, asthma, to even fatal anaphylaxis. The risk of having an allergy to royal jelly is higher in people who have other allergies.

http://www.amazon.com/PG-Tips-Black-Pyramid-Count/dp/B0001LQKBQ/ref=sr_1_2?s=grocery&ie=UTF8&qid=1396508136&sr=1-2&keywords=p.g.+tips

http://www.amazon.com/Carrs-English-Tablewater-Crackers-Sesame/dp/B007BZBOYI/ref=sr_1_11?s=grocery&ie=UTF8&qid=1396509577&sr=1-11&keywords=english+water+biscuit

http://www.amazon.com/Stakich-ROYAL-JELLY-COMPLEX-18-5/dp/B001LR3FT4/ref=sr_1_4?s=grocery&ie=UTF8&qid=1396509890&sr=1-4&keywords=pure+royal+jelly

ALMOND CROISSANTS - A nice, brisk walk through Central Park should burn off these extra calories. Just remember to stay out of The Rambles.

- 4 tsp. instant dried yeast
- 1/2 cup lukewarm water

- 3-1/2 cups bread flour
- 1/2 cup milk
- 1/3 cup sugar
- 3 Tbs. butter, melted and cooled
- 1-1/2 tsp. salt
- 1 cup butter, softened
- 1/2 cup sweet almond filling
- 1 egg
- 2 Tbs. milk
- 1/3 cup sliced almonds
- 2 Tbs. powdered sugar

Add the water and yeast to a large mixing bowl and allow it to bloom for 5 minutes. Add in the flour, milk, sugar, melted butter, and salt and mix until the dough is firm enough to form a ball, about 2 minutes.

Transfer dough in a lightly greased bowl and cover with a kitchen towel. Allow the dough to rest for about 30 minutes. Roll the dough into a 10 x 15 rectangle and then cover it loosely and allow it to rise for another 30 minutes.

Gently brush the rectangle with a quarter the softened butter and then fold the dough into thirds. Roll the long, thin rectangle back to its original 10 x 15 shape. Brush with butter and fold the dough into thirds, again, and then cover the dough and allow it to chill in the refrigerator for 30 minutes. Repeat process once more with the remaining butter.

Using a pizza cutter, cut the 10 x 15 shaped dough into 20 equal triangles. Spread a small spoonful of the almond filling across each triangle, and then roll the croissants up, starting at the wide end. Curve the ends inwards to make a crescent shape.

Place the croissants on a lightly greased baking sheet with about 2 inches apart. Cover loosely with the kitchen towel and allow them to rise for 1 hour in a warm place.

Preheat the oven to 375° F.

Whisk the egg and 2 Tbs. milk together to make a wash. Gently brush the wash onto each pastry and then sprinkle them with the sliced almonds.

Bake for about 15 minutes, until they are a nice golden brown and the almonds are slightly toasted. Go all in and sprinkle the powdered sugar over the top while the croissants are still warm. - Makes 20 pastries

PIGS IN A BLANKET - Much better than the ones off the cart on 77ᵗʰ and Central Park West.

- 1 package cocktail franks
- 1/2 cup sharp cheddar cheese, shredded
- 48 pickle chips
- 1 lb. thin sliced deli ham
- 2 packages crescent rolls
- Barbecue sauce, for dipping
- Spicy brown mustard, for dipping

Preheat oven to 350° F.

Unroll crescent rolls. Cut each crescent roll into three long strips. Sprinkle shredded cheese each strip. Top each frank with two pickle chips and wrap with a piece of ham to hold the pickles in place.

Starting at one end, roll frank in crescent dough.

Place on greased cookie sheet and bake for 10 minutes or until golden brown. Serve with barbecue sauce and mustard for dipping.

HAM AND BRIE BAGUETTE - Skip the sticky gray fish eggs and go with what you know.

- 1 fresh baked baguette
- Butter, softened
- 1/3 cup Smucker's peach preserves

- 1 (6 oz.) package deli ham slices
- 1 (5 oz.) wedge brie, sliced, room temperature

Preheat oven to 400° F.

Slice the baguette horizontally with a serrated bread knife. Spread butter on both surfaces of the cut loaf, followed by the preserves.

On bottom half of baguette, lay out slices of ham and top with slices of brie. Put the top back on to create a sandwich.

Wrap to baguette in tin foil and place in the oven, on a bake sheet, for 10 minutes.

Unwrap sandwich and cut into 2 inch pieces and secure with those frilly sandwich picks.

I AM MARY GREENE

AGT 19 YEARS

NO. 16 WATTER ST.

B L T CLASSIC - You'd have to amble on over to the Dominican's deli on the corner in order to get a sandwich this tasty.

- 12 slices bacon
- 8 slices sourdough bread
- 8 leaves iceberg lettuce
- 8 slices of ripe heirloom tomatoes
- 8 Tbs. Hellmann's mayonnaise
- Salt and pepper to taste

Cook bacon until crisp, and then drain on paper towels.

Lightly toast the 8 slices of bread. Spread 1 Tbs. mayonnaise on each slice of toasted bread. Add 1 or 2 leaves of lettuce, then 2 slices of tomato on top of lettuce. Generously season tomato slices with salt and pepper.

Arrange 3 slices of bacon evenly on top of tomato and then 1 leaf of lettuce on top of bacon. Put the remaining 4 pieces of toast on top and slice in half. - Serves 4

QUICK BLT SPREAD:

- 1 lb. bacon
- 4 Tbs. bacon drippings
- 1 large jar Hellmann's mayonnaise

Cook a whole package of bacon and then dice bacon into small bits. Place the bacon bits into a large bowl. Take 1 whole jar Hellmann's mayonnaise and empty it into the bowl and then add the drippings. Mix the bacon, mayonnaise and drippings together. Transfer the mixture back into the mayo jar, seal and refrigerate. Use the BLT spread for a quick treat.

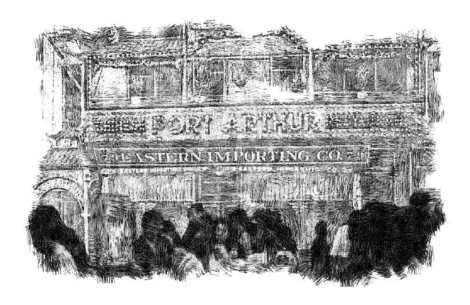

CHINESE PRESSED DUCK - One taste and you'll think you're back on Mott Street, in Chinatown.

Duck:

- 4 to 5 lb. whole duck
- 1 cup cornstarch
- 5 strips bacon
- 1 tsp. salt

- A good pinch of Chinese 5 spice
- 1/2 cup light soy sauce
- 1 tsp. sugar
- Vegetable oil, for frying

Remove neck, giblets, etc. from duck cavity. Rinse and pat dry the duck, inside and out. Place duck in a large bowl or pot. Combine salt, 5 spice, soy sauce and sugar. Pour marinade over duck and allow to soak 2 hours, rotating every 30 minutes.

Fill a wok 1/3 full with water and bring to a simmer over medium-high heat. Place a rack above simmering water. Place duck on rack, breast side up, and lay bacon strips across the breast. Cover and steam 2 to 3 hours. Keep a pot of hot water on the stove to replace any water lost while the duck is steaming. Check water level often.

Remove duck from rack and allow to cool. Remove bacon strips and set aside.

Place a large clean bath towel on a work surface. Place a cutting board on top of the towel. Put the duck, breast side down, on a cutting board. With a sharp knife, make a cut along the backbone. Using the fingers, push the meat to the side. Lift the backbone and rib cage out. Press meat down and pull the thigh, leg and wing bones out.

Once all bones have been removed, flip the duck breast side up. Take a second cutting board and cover duck completely. Gently press down until meat is compressed to about 1 inch thick.

Remove top board and sprinkle duck generously on both sides with cornstarch. Gently return duck to the wok and steaming rack. Cover and steam an additional 30 minutes and then place duck on a clean cutting board.

Empty water from the wok, dry completely and fill with oil about 1/3 of the way up. Heat the oil over medium heat to 350° F on a kitchen thermometer.

Cut duck into quarters and deep fry, a section at a time, until golden brown and crispy. Remove duck from oil and drain on paper towel. Fry reserved bacon for garnish. Cut into 2-inch pieces and serve with sweet and sour sauce.

Sweet and Sour Sauce:

- 1 cup rice wine vinegar
- 1 Tbs. Heinz ketchup
- 1 tsp. soy sauce
- 1 cup sugar
- 4 drops Sriracha hot sauce
- 1 tsp. cornstarch, dissolved in water
- 1 cup almonds, chopped

In a small saucepan, over medium heat, stir together vinegar, ketchup, soy sauce, sugar and hot sauce and bring to a simmer. Stir in cornstarch mixture to thicken. Brush some of the sauce over duck pieces. Sprinkle with nuts and crumbled bacon for garnish. - Serves 4

CHINESE COOKED SQUID - Your friends will be pushing and shouting, frantically trying to get at these Chinese delights.

- 1 tsp. Chinese five spice
- 1/2 tsp. salt
- Vegetable oil, for frying
- 3 eggs
- Cornstarch

- 1 lb. cleaned squid bodies, cut into 1/2-inch rings
- Black pepper
- 1 tsp. extra-virgin olive oil
- 4 Tbs. Chinese scallions, chopped
- 2 cloves garlic, minced
- 3 goat horn chili peppers, minced
- 1 Tbs. lemon grass, chopped
- Lime wedges, for garnish

In a small bowl, combine the five-spice powder with 1/2 tsp. of salt.

Place 1 inch of vegetable oil in a Dutch oven and heat to 350° F.

Beat the eggs in a small bowl. Place cornstarch in shallow dish or pie tin.

Working in several small batches, dip the squid in the egg; dredge the squid in the cornstarch and shaking off the extra. Carefully add the squid to the hot oil and fry about 1 minute or until crispy.

Using a set of tongs, transfer the fried squid to a paper towel lined plate to drain. Season them with a bit of the five-spice mixture and black pepper to taste. Repeat the process with the rest of the squid.

Heat the olive oil in an iron skillet, over medium-high heat. Stir-fry the Chinese scallions, garlic, and peppers for 2 minutes. Add the squid and stir-fry until just heated through. Sprinkle with more of the five-spice mixture. Transfer the squid to a serving platter and garnish with lemon grass and lime wedges. - Serves 4 to 6

COLD WATER LOBSTER TAILS WITH DRAWN
BUTTER - Imagine having this at your hospital bedside –
most unusual, but decadent and delicious.

- 4 (1 lb. each) lobster tails
- 1/4 cup lemon butter, plus 1 cup for dipping
- 4 wooden skewers soaked in water for about 30 minutes

Preheat grill.

Use some sharp scissors to cut through the ridge of the lobster tails shells from front to back. Carefully cut through the meat down to the bottom of the shells. Gently pull the shells open like a book.

Thread a skewer along the inside of the bottom shells (this keeps the tails from curling up while cooking). Brush the meat with some of the clarified lemon butter. Wrap the lobster tails in two layers of tin foil.

Cook for about 15 minutes or until the lobster meat turns firm and white.

Place the remaining clarified butter in a bowl for dipping. Remove the foil and skewers then remove the lobster meat from the shells.

Lemon Butter:

- 3 sticks unsalted butter, cut into chunks
- Zest of 3 lemons

place the butter in a 2-cup Pyrex measuring cup and heat in a microwave until melted.

Allow the melted butter set for about 10 minutes undisturbed. Using a bent spoon, remove any forth from the top of the butter.

Carefully pour the clear layer of the butter into a small bowl, leaving any of the milk solids behind in the bottom of the measuring cup. Add the lemon zest to the clarified butter and stir. - Serves 2

BROILED LAMB WITH CAPERS - No need to shout out, these recipes always draw a crowd.

- 4 thick cut lamb chops
- 1 Tbs. small capers, drained
- 5 Tbs. white wine vinegar
- 1/2 Tbs. brown sugar
- 2 Tbs. anchovy paste
- 2 tsp. coarse ground mustard
- Handful of mint
- Salt
- Pepper

Move oven rack to broiling position and preheat broiler on high.

To make the sauce, put mint leaves in between hands and rub until they break down. In a small bowl, mix the mint with the capers, vinegar and sugar. Whisk in the anchovy paste and mustard.

Grease a sheet pan and arrange the lamb chops in the pan and season with salt and pepper. Broil for 4 minutes on one side and turn them over. Baste the un-broiled side of the lamb with the sauce mixture and broil for another 3-4 minutes or until desired doneness. - Serves 4

ROAST BEEF

- 1 (4 lb.) eye of round roast
- 2 cups water
- 1 cup Creole mustard
- 4 Tbs. dry red wine
- 3 large cloves garlic, minced
- 1 tsp. dried leaf tarragon
- 1 Tbs. salt
- 3 tsp. coarsely ground black pepper
- 6 celery sticks

Preheat oven to 500° F.

Line a roasting pan with tin foil and lay the celery sticks in a row on the bottom of the pan. Place the roast, fat side up in the pan, resting on the celery sticks. Add the water to the pan. Mix the mustard, red wine, garlic, tarragon, salt and black pepper in a small bowl.

Rub roast all over with the mixture. Put roast in the hot oven and cook for 15 minutes. Reduce heat to 325° F. Roast for about 1 to 1 and 1/2 hours for rare to medium. Let the roast rest for about 10 minutes before slicing. - Serves 6 to 8

ROAST GOOSE

- 1 (10-12 lbs.) young goose
- 1-1/2 gallon sweetened ice tea
- 1 cup salt
- 1/2 cup brown sugar

- 4 bay leaves
- 1 Tbs. black pepper
- Salt and pepper to taste
- 1 apple, cubed
- 1 onion, quartered
- 1 orange, wedged
- 1 lemon, wedged
- 6 celery stalks, whole
- 6 carrots, whole

Preheat oven to 350° F.

Pour about 1 and 1/2 gallons of iced tea into plastic container big enough to fit both the goose and brine. Add the salt, brown sugar, bay leaves, and pepper; stir to blend. Place the goose into the brine mixture and make sure that it is completely submerged. Cover and refrigerate for 12 to 24 hours.

Remove the goose from the brine and dry it with some paper towels. Season the inside of the goose well with salt and pepper. Stuff the onion, apple, orange and lemon into the goose. Place the goose, breast-side up, in a large roasting pan, resting on the whole celery and carrots.

Use a small sharp knife to prick the skin. This will allow the fat to dribble out while cooking and produce a crispy skin. Season the outside of the goose well with salt and pepper, and add 2 cups of the brining liquid to roasting the pan.

Roast goose for 2 and 1/2 hours, or until it reaches an internal temperature of 175.

Remove from oven and let the goose rest for 20 minutes, cover before carving.

ROAST MUTTON & POTATOES

- 1 (8 lb.) leg of lamb
- 2 large cloves garlic, slivered
- 6 Tbs. olive oil
- 2 Tbs. dried thyme
- 2 Tbs. dried rosemary
- 2 Tbs. coarse ground black pepper
- 2 Tsp. ground coriander
- 26 new potatoes, quartered
- Salt and pepper

Preheat oven to 425° F.

Stab shallow holes in the lamb with a sharp knife and insert the garlic slivers into the meat. Rub the lamb with half of the olive oil. Combine half the thyme, dried rosemary, course pepper and coriander in a bowl and mix together. Rub the herb mixture all over the lamb.

Place the lamb in a roasting pan. Place the potatoes in a large mixing bowl. Add the remaining half olive oil, the other half of the thyme, salt and pepper. Toss them with your hands and place around the leg of lamb.

Place in oven for 45 minutes and then reduce heat to 375. Cook the lamb and potatoes for 30 minutes more*. Remove from oven, cover with tin foil and rest meat for 20 minutes before carving.

*For rare, roast for 12 minutes, medium 16 and well done 20 minutes per pound.

BOILED HAM & CABBAGE

- 1 cured ham, (6 to 8 lbs.)
- 20 whole cloves
- 6 small onions, peeled
- 6 small potatoes
- 6 carrots cut into chunks
- 12 stalks celery cut in chunks

- 1 large cabbage, cut into 8 wedges
- Fresh ground black pepper
- Cold water

Stick the cloves in the surface of the ham, each about 4 inches apart.

Put ham and onions into a large stockpot and cover with cold water. Bring pot to a boil over medium heat. Reduce heat and simmer for about 20 minutes. Add the potatoes, carrots and celery and bring broth to a boil again. Reduce heat and simmer another 20 minutes. Add the cabbage wedges and bring to a boil one more time. Reduce heat and simmer yet another 20 minutes until cabbage is fully cooked.

Carefully lift ham out onto a platter, surround it with the vegetables and pour some of the broth over everything. - Serves 10 to 12

ROASTED VEGETABLES

- 6 potatoes
- 2 red onions
- 2 zucchini
- 2 yellow squash
- 10 carrots
- 8 oz. button mushrooms
- 1 Tbs. thyme
- 2 Tbs. rosemary
- 1 tsp. dried basil
- 3 cloves minced
- 1/4 cup olive oil
- 4 Tbs. balsamic vinegar

Preheat oven to 450° F.

Chop all the vegetables into bite sized chunks. Mix thyme, rosemary, basil, garlic, olive oil, balsamic vinegar, salt, and pepper together in a bowl.

Put the chopped vegetables in a large plastic bag, and then pour the oil/vinegar/herb mixture over the vegetables. Seal bag and massage until all the vegetables are coated evenly.

Line a roasting pan with tin foil, and lightly spray with cooking spray. Dump the bag and spread the vegetables evenly on the pan. Roast for 45 minutes, stirring every 15 minutes.

Dish will be done when the potatoes are fork tender. Remove from oven and transfer to a platter. Top with butter and salt and pepper to taste. - Serves 8 to 10

NEW YORK STEAMED "BRAVE" OYSTERS - The ideal snack after a tedious ride on the Chauncey M. Depew elevated tram.

- 24 fresh whole oysters
- 1 lemon, cut into 8 wedges
- Tabasco sauce
- Sprigs of fresh parsley

To make a steamer, use a large metal colander as a basket. Place the metal colander inside of a large stockpot, with the colander handles resting on the edges of the pot. Fill the pot with enough water to allow a good amount of steam, but not so much that the water will touch the bottom of the colander. Bring water to a gentle simmer, over medium to medium high heat and cover with a large stainless steel bowl, inverted, (as a lid).

Clean the outside of oysters well, removing any noticeable debris from the shells. Discard any oysters that have opened or look damaged and cracked.

Place the oysters in the steamer in a single layer. Do not crowd or stack the oysters (if necessary steam the oysters in several batches). Place the lid on the steamer.

Steam until all of the oysters have opened. Once the last shell has opened, continue to steam for an additional 5 minutes. If, at this time, any of the oysters didn't open, throw them away.

Transfer the steamed oysters to a serving platter (again, chuck any oysters that have not opened). Garnish platter with parsley sprigs and serve immediately with lemon wedges and Tabasco sauce. - Serves 2 to 4

BUTTERED RAG CORN ON THE COB - A classic bit of New York street food before catching Scout of the Plains at The Windsor perhaps?

- 6 ears of fresh corn, husked and cleaned
- 1 stick butter, melted
- Paper towels
- Tin foil
- Salt and pepper

Melt butter in a covered heat proof bowl in a microwave. Lay out 6 sheets of heavy duty tin foil about 8 inches long. Tear off 6 sheets of heavy duty paper towels. Soak each paper towel sheet in melted butter and lay the sheet in the middle of the foil. Generously salt and pepper the butter soaked towel. Lay corn cob on the lower edge of the towel.

Tightly roll the corn in the tin foil and seal the ends. Place on preheated grill and rotate every 5 minutes for a total cooking time of 20 minutes. The corn can also be cooked in an oven at 400° F for 30 minutes. - Serves 3 to 6

BREADCRUMBS - Hansel and Gretel would be proud.......
now where is that triceratops?

- 1/2 tsp. salt
- 1/2 tsp. parsley
- 1/2 tsp. black pepper
- 1/2 tsp. garlic powder
- 1/4 tsp. onion powder
- 1/4 tsp. oregano
- 1/4 tsp. basil
- 6 slices stale bread, cut into 1-inch pieces

Preheat the oven to 325° F.

Place everything in a food processor and pulse until coarse crumbs form, about 2 minutes. Spread the crumbs evenly on a bake sheet and bake until the crumbs are crisp, about 5 minutes.

For croutons:

Cut the bread into 1/2-inch cubes. In a large bowl, combine 1/4 cup melted butter and the seasoning mixture. Add the bread cubes and toss in the coating. Arrange in a single layer on a baking sheet. Bake bread cubes for 15-20 minutes or until lightly browned.

FRENCH CHOCOLATE TRUFFLES - A Tiffany lamp, some obscure books and thee.......

- 2/3 cup heavy cream
- 12 oz. Valrhona* semi-sweet chocolate broken into chunks
- 1 tsp. pure vanilla extract
- 1/3 cup Valrhona* premium cocoa powder

Place cocoa powder in a small, shallow bowl.

Bring whipping cream just to a boil in a small saucepan over medium heat,. Remove the pan from the heat. Add the chocolate chunks and vanilla extract and stir until smooth.

Chill the chocolate cream in the fridge until its firms up enough to roll into balls.

Scoop out small spoonfuls of the mixture and roll them into a ball. Roll the ball in the cocoa powder and chill.

*http://www.worldwidechocolate.com/shop_valrhona_blo cks_cocoa_powder_butter_praline_xocopili.html#v1

POTATOES & CABBAGE - Put on administrative leave? Well, go home a boil some of this.

- 1 head of cabbage
- 4 potatoes
- 1/4 cup vegetable oil
- 1/4 cup butter, divided

- 1/2 tsp. garlic powder
- 1/2 tsp. onion powder
- 1 tsp. salt
- 2 tsp. black pepper

Peel away any dirty or bruised outer leaves from cabbage. Rinse the cabbage in cold water. Remove whole leaves from cabbage and throw away the core.

Wash, peel, and slice potatoes into 1/2 inch slices. In a large iron skillet, over medium heat, melt half the butter and oil together and stir. Add potatoes and cabbage leaves and cook, covered, for 20 minutes, stir occasionally. Add garlic powder, onion powder, salt and pepper and stir to coat. Add the remaining butter, stir and cover. Cook additional 10 minutes, or until tender. - Serves 4

DOUBLE CORNED BEEF WITH SWISS ON RYE WITH MAYO - Craving a dilly of a deli sandwich?

- 8 slices rye bread
- 1 lb. thinly sliced corned beef
- 8 oz. thinly sliced Swiss cheese
- 1 sweet onion, thinly sliced and sautéed
- 1/2 stick butter, softened
- Dijon mustard
- Hellmann's mayonnaise

Preheat oven to 500° F.

Place a cookie sheet in the oven to heat.

Place 4 slices of bread on a cutting board. Smear softened butter on the bread and flip the bread over. Generously spread the Dijon mustard on two of the slices.

Divide the sliced corned beef evenly on top of the mustard side bread slices. Top with Swiss cheese and sautéed onion. Top each with remaining 4 rye bread slices and smear the top of the bread with more softened butter.

Remove the hot cookie sheet from the oven with an oven mitt. Place the buttered sandwiches on the hot sheet and slide it in the oven for 3 to 5 minutes. Flip sandwiches and cook 3 to 5 more minutes. Remove the sandwiches and open. Spread with mayo, replace top, cut in half, and serve.
- Makes 4 sandwiches

DOUGHNUTS - Enjoy the break, stay in the moment.

Glaze:

- 1/2 cup butter
- 3 cups powdered sugar
- 2-1/4 tsp. pure vanilla extract
- 6 Tbs. evaporated milk

Melt the butter and stir in powdered sugar and vanilla until smooth. Add milk, a bit at a time, until desired consistency is reached. Set glaze aside until needed.

Doughnuts:

- 3 packages instant active yeast
- 1/2 cup water, warm
- 2 -1/4 cups milk, scalded, then cooled
- 3/4 cup sugar
- 1-1/2 tsp. salt
- 3 eggs
- 1/2 cup shortening
- 7-1/2 cups all purpose flour
- Vegetable oil for frying

Proof the yeast by adding it to the warm water and letting bloom for 10 minutes. Place milk in a heat-proof bowl and scald it in a microwave. Allow milk to cool back down until it feels warm.

Use a standing mixer with a dough hook to make this dough. Combine yeast, milk, sugar, salt and eggs, shortening and 3 cups of the flour. Beat on low for 30 seconds and then bump the speed up to medium and mix for about 2 minutes, scraping bowl occasionally. Slowly add the rest of the flour and mix until smooth. Cover the mixing bowl with plastic wrap and let the dough rise until it doubles in volume.

After the dough has risen, empty the dough out onto a lightly floured surface and roll the dough around to coat the entire dough ball. Flour your rolling pin and very gently roll dough out to 1/2-inch thick. Cut dough out with a floured doughnut cutter. Cover and let the doughnuts rise until they've doubled, about 30 minutes.

Using deep fat fryer heat the oil to 350° F.

Carefully place the doughnuts in the oil, 2 or 3 at a time. Cook on each side for about 45 seconds. Use chopsticks or a slotted spoon to flip the doughnuts and remove them from the oil. Place doughnuts on a wire rack on top of some paper towels to drain.

Once all the doughnuts are fried, dip them in the glaze and set them back on the rack to set. - Serves 24 people or 2 cops

"A large oilcloth had been spread over it, covering
something large and rather bulky."

STILL LIFE WITH CROWS

BUTTERFLIED PORK CHOPS

MAISIE'S MEATLOAF

MAISIE'S PORK & BEANS

MAISIE'S DOUBLE-DIPPED FRIED CHICKEN

MAISIE'S SWEET POTATO FRIES

MAISIE'S GREEN GODDESS DRESSING

MAISIE'S FRIED STEAK

MAISIE'S CHICKEN FRIED STEAK

MAISIE'S BROILED STEAK

MAISIE'S GRILLED STEAK

MAISIE'S BROASTED STEAK

MAISIE'S POT ROASTED STEAK

MAISIE'S VELVEETA STEAK FRIES

STEAK TARTARE A LA PENDERGAST

PEACH COBBLER

SHOOFLY PIE

BOILED EGG, TOAST O.J. AND TEA

WAGON WHEEL'S CHOCOLATE ÉCLAIRS

ROAST BEEF SANDWICH

GASPARILLA'S BURGOO

ROASTED TURKEY DINNER

ALLIGATOR

CHICKEN

IGUANA

SNAKE

PRALINES

BACCELLI E PECORINO ANTIPASTO PLATE

PIZZA

EGGS AND BACON

STEWED TOMATOES

CAP'N CRUNCH CHEESECAKE

EARS OF CORN

ROASTED BUFFALO STEAKS

BEANS AND STEW MEAT

GINGER SNAPS

TEA CAKES

GRILLED CHEESE AND TOMATO BUTTERFLIED PORK CHOPS - Serve this with a toe-tag, if you dare.

- 4 (8oz.) boneless pork chops, about 1 inch thick
- 8 slices sharp cheddar cheese, 1/2 inch thick
- 8 sun dried tomatoes, in oil, drained
- 3 Tbs. olive oil
- 2 tsp. fresh sage, chopped
- Salt and pepper

Preheat oven to 400° F.

Using a small, very sharp knife, slice pork chops almost in half, along the side, being careful not to cut all the way through. Open the pork chop like book. Place two slices of cheese and 2 tomatoes on bottom half of each pork chop. Fold closed and secure with toothpicks.

Place a large iron skillet over medium-high heat. Brush pork chops with oil and season with sage, salt and pepper on both sides.

Sear the pork about 3 minutes on one side, flip and then transfer skillet to the oven. Cook for 8 to 10 minutes or until internal temperature reads 145° F on a kitchen thermometer.

Remove pork chops from oven, using an oven mitt. Cover the skillet loosely with tin foil and let rest 5 minutes. Be sure to remove toothpicks before serving. - Serves 2 to 4

MAISIE'S MEATLOAF - This must be Medicine Creek's most famous blue plate special.

- 1-1/2 lbs. ground beef, lean
- 1 cup milk
- 1 Tbs. Worcestershire sauce
- 1/4 tsp. dried sage
- 1/2 tsp. salt
- 1/2 Tbs. yellow mustard
- 1/4 tsp. black pepper
- 1/8 tsp. garlic powder
- 1 egg, beaten
- 3 slices toast, torn into small pieces
- 1/4 cup onion, chopped
- 1/2 cup Heinz ketchup
- 1/4 cup brown sugar

Preheat oven to 350° F.

Mix all ingredients, except ketchup and brown sugar, well with your hands. Shape into a 9 x 5 loaf in a roasting pan.

Mix the ketchup and brown sugar together in a small bowl and spread over the top.

Bake 1 hour and 15 minutes. Remove from oven and let rest 20 minutes before transferring to a platter for slicing. - Serves 4 to 8

MAISIE'S PORK & BEANS - No legumes in this recipe!

- 1 lb. dry red kidney beans
- 1/3 cup molasses
- 4 Tbsp. Dijon mustard
- 1/8 tsp. ground cloves
- 3/4 cup Heinz ketchup
- 1/2 cup dark brown sugar
- 1 tsp. fresh ground black pepper
- 2 cups hot water
- 1/2 lb. salt pork, cut into 1 inch pieces
- 1-1/2 cups chopped

Examine the dry beans for any rocks or stems. Empty the beans in a large pot and cover with water about 2 inches above the level of the beans. Place the pot over high heat. Bring to a boil, remove from heat and let the beans soak for 2 hours, then drain.

Mix the molasses, mustard, ketchup, brown sugar, pepper and ground cloves with 2 cups of water.

In a crock pot, place half of the salt pork in the bottom of the crock. Make a layer of half the drained beans. Now add all of the onions, then top with another layer of beans and the rest of the salt pork. Pour the molasses/water mixture over the beans.

Set the slow cooker to low and cook for 8 hours until the beans are tender. Check the level of the liquid every hour and add more water to cover, if needed. Beans should be fork tender. After cooking the full 8 hours, taste and adjust salt to taste. - Serves 6 to 8

MAISIE'S DOUBLE-DIPPED FRIED CHICKEN IN CORN BATTER - You might want to double up on this Cry County favorite.

- 3 lb. frying chicken cut into 8 pieces
- 2 cups buttermilk
- 1/4 cup sweet tea
- 2 tsp. Picapeppa pepper sauce*
- 2-1/2 cup flour
- 1/2 cup cornmeal
- 1/2 tsp. baking powder
- 1 Tbsp. salt
- 1 Tbs. fresh cracked black pepper
- 1 Tbs. dry oregano
- 1 Tbs. garlic powder
- 1 tsp. paprika
- 1 tsp. cayenne
- Peanut oil for frying

Rinse the chicken pieces and pat dry with paper towels. In a large Ziploc bag, combine the buttermilk, sweet tea, and pepper sauce. Place chicken pieces in the bag and place the bag in the refrigerator for 12 to 24 hours.

Remove the chicken from the bag and pour the liquid into a shallow bowl. Season the flour/cornmeal with the baking powder, salt, pepper, oregano, garlic, paprika, and cayenne. Dredge the marinated chicken pieces in the flour/cornmeal mixture until well coated. Then, dip chicken in the liquid again, followed by another coat of seasoned flour. Allow the chicken dry out while preparing the oil.

Heat the peanut oil in a large electric skillet to 350° F. There should be about 1 inch of oil in the pan (about 3 cups).

Once the oil has reached 350° F, carefully add in the chicken 4 pieces at a time, skin-side down. Fry for 5 minutes, then turn the chicken over and fry the other side 5 minutes. Turn chicken once again, frying a total of 15 minutes.

Remove chicken to a platter lined with paper towel to drain. - Serves 2 to 8

*http://www.amazon.com/Pickapeppa-Sauce-5oz/dp/B0001CVIE4/ref=sr_1_1?ie=UTF8&qid=1398935050&sr=8-1&keywords=picapepper+sauce

MAISIE'S SWEET POTATO FRIES - Swivel back and watch the action when you set these out for your guests.

- 4 large sweet potatoes, peeled and cut into steak fries
- 2 tsp. salt
- 2 tsp. garlic powder
- 2 tsp. pumpkin pie seasoning
- 1 tsp. brown sugar
- Olive oil, to coat
- Hellman's mayonnaise
- B B Q sauce

Preheat oven to 425° F.

Put cut sweet potatoes into a large Ziploc bag with olive oil, add salt, garlic, brown sugar and pumpkin pie seasoning and shake the bag to coat. Place the fries onto cookie sheet, making sure that they don't touch each other. Put the fries in oven for 10 minutes. Remove the cookie sheet and then flip the fries over. Place back in the oven for 10 more minutes. They should be soft on the inside, with a nice browned outside. Serve with a sauce of equal parts BBQ sauce and mayonnaise. - Serves 2 to 4

MAISIE'S GREEN GODDESS DRESSING - My goodness, this dressing is truly heavenly.

- 1 clove garlic, minced
- 1 cup Hellmann's mayonnaise
- 1 cup sour cream
- 1 ripe avocado, peeled and pitted
- 1/2 cup chopped parsley
- 1/4 cup chopped tarragon
- 3 Tbs. chopped chives
- 2 Tbs. lemon juice
- 1 tin anchovies
- Salt and black pepper to taste

Put all of the ingredients in a food processor and pulse until dressing is smooth. - Makes about 3 cups

MAISIE'S FRIED STEAK

- 2 (16 oz) rib-eye steaks, 1-1/2 inches thick
- Vegetable oil, to coat
- Salt and pepper, to taste

Pat steaks dry using balled up paper towels. Lay steaks in a shallow dish, add oil and massage the oil into the steaks. Generously season both sides with salt and freshly ground black pepper to taste. Let the steaks sit at room temperature for about 30 minutes.

Place a large iron skillet in the oven and heat to 500° F. When oven has reached the proper temperature wait an additional 5 minutes before removing skillet from the oven. Transfer the skillet to the stove top with the burner set to high.

Place steaks in hot skillet and sear them for 2 minutes without moving. Flip steaks and sear for another 2 minutes without moving. Transfer skillet to the oven, and cook 3 minutes. Remove skillet, flip steak and cook 3 minutes longer for medium rare.

When steaks are done, remove skillet and transfer the steaks to warmed plates. Tent steaks loosely with tin foil and let them rest for about 5 minutes before serving. - Serves 2

MAISIE'S CHICKEN FRIED STEAK

- 6 cube steaks
- 1 cup all purpose flour
- 1 tsp. salt
- 1 tsp. pepper
- 1 tsp. paprika
- 2 cups hot milk
- 3 eggs, beaten
- 4 to 6 Tbs. oil
- 3 Tbs. butter

Place the flour, hot milk and the beaten eggs in 3 separate bowls. Mix salt, pepper, and paprika into the flour and blend. Soak the cube steaks in hot milk, and then dredge it in the seasoned flour. Dip floured steaks in beaten eggs, then again in the seasoned flour.

Heat half the oil in a large iron skillet on medium heat. When the oil is hot, carefully place 3 of the cube steaks in the skillet. Brown the cube steaks 4 minutes each side then remove the steaks from the skillet. Add the remaining oil, and when oil is back up to temperature, repeat the cooking process with the last 3 steaks. Put all the steaks on a wire rack set in a pan and place into a warm oven.

Add the butter to the hot oil. Add 3 Tbs. of the seasoned flour, stir to make a paste or roux and cook for 1 minute. Slowly add the hot milk used for soaking the steaks and whisk until the mixture starts to boil and thicken. Re-season with lots of pepper. Serve chicken fried steak, with the white gravy on top. - Serves 2 to 6

MAISIE'S BROILED STEAK

- 2 (10 oz.) rib-eye steaks
- 2 Tbs. black pepper
- 1 Tbs. salt
- 2 tsp. cayenne pepper
- 1 tsp. chili powder
- 1 tsp. paprika
- 1 tsp. sugar
- 1 tsp. cumin, ground
- 1 tsp. garlic powder
- 1 tsp. onion powder
- Olive oil
- Butter

Let the steaks reach room temperature and, using a paper towel, dab away any excess moisture. Mix all the spices together in a small bowl.

Move oven rack to the broiling position and turn oven to high broil setting. Preheat a large iron skillet by setting it under the broiler for about 20 minutes.

Rub steaks with olive oil and then massage in all the seasonings. Once the skillet is hot, carefully remove it from the oven, lay the steaks in the skillet and return to the broiler. Close the oven and cook for 3 minutes on one side, flip steaks with tongs and sear the opposite side for 3 minutes more.

Now turn the oven to 500° F and allow the steaks to cook 5 to 7 minutes. Remove steaks from the oven, place a pat of butter on each steak and let the steaks rest for 5 minutes. - Serves 2

MAISIE'S GRILLED STEAK

- 3 lb. skirt steak
- 1 Tbs. ground mustard
- 1 Tbs. onion powder
- 1 Tbs. garlic powder
- 1 Tbs. salt
- 1/2 tsp. cayenne
- 1/4 tsp. allspice

Mix all the spices together in a small bowl. Rub the skirt steak with the spice mix and let steak rest at room temperature for 20 minutes.

Set a gas grill to high and allow the grate to get extremely hot. Grill 3 to 4 minutes per side until meat is well seared and medium-rare. Place steak to a cutting board; let rest for 10 minutes. While the meat is resting, prepare the horseradish sauce. Slice the meat extra thin and serve with horseradish sauce. - Serves 4 to 6

Horseradish Sauce:

- 4 Tbs. sour cream
- 1 Tbs. prepared horseradish
- Salt and freshly ground black pepper to taste
- 1 tsp. lemon juice
- 2 tsp. olive oil

Mix all ingredients together in a small bowl.

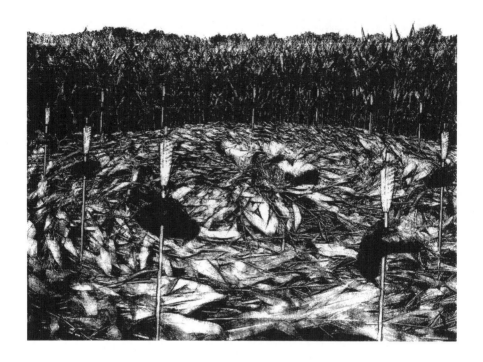

MAISIE'S BROASTED STEAK

- 1 cup water
- 3 Tbs. green chili paste
- 1/2 Tbs. salt
- 2 Tbs. baking powder
- 1 Tbs. ginger
- 1 Tbs. garlic paste
- 2 (12 oz.) New York strip steaks, cut into 4 pieces each

- Vegetable oil for frying

- 1/2 cup corn flour
- 2 cups white flour
- 1/2 Tbs. salt
- 2 tsp. white pepper

In a large Ziploc bag, add water, green chili paste, and 1/2 Tbs. salt, baking powder, and ginger and garlic paste and squeeze the bag to combine. Place the cut steaks in the bag, shake and massage to coat, seal and refrigerate for 4 hours.

Preheat oil or fryer to 350° F.

In a medium bowl, blend the corn flour, white flour, the rest of the salt and 2 tsp. white pepper together. Dredge the steaks in the flour mixture.

Deep fry the coated steaks until just golden brown. - Serves 4

MAISIE'S POT ROASTED STEAK

- 4 (7 oz.) chuck steaks
- 4 Tbs. olive oil
- 1 large onion, cut into wedges
- 1 garlic clove, crushed
- 12 oz. can of beef stock
- 1 Tbs. tomato paste
- 1/2 tsp. dried thyme
- 1 bay leaf
- 1 tsp. flour
- 1/2 tsp. mustard powder
- Salt and black pepper

Preheat the oven to 325° F.

Season both sides of steaks generously with salt and pepper. Heat half of the oil in a large iron skillet. Sear the steaks over a medium-high heat for 2 minutes on each side. Transfer steaks to a lidded casserole dish. Return the skillet to the stove and reduce the heat to medium. Add the remaining oil and fry the onion for five minutes. Stir in the garlic and cook for one minute. Add the flour and mustard powder and stir for 1 minute more. Pour in the stock, tomato paste, thyme and bay leaf. Bring the mixture to the boil. Pour the gravy over the steaks. Cover the casserole dish and transfer it to the oven. Cook for 1 and 1/2 hours or until tender. - Serves 4

MAISIE'S VELVEETA FRIES - Rich and velvety smooth, just like a certain Special Agent we know.

- 8 baking potatoes
- Oil for frying
- Salt and pepper to taste
- 1 (12 oz.) block Velveeta cheese

Preheat the deep fryer to 300° F degrees.

Cut the potatoes into long, 1/4 x 1 inch planks. Add the French fries to the basket, a batch at a time, and cook for 3 minutes. Remove and drain onto paper towels. Repeat until all potatoes are par-fried.

Turn fryer up to 350° F. Cook fries until golden brown. Remove; drain on paper towel and season with salt and pepper to taste.

While the fries are cooking cut the Velveeta cheese into 1 inch cubes, place in bowl, cover with plastic wrap and microwave, one minute at a time until melted, stirring occasionally.

When the potatoes are done, serve immediately with the cheese sauce poured over the top or in a bowl for dipping. - Serves 2

STEAK TARTARE A LA "PENDERGAST" - Just say no bun, thank you.

- 2 lbs fresh top sirloin
- 2 egg yolks
- 1 Tbs. garlic, finely minced
- 2 Tbs. parley, minced
- Salt and pepper
- Buttered toast points

Trim and grind the meat twice*. In a medium bowl, mix the egg yolks and garlic. Add the meat and half the parsley. Season the mixture with salt and pepper. Fold lightly for a few seconds. Divide the tartare into 4 portions, lightly mold the portions into loose balls and place on 4 chilled plates. Garnish with the remaining minced parsley, with toast points to the side. Serve immediately; with a 1997 Leo' Ville Poyferre'. - Serves 4

*You can cut the sirloin into 1-inch cubes then partially freeze the cubes for about 20 minutes. Fill a food processor about half full and grind the cubes in 15 one-second pulses, or to a medium grind. Empty into a bowl and repeat with the remaining meat. Check the ground meat for any large pieces or gristle and remove.

FRESH PEACH COBBLER - Desserts not your strong point?
Fresh or canned, yes you can.

- 3 large peaches, peeled and sliced
- 1-1/2 cups sugar, divided
- 1/2 cup butter, melted
- 1 cup all purpose flour
- 2 tsp. baking powder
- 1/4 tsp. salt
- Dash ground nutmeg
- 1 cup milk

Preheat oven to 375° F.

In a bowl, toss the fresh peaches in 3/4 cup sugar; and set aside.

Pour butter into an 8 x 8 bake pan.

Sift the flour, baking powder, salt, nutmeg and remaining sugar in a separate bowl ; stir the milk in just enough so everything is combined. Do not over mix.

Pour the batter over butter in the pan. Top with the peaches and bake for 45 minutes or until golden brown. - Serves 6

COBBLER WITH CANNED PEACHES

- 3/4 cup plus 2 Tbs. sugar
- 1 cup Bisquick
- 1 stick butter, melted - divided
- 2 cans sliced peaches, un-drained + 1/4 cup milk
- Cinnamon

Preheat the oven to 350° F.

Grease an 8 x11 baking dish with cooking spray and set aside.

In a medium mixing bowl mix 3/4 cup of the sugar, the flour, and half the melted butter together. Sprinkle one-third of this mixture on the bottom of the baking dish. Add the peaches, peach juice and milk; stir.

Top the peaches with the remaining sugar/flour mixture. Sprinkle the crust with the remaining 2 Tbs. of sugar, the remaining butter and then dust the top with cinnamon.

Bake for 30 to 45 minutes or until brown and bubbly. Serve hot with vanilla ice cream. - Serves 6

SHOO-FLY PIE - Go ahead and go there..........you'll be glad you did.

- 1 (9 inch) pre-made pie crust
- 3/4 cup dark molasses
- 3/4 cup very hot water
- 1/2 tsp. baking soda
- 1-1/2 cups flour
- 1/4 cup butter
- 1/2 cup brown sugar

Preheat oven to 400° F.

In a small bowl, dissolve baking soda in hot water and add molasses.

In a separate bowl, combine sugar and flour and rub in the shortening to make crumbs.

Pour 1/3 of the liquid into an unbaked crust then add 1/3 of the crumb mixture. Top that with 1/3 of the liquid and then the crumbs. Pour on the last 1/3 of the liquid and top with the remaining crumbs.

Bake pie for 15 minutes. Lower temperature to 350° F. Bake an additional 20 minutes or until crust is a golden brown. - Serves 8

BOILED EGG, TOAST, O.J. AND TEA - To make everything cheery, add an ironed lace tablecloth and a vase of marigolds.

- 6 extra large eggs, at room temperature
- Salt and freshly ground pepper
- 6 slices of toast, buttered

Place the eggs in a large saucepan; fill the pot with water, covering the eggs by 1 inch.

Remove the eggs and set them aside. Set the pot over high heat, and bring to a full boil.

Turn off heat, add the eggs back to the water, and cover the pot with its lid. Let the eggs steep for 5 minutes. Remove the eggs from water with a slotted spoon. Serve immediately in egg cups. Remove the tops and season the eggs with salt and pepper. Serve along with buttered toast, orange juice and hot tea. - Serves 3 to 6

CHOCOLATE ÉCLAIRS - Keep your motor running by refueling on these beauties?

Batter:

- 1/2 cup butter, cubed
- 1 cup water
- 1 cup all purpose flour
- 1/4 tsp. salt
- 4 eggs

Filling:

- 3 cups milk
- 3/4 cup sugar
- 1/2 tsp. salt
- 6 Tbs. all purpose flour
- 3 eggs beaten
- 2 tsp. pure vanilla extract

Icing:

- 2 oz. semi-sweet chocolate
- 2 Tbs. butter
- 1 cup powdered sugar
- 2 Tbs. hot water

Preheat oven to 450° F.

For the pastry: In a large saucepan, bring water to a boil. Add butter and stir until the butter melts. Reduce heat to low and add the flour and salt. Stir the mixture until it forms a ball. Remove from the heat. Add eggs, one at a time, blend until eggs are well incorporated. Put the batter in a 1 gallon Ziploc bag; remove excess air from the bag and seal.

Cut a 1-1/2 inch hole in one corner of the bag and pipe the batter into 4-inch long strips, 2 inches apart, on a greased cookie sheet. Bake for 15 minutes, then reduce heat to 325° F and bake 20 minutes longer. Remove the pastries from the oven and cool them completely on a wire rack.

For the filling: Combine the milk, sugar, salt and flour in a medium saucepan and cook over medium-low heat until thickened. Remove from heat (but leave the burner on) and pour a bit of the hot liquid into the eggs in a small bowl. This will temper the eggs. Add the egg mixture back to the saucepan and continue cooking until the mixture is thickens and creates a custard. Remove from heat and add vanilla. Place the filling in a Ziploc bag, seal and cool the filling in the refrigerator for 2 hours.

Now for the icing: Melt chocolate and butter together in the same saucepan used before for the filling (cleaned out of course), over low heat. Stir in the powdered sugar. Add hot water until icing is smooth.

To put the éclairs together just poke a small hole into each end of the pastry with your pinky finger. Cut a small hole in the corner of the filling bag and gently pipe the custard into the éclairs. Spread the icing over the top of the éclairs. Chill until serving.

ROAST BEEF SANDWICH - There won't be any need for a doggie bags when you fix this scrumptious sandwich.

- 2 lbs. roast beef (rare)
- 1/2 cup sour cream
- 1/4 cup Hellmann's mayonnaise
- 1 Tbs. A-1 sauce
- 2 tsp. prepared horseradish
- 1/8 tsp. salt
- 1/8 tsp. pepper
- 12 slices rye bread
- 6 lettuce leaves
- 12 tomato slices
- 1 small onion thinly sliced

Using about 2 lbs. of Maisie's roast beef recipe, place the meat in the freezer for 20 minutes.

Remove the meat and slice as thin as possible. In a small bowl, combine the sour cream, A-1 sauce, horseradish, salt and pepper.

Spread the sauce over six slices of bread; layer with beef, lettuce, tomatoes and sliced onion. Top with the remaining bread. - Serves 6

GASPARILLA'S BURGOO – There's no need to go hunting for these ingredients, that is, unless you want to.

- 2 lbs. boneless chicken breast, skin removed (3 rabbits or 4 squirrels if you can find 'em)
- 1-1/2 cups onions, coarsely chopped
- 1 cup carrots, diced
- 1 cup celery, diced
- 1 cup green bell pepper, diced
- 4 garlic cloves, chopped
- 1 (14 oz.) can diced tomatoes
- 1 tsp. black pepper
- 1/2 tsp. dried thyme
- 2 bay leaves
- 2 cups chicken stock
- 3 large potatoes, diced into 1-inch cubes
- 1 can lima beans
- 1 can corn
- 1 Tbs. cornstarch

Cut chicken into large chunks (quarter squirrels or rabbits, if using). Add the meat, onions, carrots, celery, peppers, garlic, tomatoes, potatoes, spices and stock to a slow cooker. Cover and cook on the low setting for 6 hours.

After 5 hours, add the canned lima beans and corn, stir and cook an hour longer. Mix the cornstarch with 1/4 cup water, and add it to the burgoo. Stir well and cook 15 more minutes to thicken before serving. - Serves 8

TURKEY DINNER MEDALLIONS - It's like going to the Annual Turkey Bake at the Lutheran church.

- 4 turkey cutlets
- 2 Tbs. lemon juice
- 1/4 tsp. tarragon
- 1/4 tsp. oregano
- 1/4 tsp. cumin
- 1/4 tsp. paprika
- Salt and pepper to taste
- Water
- Mashed potatoes
- 1 can French cut green beans
- Prepared brown gravy
- Prepared cranberry sauce

In a medium bowl, mix the lemon juice and all the herbs & spices. Add cutlets and coat with the mixture. Let the cutlets marinate for 20 minutes.

Bring a large pot of water to a boil.

Roll out a sheet of plastic wrap at about twice the length of the turkey cutlet. Place one cutlet on the plastic wrap in the middle.

Spread about 3 Tbs. of the mashed potatoes on the cutlet then about 3 Tbs. of the green beans. Salt and pepper to taste.

Roll up the turkey cutlet in the plastic wrap tightly. Press as much air out of the turkey as you can as you roll it. Once the cutlet is rolled up, roll it back and forth on several times to tighten it like a sausage. Tie the loose ends in a knot. Repeat with the 3 other cutlets.

Once the water has reached a boil, turn off the heat and drop the rolled-up turkey pouches in the pot. Cover the pot and let the turkey steep for 30 minutes.

Remove the turkey from the water. Cut off the knotted ends of the plastic wrap, and unwrap. Slice the turkey into 6 slices and place the turkey medallions on a plate with hot brown gravy and cranberry sauce. - Serves 4

ALLIGATOR BITES - Tastes like chicken......

- 1-1/2 lb. alligator tail meat, cut into 2-inch cubes
- 2 egg whites
- 2 Tbs. Cajun seasoning
- 1 tsp. cayenne pepper
- 2 tsp. Tabasco sauce
- 1 tsp. baking powder
- 2 tsp. cornstarch
- 1/2 bottle of beer
- 2 cups flour
- 1 cup corn meal
- 1 quart vegetable oil

Preheat oil to 375° F.

In a bowl, add beer, egg whites, Cajun seasoning, cayenne pepper, Tabasco sauce, baking powder and cornstarch. Beat together until well mixed. Place the chunks of alligator in the beer/egg mixture and soak for 10 minutes.

In a separate bowl mix the flour and yellow corn meal together. Dredge the chunks well in the flour.

Fry in the hot oil until the alligator floats to the top, about 5 minutes. Serve them with this remoulade. - Serves 6

- http://buyexoticmeats.com/snmeforsa.html

Remoulade:

- 1-1/2 cup Hellmann's mayonnaise
- 1/2 cup sliced green onion
- 2 Tbs. garlic, finely minced
- 1/2 cup spicy mustard
- 1/2 cup Heinz ketchup
- 1 tsp. Cajun seasoning
- 1 Tbs. lemon juice
- 1 Tbs. Worcester sauce
- 2 Tbs. horseradish
- 2 tsp. Tabasco sauce
- 1/2 tsp. salt
- 1/4 tsp. cayenne pepper

In a small bowl, combine all ingredients.

SLOW ROASTED HONEY CHICKEN - Tastes like alligator.....

- 4 Tbs. honey
- 4 Tbs. olive oil
- 1/2 tsp. ground cinnamon
- 1/2 tsp. smoked paprika
- 1/4 tsp. nutmeg
- Salt and black pepper
- 4 to 6 lb. whole chicken
- Half a lemon
- Half an onion
- Dried thyme

- Salt and black pepper

Mix together the honey, olive oil, cinnamon, smoked paprika, nutmeg and some salt and pepper in a small bowl.

Preheat oven to 275° F.

Remove the pack of giblets from the chicken. Rinse chicken and pat dry with paper towels. Place chicken in a tin foil lined roasting pan, fitted with a V shaped roasting rack.

Sprinkle the cavity of the chicken with salt and pepper. Stuff the cavity with the onion and lemon halves and sprinkle salt, pepper, and thyme all over the outside of the bird. Tie the drumsticks together using butcher's twine and fold the wing tips under. Brush the outside of the chicken with about half of the honey glaze.

Bake, uncovered, for 2 and 1/2 hours, remove pan from oven and brush on the remaining glaze. Return pan to oven for an additional 2 hours more or until a kitchen thermometer reads 165° F when inserted in the thickest part of the thigh. Remove chicken and allow it to rest for 10 minutes before carving. - Serves 2 to 4

IGUANA STEW - Tastes like, well, tastes like iguana...

- 2 lb. boneless iguana meat* cut into large chunks or 2 lb. boneless skinless chicken thighs cut into large chunks

Spice Rub:

- 1 cup cilantro, chopped
- 6 cloves garlic, minced
- 2 jalapeno peppers, seeded and minced
- 2 Tbs. fresh thyme, chopped
- 3 tsp. vegetable oil
- 1/2 tsp. salt
- 1 tsp. pepper or to taste

In The Pot:

- 4 Tbs. vegetable oil
- 5 Tbs. molasses
- 1 large white onion, diced
- 1 can coconut milk
- 3 Tbs. tomato paste
- 1/4 cup water or ginger beer
- 1/2 tsp. allspice
- 1/4 tsp. nutmeg
- 1/4 tsp. cinnamon
- Salt and pepper to taste
- 3 large potatoes, peeled, cubed
- 2 mango, peeled, cubed
- 2 large sweet potatoes, peeled, cubed
- 3 - 4 carrots, peeled, sliced
- 2 plantain, peeled, sliced

Preheat oven to 375° F.

Mix the cilantro, garlic, peppers, thyme, oil and salt and pepper together into a paste in a large bowl. Spread the paste over the meat and place in a large Ziploc bag. Place the bag in the refrigerator over night.

In a large Dutch oven over medium heat, heat the oil and molasses, until bubbling. Brown the iguana or chicken in the molasses mixture, 5 chunks at a time. Place the browned meat on a plate and set aside.

Add the onions to the Dutch oven and then add the water or ginger beer and scrape the bottom of the pot to deglaze.

Cook onion until soft and add the coconut milk, tomato paste, allspice, nutmeg and cinnamon and cook 5 minutes. Add salt and pepper to taste.

Place all the browned meat back in Dutch oven and then add all the vegetables. Cover and place in the preheated 375° F oven for 1-1/2 to 2 hours, or until vegetables are fork tender. Salt and pepper to taste. - Serves 6

*http://www.exoticmeatmarkets.com/iguanameat.html

SNAKE STIR FRY - Also tastes like alligator.....

- 1 lb. snake meat, cut into 1 inch pieces *
- 1 clove garlic, minced
- 3 tsp. olive oil
- 3 Tbs. honey
- 2 Tbs. light soy sauce
- 1/8 tsp. salt
- 1/8 tsp. pepper
- 1 pack Byrd's-Eye frozen stir-fry vegetable blend
- 2 tsp. cornstarch
- 1 Tbs. water

In a large nonstick skillet or wok at medium-high stir-fry snake meat and garlic in 2 tsp. oil for 1 minute.

Add the honey, soy sauce, salt and pepper. Cook and stir until the snake is lightly browned. Remove and cover with tin foil to keep warm.

In the same pan, add the remaining oil and heat. Add the stir-fry vegetables and cook for 5 minutes or until tender.

Return the snake to the pan, stir to coat. Mix the cornstarch and water together and slowly stir it into the snake mixture. Bring to a simmer and allow sauce to thicken slightly. Serve with rice. - Serves 2

- http://buyexoticmeats.com/snmeforsa.html

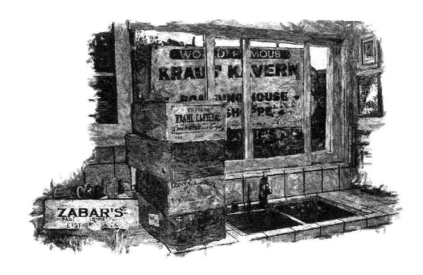

SWEET & SALTY PRALINES - Envision mint juleps and cypress trees, while you appreciate these sweet New Orleans indulgences.

- 1-1/2 cups light brown sugar
- 2/3 cup heavy whipping cream
- 1/8 tsp. salt
- 2 Tbs. butter
- 1-1/2 cups pecan halves
- 1 tsp. pure vanilla extract
- Sea salt

In a large Pyrex bowl, combine sugar, heavy cream, salt, butter and the pecans.

Microwave the mixture for 5 minutes on high, stirring once and cook 4 minutes longer. Let the mixture cool 3 minute.

Stir in the vanilla and continue to stir 3 minutes more. Drop spoonfuls onto buttered waxed paper. Sprinkle with sea salt and allow to cool.

BACCELLI E PECORINO ANTIPASTI PLATE - Baldacci's, Zabar's.....Who eats lunch at one o'clock............You do.

- 2 cups of shelled and cooked fava beans or 1 can (19 oz.) fava beans (rinsed)
- 1 head of arugula
- 1 Tbs. lemon juice
- 3 Tbs. extra-virgin olive oil
- 1 clove garlic, chopped
- 2 Tbs. chopped fresh oregano
- 2 Tbs. Italian parsley
- 2 Tbs. chives
- Red pepper flakes, to taste
- Salt and black pepper to taste
- 7 oz. wild boar salami, thinly sliced *
- 16 oz. Pecorino cheese, half shaved, half sliced *
- 4 oz. Miele al Tartufo Bianco *
- 7 oz. prosciutto Di San Daniele, thinly sliced *
- Balsamic Syrup*

In a bowl, whisk the lemon juice with the extra-virgin olive oil, add the beans, garlic, oregano, parsley, chives and pepper flakes. Toss to combine. Salt and pepper to taste.

Place 3 leaves of arugula in the center of a plate and add the fava bean mixture. Shave some of the Pecorino cheese over the beans. Surround salad with salami, prosciutto and sliced cheese. Drizzle cheese with truffle honey and lightly add balsamic syrup to taste. - Serves 2 to 6

* http://www.murrayscheese.com/prosciutto-di-san-daniele-4oz.html#

*http://www.murrayscheese.com/cheese/parmigano-pecorino-grating/pecorino-oro-antico.html

* http://www.amazon.com/Savini-Tartufi-Miele-Tartufo-Bianco/dp/B0030IU662

*http://www.murrayscheese.com/creminelli-wild-boar-salami.html

* http://www.amazon.com/Acetum-Blaze-First-Balsamic-7-3-Ounce/dp/B0002F7MX6/ref=sr_1_1?ie=UTF8&qid=1371423484&sr=8-1&keywords=Balsamic+Syrup

KANSAS STYLE PIZZA – Just like Chicago and New York, Medicine Creek has its very own style of pizza. Who knew?

Seasoning:

- 1/2 Tbs. oregano
- 1/2 Tbs. basil
- 1 tsp. thyme
- 4 Tbs. Parmesan cheese, grated

Combine all 4 ingredients in a small mixing bowl and blend well.

Sauce:

- 4 medium ripe tomatoes, diced and crushed
- 5 Tbs. tomato paste
- 3/4 Tbs. sugar
- 1/2 tsp. basil
- 1/2 tsp. salt
- 1/2 tsp. black pepper
- 1/4 tsp. thyme

To make the sauce, combine all ingredients in a large bowl and mix well.

Cheese:

- 1 cup extra sharp cheddar cheese, shredded
- 1/2 cup Swiss cheese, shredded
- 1/2 cup provolone cheese, shredded
- 3 tsp. Liquid Smoke

Place the Liquid Smoke in the bottom of a large stainless steel bowl. Use a paper towel and coat the inside of the bowl. Add the cheeses and toss until cheeses and Liquid Smoke are completely incorporated.

Crust:

- 2-1/4 cups all purpose flour
- 1/2 tsp. salt
- 1 tsp. baking powder
- 2 tsp. olive oil
- 2 tsp. dark corn syrup
- 1/2 cup water

For the crust, mix all ingredients together until thoroughly combined. Divide the dough in half, place on a lightly floured work surface, shape into round balls then roll them out into very thin, 14 inch rounds. Place the crusts on 12 inch pizza pans, sprayed with cooking spray, and tuck the edges under.

Adjust the oven rack to the lowest position and preheat oven to 450° F.

Place half the sauce on each pizza and spread it out all the way to the edge of the crust. Sprinkle half the cheese on top of the sauce.

Place pizza on the lowest rack and bake 10 to 12 minutes or until cheese is lightly brown and bubbly.

Once cooked to desired crispness, remove the pizza, allow it to cool about 5 minutes and cut into 3x3 inch squares. Sprinkle the pizza slices with seasoning mixture. - Makes 2 pizzas

EGGS AND BACON - Ah, nothing like a hearty breakfast a la Castle Club to start your day.

- 6 eggs
- 6 slices of bacon
- 6 slices of bread
- Shredded cheddar cheese

Preheat oven to 400° F.

Lay the bacon out flat on a plate and cover with a paper towel. Put the plate in the microwave and cook for 2 or 3 minutes, just enough so that bacon is cooked but bendable.

Cut out 6 rounds from the bread with a juice glass or round cookie cutter. Spray a muffin tin with butter flavored cooking spray and lay the bread rounds into the tin.

Wrap the bacon around the inside edge of each muffin cup and sprinkle cheddar cheese on top of the bread rounds.

Crack the eggs into each muffin cup. Salt and pepper to taste. Bake for 15 minutes or until the whites have set and the yolk are to your liking. - Serves 3

STEWED TOMATOES WITH GRILLED CHEESE
CROUTONS - Some real, small town, bowling alley chow, with an elegant twist. Why not?

- 2 lbs. fresh ripe tomatoes
- Boiling water
- 4 Tbs. butter
- 4 tsp. sugar
- 1/2 tsp. salt
- 1/4 tsp. freshly ground pepper
- 8 basil leaves, chopped
- 6 slices of bread cut into 2-inch cubes
- 1 Tbs. butter
- 1/2 cup extra sharp cheddar cheese, finely shredded
- Garlic salt
- 1/4 cup fresh chives, chopped

Using a slotted spoon, place whole tomatoes in a pot of boiling water for about 30 seconds. Once all the tomatoes have been scalded, the skin will just slide right off the tomatoes. Next core and roughly chop up the tomatoes.

Put tomatoes, 3 Tbs. butter and sugar into a saucepan. Heat until simmering, and then reduce heat to low. Let them cook for about 30 minutes or until tomatoes are soft and have cooked down a bit. Add chopped basil and then salt and pepper to taste.

Melt 1 Tbs. butter in a medium pan over medium heat. Add the cubed bread and let them get lightly toasted. Flip the pieces over to toast other sides. Sprinkle with cheddar cheese and garlic salt and remove from heat.

Serve the stewed tomatoes with several cheese croutons floating on top, garnish with chopped chives. - Serves 4

STEWED TOMATOES

- 10 large ripe tomatoes
- Boiling water
- 3 Tbs. butter
- 1 large white onion, thinly sliced
- 1 clove garlic, crushed
- 3/4 cup chopped celery
- 1/2 cup chopped green bell pepper
- 3 Tbs. light brown sugar
- 2 bay leaves
- 1 tsp. salt
- 1/4 tsp. pepper
- 1/8 tsp. red pepper flake
- 1 tsp. dried basil
- Fresh parsley, chopped

Bring some water to a boil in a medium saucepan. Core the tomatoes and place them in boiling water for about 15 to 20 seconds. Remove the tomatoes with a slotted spoon and then put them into a bowl of ice water. Remove the skin from the tomatoes. Cut tomatoes in quarters. In crock pot add all the ingredients. Cover and cook on low for 4 hours. Be sure to remove the bay leaves before serving. - Serves 4 to 6

CAP'N CRUNCH CHEESECAKE - A real Trailer Park treat. This isn't your mother's cheesecake.

Crust:

- 4 cups Cap'n Crunch
- 6 Tbs. unsalted butter, melted
- 1/8 tsp. salt

Filling:

- 2 packages (8 oz. each) cream cheese, softened
- 2/3 cup sugar
- 3 large eggs
- 1/2 tsp. pure vanilla extract

Topping:

- 3 Tbs. sugar
- 8 oz. sour cream
- 1 tsp. pure vanilla extract

Preheat oven to 350° F.

Place Cap'n Crunch in a food processor and pulse until finely ground. In a medium bowl, combine the crumbs, butter, and salt and stir until the mixture is moistened. Press the mixture in the bottom and about 1 inch up the sides of a well greased 9 inch pie pan. Bake for 8 minutes and remove from oven.

Beat cream cheese, sugar, eggs, and the 1/2 tsp. vanilla with mixer until smooth. Pour into the 9 inch pie pan on top of the crust. Bake about 25 minutes. Turn the oven off and remove cheesecake. Allow the cheesecake to cool for about 5 minutes.

Combine sugar, sour cream, and vanilla. Spread over the warm cheesecake and return to the warm oven for 5 minutes. Cool and then refrigerate at least 2 hours. - Makes 12 slices

EARS OF CORN - To really confuse things, tie on some tags with some weird code written on it, just for fun.

- 12 ears corn on the cob, in the husks
- Salted water
- Melted butter and a pastry brush
- Old Bay seasoning

Preheat oven to 350° F.

Soak the ears in the salted water for about 20 minutes. Place the ears of corn directly on the middle rack in oven and bake for 30 minutes.

Remove corn cobs. Pull back husks, brush with butter and sprinkle with Old Bay. Peeled back husks can be used as handles. - Serves 6

THE FORTY-FIVE'S WHISKEY GRILLED BUFFALO STEAKS - Whiskey over here, amigo, it helps with the digestion.

- 4 (10 oz.) buffalo steaks
- 3/4 cup good whiskey
- 1/3 cup vegetable oil
- 4 cloves garlic, minced
- 1 tsp. onion powder
- 1/2 tsp. salt
- 1/4 tsp. black pepper

Place steaks in a large Ziploc bag. Combine remaining ingredients in a small bowl and pour over the steaks.

Seal the bag and allow steaks to marinate about 30 minutes or until steaks reach room temperature.

Preheat grill for medium heat. Remove steaks from bag and place steaks onto grill (be careful, that whiskey will flare up) and cook for 5 minutes per side. Remove from heat and serve rare. - Serves 4

ROASTED BUFFALO STEAKS

- 3 lbs. of top round buffalo steaks, sliced thin
- 1/4 cup flour
- 2 Tbs. olive oil
- 2-1/2 cups beef stock
- 3 Tbs. Worcestershire sauce
- 1 -1/2 lbs sliced onions
- Salt and pepper to taste

Preheat oven to 375° F.

Pound out the buffalo steaks to tender. Dredge well in flour, salt and pepper.

In heavy iron skillet heat oil, add the steaks and brown on both sides.

Remove the meat and the add stock and bring it to a boil. Add Worcestershire sauce, salt and pepper to taste. Add half the onions to the pan, then the browned steaks and then the rest of onions.

Tightly cover the skillet with tin foil or a lid, and place the skillet in preheated oven and bake for 2 hours. - Serves 4 to 6

BEANS AND STEW MEAT - The only thing you'll be cursing is the fact that you have to share this marvelous dish.

- 1 cup dried pinto beans
- 1 lb. stew meat (beef, buffalo or venison) cut into 1 inch chunks)
- 2 cups cold water
- 1/2 cup chopped carrot
- 2 cloves garlic, minced
- 1 tsp. chili powder
- 1/2 tsp. salt
- Dash cayenne pepper
- 1 can corn, drained
- 1 large onion, chopped
- 1 medium green pepper, chopped
- 1 can diced tomatoes
- 3 tsp. balsamic vinegar
- Salt and pepper to taste

First check the beans for stones and twigs. Rinse them well in cold water. Place the beans in a large stockpot. Add enough water to cover the beans by about 3 inches. Bring pot to a boil for about 5 minutes. turn off the heat, cover the pot and let it stand for 1 hour.

Drain the beans in a colander then return them to the pot. Add the stew meat, 2 cups cold water, carrot, garlic, chili powder, salt and cayenne pepper. Bring the pot back to a boil. Reduce the heat, cover and let it simmer for 1 hour.

Add the corn, onion and green peppers. Cover and cook for another 30 minutes or until beans are nice and tender. Stir in the tomatoes and vinegar at the last minute. Salt and pepper to taste. - Serves 4 to 6

GINGER SNAPS - Serve these by the fire on a winter's night, with a nice pot of tea. What could possibly go wrong?

- 2-3/4 cups self rising flour
- 1 tsp. baking soda
- 1 tsp. cinnamon

- 1 tsp. ginger
- 1/4 tsp. cloves
- 1 cup brown sugar
- 3/4 cup butter, softened
- 1 egg
- 1/4 cup molasses
- White sugar

Mix flour, baking soda, and spices in a bowl and set aside. Beat sugar and butter together until creamy. Beat the egg and molasses into the butter mixture. Stir in the flour mixture with a wooden spoon until blended. Cover with plastic wrap and chill for at least 2 hours.

Preheat oven to 375° F.

Using your hands, shape the cookie dough into 1-inch balls, roll them in white sugar, and place on lightly greased cookie sheets about 2 inches apart.

Dip the bottom of a juice glass in white sugar and use the glass to flatten each dough ball to about 1/4 inch thick.

Bake for about 8 to 10 minutes, cool until cookies set.

TEA CAKES - Set these out at your next tea party, just remember not to slump at the table.....or bleed on it, for that matter.

- 1 cup butter, softened
- 1/2 cup powdered sugar
- 1 tsp. pure vanilla extract
- 2-1/4 cups flour
- 3/4 cup pecans, finely chopped
- 1/4 tsp. salt
- Powdered sugar

Preheat oven to 400° F.

Mix the butter, powdered sugar and vanilla in large bowl. Stir in the flour, nuts and salt. Shape dough into 1-inch balls by rolling them in your palms.

Place the dough balls about 2 inches apart on ungreased cookie sheet. Bake for 10 minutes. Remove cookies from cookie sheet and cool slightly on wire rack. Roll the warm cookies around in a bowl of powdered sugar, let cool completely and then roll in powdered sugar again.

"Muuuuuuuhhhhhhhhhhh!"

WHEEL OF DARKNESS

BUTTER TEA

TSAMPA

TIBETAN FLAT BREAD

BERRY RAT

DOVER SOLE

OYSTERS ROCKEFELLER

TOURNEDOS OF BEEF ROSSINI

CORNED BEEF AND CABBAGE

SHEPHERDS PIE

YELLOW SHEET CAKE

ASSORTED HORS D'OEUVRES

ANTIPASTI

SQUAB WITH APPLES

PHEASANT

CAVIAR

TRUFFLE PÂTÉ

CRÈME BRULEE

WATERCRESS SALAD

BUTTER SCONES

TIBETAN BUTTER TEA (PO CHA) - To help you along your journey of meditation and enlightenment.

- 8 cups water
- 4 Tbs. loose black tea
- 1 tsp. salt
- 2 Tbs. unsalted butter
- 1-1/2 cup half and half

Combine water and tea in a medium pot, bring to a boil. Boil tea for 5 minutes and then turn off the heat and let steep for 5 minutes more. Strain the tea into a large pot and discard the tea leaves. Bring tea back to a boil and then decrease the heat to simmer. Add salt, butter, and half-and-half* and stir until dissolved. Carefully pour liquid into a heat proof blender or food processor and churn for 3 minutes. Serve the tea in small bowls.

   *To achieve the gamey taste of nak butter, add 1 tsp. plain goat cheese.

TSAMPA – (PA)

- Tsampa flour*
- Butter Tea
- Sugar
- Butter

Put barley flour in a tea bowl and then pour hot butter tea on top. Drink several cups, if desired. Upon drinking the final bowl, leave a very thin layer of liquid behind. The tea has soaked into the upper most layer of the flour enough to make perfect tsampa. Add a pat of butter and a pinch of sugar and stir it into the flour/tea mixture with a finger.

When the paste begins to thicken, place all four fingers in the bowl. Pull in the mixture forward with the fingers and squeeze it against the palm. The tsampa will begin to become firmer and denser. Rotate the bowl with the hand holding it from underneath and keep working on all areas of the tsampa. Use index finger to push down any tsampa that runs up the edge of the bowl.

When the tsampa is dry enough, scoop it out of the bowl and massage it in your hand, squeezing it into a small loaf shape. The bowl should be free of any residual tsampa and ready for more butter tea. Eat the tsampa like a teacake or biscuit.

*http://www.tibetantsampa.com/category-s/1825.htm

TIBETAN FLAT BREAD - Simple, straight-forward, and a gift.

- 1 cup all purpose flour
- 1/2 cup buckwheat flour
- 1 tsp. salt
- 2 tsp. baking powder

- 1 cup water
- 2 Tbs. vegetable oil
- 2 Tbs. water (for steaming)

Combine flours, salt and baking powder in a medium bowl. Add water and mix until well blended.

Coat the inside of an iron skillet with oil and pour in the dough. Oil a hand and pat the dough to form a round. Pour 2 Tbs. of water around the outside edge, between the dough and the edge of the pan.

Place the skillet on the stove and turn heat to medium. Cover the skillet and lower heat to medium-low and steam for 10 minutes. Remove lid and carefully flip the bread. Cover once more and cook 5 minutes. Remove from skillet and cut the bread into wedges. - Serves 8

BERRY RAT - Climb, walk or crawl, but definitely take some time to try this berry packed entrée.

- 1-1/2 cups pita bread crumbs, stale or toasted
- 1-1/2 cups goat cheese
- 1/2 cup cottage cheese
- 2 eggs, beaten
- 1/4 cup parsley, coarsely chopped
- 1/4 cup green chilies, finely chopped
- 3/4 cup fresh mixed berries (blueberries, raspberries, blackberries)
- 1 Tbs. finely chopped rosemary
- 16 boneless chicken thighs with skin

- 1/4 tsp. turmeric powder
- 1/4 tsp. curry powder
- Salt and black pepper

Preheat oven to 450° F.

Combine the bread crumbs, goat cheese, cottage cheese, eggs, parsley, chilies, berries and rosemary in a medium bowl.

Place the chicken thighs, skin side down, on a clean work surface covered in plastic wrap and season with salt and black pepper. Place some filling on each thigh. Bring the sides of the thighs up and over the filling then tie tightly in 3 places with kitchen string. Season the skin of the chicken thighs with turmeric, curry powder, salt and pepper.

Arrange the chicken thighs skin side up on a tin foil lined, baking sheet sprayed with cooking spray. Bake chicken for about 35 minutes or until the skin is brown and crispy. Let the chicken rest for 10 minutes then cut and discard the strings. - Serves 8

DOVER SOLE - Next stop, The King's Arms, Deck Two

- 2 Dover sole fillets
- 1 cup crushed roasted pecans
- 1 clove garlic, peeled
- 1 tsp. salt
- 1 tsp. pepper
- Zest of one I lemon
- 1 egg
- 1/4 cup milk

Preheat oven to 350° F.

Place pecans, garlic, and lemon zest in a food processor and pulse to a medium ground and then transfer the mixture to a shallow dish or pie plate.

Crack egg into a large bowl. Add milk, salt and pepper and beat with a fork until well combined. Dip the fish fillets in the egg and then into the pecan mixture. Coat well and transfer to a parchment paper lined bake sheet. Spread any extra pecan mixture over the fish and pat down firmly.

Bake fish fillets for about 15 minutes or until completely cooked. Squeeze lemon juice over the fish before serving. - Serves 2

OYSTERS ROCKEFELLER

- 36 fresh oysters
- 1-1/2 sticks butter

- 3 cups fresh spinach leaves
- 1/2 cup toasted French bread crumbs
- 4 Tbs. chives
- 3 Tbs. fresh celery leaves
- 3 Tbs. tarragon
- 3 Tbs. parsley, minced
- 3 Tbs. fresh chervil
- Tabasco Sauce to taste
- 1/2 tsp. Herbsaint or Absinthe*
- 1/2 tsp. salt
- Rock Salt
- Lemon wedges and parsley sprigs for garnish

Using an oyster knife, pry open the oyster shells from the back hinge. Remove oysters and place then in a bowl with any oyster juice (liquor). Pick 36 of the shells that are in the best shape and throw the rest away.

Melt the butter in a large saucepan over medium heat. Add the spinach, bread crumbs, chives, celery leaves, tarragon, parsley, chervil, Tabasco Sauce, Herbsaint, and salt. Cook for about 15 minutes, stirring constantly. Remove spinach mixture from heat, pour into a food processor and puree. Let the spinach mixture cool to room temperature.

Position the oven rack to the broiler position and turn broiler on. Spread a thin layer of rock salt on an oven proof platter. Set oysters shells in the rock salt and level them out.

Place an oyster and some of the oyster juice in each shell. Add a spoonful of spinach mixture over each oyster. Broil the oysters, watching carefully, until spinach starts to bubble and brown slightly, about 5 minutes. Garnish the platter with the parsley and lemon wedges. - Serves 6 to 10

* Herbsaint and Absinthe are aniseed flavored spirits

http://www.drinkupny.com/Legendre_Herbsaint_Liqueur_d_
Anis_Veritas_p/s1014.htm

TOURNEDOS OF BEEF ROSSINI

- 4 slices country white bread, crust trimmed
- 4 (5 oz.) fillets of beef
- 5 Tbs. clarified butter
- 4 slices fresh foie gras
- 8 slices black truffle
- Salt and freshly ground black pepper to taste
- 1/3 cup Madeira
- 1/4 cup veal glaze

Trim the bread to the size of the fillets of beef and trim any fat from the beef. Heat 3 Tbs. of the clarified butter in a large iron skillet, over medium-high heat. Grill the bread slices in the skillet, on both sides until they are golden. Place a slice in the center of each plate.

Add 1 more Tbs. of clarified butter to the skillet, and sauté the foie gras briefly on each side, until lightly browned. Remove and set aside. Next sauté the truffle slices in the accumulated butter and duck fat in the pan for about 30 seconds. Remove the truffles and set aside.

Add the remaining butter to the pan, and sauté the beef to the desired degree of doneness, turning it once to brown both sides. Season the beef with salt and pepper. Place the beef on the bread slices, and top with a slice of foie gras and two truffle slices.

Deglaze the pan with the Madeira over high heat, stirring and scraping to loosen any browned bits. Cook until the wine is reduced by half.

Stir in the veal glaze, cook until the sauce becomes thick, about 1 minute. Adjust the sauces seasonings and pour the sauce over the beef. - Serves 4

CORNED BEEF AND CABBAGE - Let's see how the other half lives. Deck C anyone?

- 2 bottles stout
- 3 Tbs. dark brown sugar
- 3 lbs. uncooked corned beef brisket
- 2 Tbs. pickling spice
- 1 red onion, cut in chunks
- 6 cloves garlic, peeled and crushed
- 3 Tbs. vegetable oil
- 1 head cabbage, cut in 6 to 8 wedges
- 6 carrots, cut into 2 inch chunks
- 1 lb. of red potatoes, cut into 1-inch chunks
- 2 Tbs. fresh parsley, chopped

Preheat oven to 300° F.

Add beer and brown sugar to a Dutch oven over medium-high heat and stir to blend. Carefully place the brisket into pot and pour in enough water to cover meat completely. Add pickling spice, onion and garlic and simmer for 5 minutes.

Cover pot and place in oven to roast for 2 hours. Remove pot from oven and flip the brisket, cover and return to oven for 3 more hours.

30 minutes before the meat is done, place a second pot over medium-high heat. Add oil, cabbage wedges, carrots and potatoes and cook, undisturbed, until browned, about 5 minutes. Turn the vegetables and cook an additional 5 minutes. Take 3 cups of the brisket broth from the oven and pour it over the vegetables. Bring the pot to a simmer and cover. Turn heat down to low and let it cook 10 minutes.

Carefully remove cabbage and set aside. Replace lid and cook carrots and potato for an additional 10 minutes.

Remove the brisket from the oven, slice and place on a warmed platter. Surround with the vegetables and pour half the sauce over the meat. Garnish with chopped parsley. - Serves 6 to 8

SHEPHERD'S PIE

- 5 large potatoes, peeled and diced
- 4 Tbs. butter
- 3 Tbs. milk
- Salt and pepper
- 2 large onions, chopped
- 2 lbs. ground beef or ground lamb
- 2 large carrots, grated
- 2 (12 oz.) cans Swanson's beef broth
- 1 Tbs. cornstarch
- 1 can peas, drained
- 1/8 cup Worcestershire

Preheat oven to 400° F.

Place the potatoes in a large pot or Dutch oven. Cover the potatoes with lightly salted water and bring to a boil. Reduce the heat to a simmer and cook until tender. Drain the potatoes in a colander and return potatoes to the pot. Add butter and milk; mash and whip the potatoes using an electric mixer. Salt and pepper to taste and set aside.

Place an iron skillet over medium-high heat. Add the ground meat and onions; season with salt and pepper. Once the meat has browned, add the carrots and stock. Mix the cornstarch with 1/4 cup of water and pour into the skillet. Cook meat mixture for 10 minutes longer. Remove the skillet from the heat, add peas and Worcestershire sauce and stir to combine.

Cover the beef mixture completely with the whipped potatoes and place the skillet in oven and bake for 30 minutes, until potatoes are golden brown. Allow the pie to cool about 15 minutes before serving. - Serves 6

YELLOW SHEET CAKE

- 4 eggs, room temperature
- 2-3/4 leveled cups all purpose flour
- 2 leveled tsp. baking powder
- 1/2 tsp. salt
- 1 cup milk
- 1 tsp. pure vanilla extract
- 3/4 cup butter
- 1-1/3 cups sugar

Cake:

Preheat oven to 350° F.

Grease a 13 x 9 inch baking pan with softened butter and sprinkle with flour. Tilt pan back and forth to spread flour over butter coating and shake out excess into the sink.

Sift flour, baking powder and salt through a wire strainer, into a bowl.

Whip the butter in large mixing bowl on medium speed, for 1 minute. Gradually add sugar while continuing to mix. Whip for 10 minutes until light and fluffy. Add eggs one at a time, beating and scraping bowl.

Mix in two-thirds of flour mixture to the bowl. At low speed, mix until flour mixture is just incorporated. Add milk and vanilla, mix for 30 seconds, and then slowly add the remaining flour. Pour batter into prepared pan and spread it out.

Place the pan in the oven and bake 35 to 40 minutes or until toothpick inserted in cake comes out clean. Cool cake completely before icing.

Icing:

- 2 sticks butter softened
- 4 cups powdered sugar, sifted
- 1/4 tsp. salt
- 1 Tbs. pure vanilla extract
- 3 Tbs. milk

Beat the butter for 3 minutes at medium speed. Add powdered sugar and reduce to lowest speed until the sugar has been well incorporated in the butter. Increase the mixer speed back to medium and add vanilla, salt, and milk and beat for 5 minutes. If frosting is too thick, add a little bit more milk. - Serves 12

SHIPBOARD HORS D' OEUVRES - Indulge; it's going to be an interesting night.

Mushroom Caps:

- 40 button mushrooms caps
- 4 slices lightly toasted wheat bread, cut into cubes
- 1 shallot
- 1 green pepper
- 4 oz. cream cheese
- 1/4 cup finely chopped parsley
- 1/4 cup Parmesan, freshly grated
- 1 tsp. salt
- 1/4 tsp. white pepper

Place oven rack on broiler position and preheat the oven to 350° F.

Place bread in a food processor and pulse to fine crumbs. Transfer the crumbs to a medium mixing bowl. Place the shallot, green pepper, and cream cheese in the food processor and pulse until well combined. Transfer cream cheese mixture to the bowl of bread crumbs and fold until well combined. Stir in the cilantro, half the Parmesan cheese, salt, and pepper.

Place mushroom caps on a large cookie sheet. Place a heaping spoonful of the bread crumb mixture into each mushroom cap.

Bake for 15 minutes or until mushrooms are soft and filling begins to bubble. Remove mushrooms from oven and turn the oven to broil. Sprinkle the mushrooms with the remaining Parmesan cheese and place mushrooms back in oven. Broil the mushrooms until the cheese is just browned, about 1 minute. Serve immediately. - Serves 8 to 10

Asian Chicken Wings:

- 3 lbs. chicken wings, separated at the joint, wing tips discarded
- 1/2 cup soy sauce
- 1/2 cup fresh lime juice
- 3 Tbs. Thai fish sauce
- 4 cloves garlic, peeled and crushed
- 1 fresh red Thai chilies, thinly sliced
- 2 tsp. sugar
- 2 ripe mangoes, cut into 2 inch chunks
- 1/2 Tbs. salt
- Vegetable oil, for frying
- 1/2 cup cornstarch
- 1/2 cup rice flour
- 1/4 cup chopped mint
- Hot and Sour Sauce

Place soy sauce, lime juice, fish sauce, garlic, chilies, and sugar in a medium saucepan over medium heat. Bring the mixture to a boil, then remove from heat and let it cool completely. Place the chicken wings in a large Ziploc bag and pour sauce mixture over chicken. Seal and massage bag until chicken is well coated. Refrigerate and allow chicken to marinate for at least 2 hours.

Season mango with salt in a medium bowl, cover and set aside.

In a Dutch oven, add 3 inches of vegetable oil. Over medium-high heat, heat the oil until it reaches 375. A deep fat fryer can also be used, set to 375.

Mix together cornstarch and rice flour in a second large Ziploc bag. Remove chicken from marinate and, working in small batches, drop chicken into the cornstarch mixture. Seal the bag and shake to coat. Remove chicken and carefully add it to the hot oil. Cook the chicken for about 10 minutes until crisp and cooked through. Transfer the chicken to paper towels to drain and repeat steps until all the chicken is cooked.

Place a small bowl of hot and sour sauce in the middle of a large platter, Arrange chicken on platter and garnish with salted mango slices and mint leaves. - Serves 8 to 10

Mini Crab Muffins:

Crab:

- Vegetable oil
- 1 (12 oz.) can lump crabmeat, drained
- 1/2 tsp. Old Bay seasoning
- 1 Tbs. Melted butter or vegetable oil
- 1/2 cup shallots, minced
- 1 cup red/yellow/green pepper, finely chopped
- 1 cup (4 oz) shredded Swiss cheese

Batter:

- 1/2 cup Bisquick
- 1/2 cup milk
- 2 eggs

Sauce:

- 1/2 cup Hellmann's mayonnaise
- 1/2 tsp. Old Bay seasoning
- 1 Tbs. fresh lemon juice

Garnish:

- Zest of the lemon
- Parsley, chopped

Spray 2 mini muffin tins with butter flavored cooking spray.

Preheat oven to 375° F.

In a medium mixing bowl, combine crabmeat and Old Bay; set aside.

In an iron skillet, heat oil over medium-high heat until hot. Add the shallots and tri-colored bell peppers and cook about 5 minutes. Remove from heat and add the crabmeat and Swiss cheese to the skillet. Fold everything together until well combined.

In the same medium bowl, stir the batter ingredients together with whisk until just blended.

Scoop about 1 Tbs. of the batter into each muffin cup. Top with about 1 Tbs. of the crab mixture. Spread another 1 Tbs. of the batter onto crab.

Bake about 10 minutes or until the tops are golden brown.

While crab cakes are cooking go ahead and whip up the sauce.

Cool 5 minutes. With thin knife, loosen sides of crab cakes from pan; remove cakes from pan and place top sides up on wire rack.

Serve each mini crab cakes topped with generous amount of the sauce and top with the lemon zest and chopped parsley.

ANTIPASTO PLATE

- 1 lb. provolone cheese, sliced
- 1/4 lb. Genoa salami, sliced
- 1/4 lb. hard salami, sliced
- 1/4 lb. prosciutto, cut in thin strips
- 12 oz. ball of mozzarella cheese in brine

- 1 wedge Parmesan cheese
- 1 large tomato
- 1 jar roasted red peppers, drained and coarsely chopped
- Artichoke hearts, drained and coarsely chopped
- Balsamic vinegar
- Olive oil
- Course ground back pepper
- Black olives, whole
- Italian green olives, whole
- 1 jar pepperoncini
- Marinated mushrooms, whole
- Fresh Italian parsley, chopped
- 1 large loaf crusty bread, sliced

Take a large pizza pan (16") and rub it generously with olive oil, then sprinkle it with sea salt.

Place slices of provolone cheese around the whole pan, overlapping the provolone slices about 1 inch. Place the Genoa salami in the same way on top of the cheese, overlapping again, 1 inch. Next layer the hard salami on top of the Genoa salami in a wider pattern.

Tear the mozzarella into small chunks and place around the pan randomly. Slice the Prosciutto into fine strips and sprinkle it around the pan as well. Next add the coarsely chopped tomato, roasted red peppers and artichoke hearts. Next add fresh ground pepper and fresh chopped parsley. Drizzle on the balsamic vinegar and olive oil and grate a fair amount of Parmesan cheese over the whole thing. Garnish with chopped Italian parsley.

Take a small bowl and place it upside down in the center of the assembled antipasto. Using a pizza cutter or sharp knife, cut around the edge of the bowl. Remove the bowl and the small circle of antipasto.

Now take the pizza cutter and slice through the entire layer (just like slicing a pizza), creating pie shaped slices about 2 inches wide at the outside edge. Be sure to cut all the way through.

Place a bowl full of the olives, mushrooms and pepperoncini in the center and serve with a metal pie server. Place a basket with the crusty bread to the side. - Serves 12 to 16

SQUAB WITH APPLES

- 2 large apples, peeled, cored and cut in quarters
- 4 squab, cleaned, rinsed and pat dry (Cornish hens can be used, just roast about 10 minutes longer)
- Salt and pepper
- 2 Tbs. dried thyme
- 4 bay leaves
- 4 garlic cloves, peeled
- 4 small onions, peeled
- 8 small red potatoes
- 2 Tbs. olive oil
- 4 Tbs. dry Amontillado sherry
- 3/4 cup Swanson's chicken broth
- 4 Tbs. butter

Preheat oven to 450° F.

Season the birds inside and out generously with salt, pepper and dried thyme. Place a bay leaf and a clove of garlic inside each bird and truss legs together with kitchen twine.

Place the birds in a large roasting pan, breast side up and arrange the onions, potatoes and apples around them. Drizzle olive oil over the birds, potatoes and onions.

Place the roasting pan in the oven and roast for 20 minutes. using a turkey baster, baste the birds about every 5 minutes with the pan drippings to keep the birds moist.

Remove the pan from the oven and drain the accumulated fat. Remove apples and set them aside. Add the sherry and chicken broth to the pan and return it to oven. Cook 15 minutes longer then remove pan from oven.

Carefully lift squab with a knife inserted in the cavity. Tilt each bird to allow any juices flow back into pan. Arrange squab, potatoes and onions on a serving platter and remove twine from the birds. Add the apples to the platter and cover with tin foil to keep warm.

Place the roasting pan on top of the stove over medium-high heat. Bring the drips to a simmer and add the butter. Blend the butter into the drips while at the same time scraping up all the brown bits from the pan. Pour gravy over the roasted birds just before serving. - Serves 4

PHEASANT UNDER GLASS

Stuffing:

- 2 cups cooked wild rice
- 1/2 cup shiitake mushrooms, chopped
- 1/2 cup white onion, minced
- 2 Tbs. butter
- Salt and pepper to taste

In a large pan over medium heat; sauté mushrooms and onions in the butter for about 5 minutes or until just tender. Stir in the cooked wild rice. Salt and pepper to taste and set aside.

Sauce:

- 2 Tbs. butter
- 1 large shallot, minced
- 4 shiitake mushrooms, sliced thin
- Juice of half a lemon
- 2 morel mushrooms, sliced thin
- 1 cup Swanson's chicken broth
- 1 cup dry white wine
- 3 Tbs. cognac
- 3 Tbs. heavy cream mixed with 1 tsp. cornstarch
- Salt and pepper to taste

In a medium saucepan, sauté the shallots, morel and shiitake mushrooms in butter for 5 minutes. Remove the mixture from the saucepan and add the chicken broth and 1/2 cup of white wine. Simmer until the liquid reduces by half. Add the cream, lemon juice and cognac. Increase heat to medium-high and stirring constantly, bring the sauce up to the boil until it thickens.

Pheasants:

- 2 pheasants (about 2 lbs. each)
- 4 Tbs. olive oil
- Salt and pepper
- 4 thick slices of crusty bread, toasted

Preheat oven to 400° F.

Stuff the pheasants with the wild rice stuffing and truss the legs closed with kitchen string (tuck the wings under the backs so they will not over cook). Pour 2 Tbs. olive oil over each bird and massage, coating the birds well. Season the birds generously with salt and pepper.

In a roasting pan sprayed with cooking spray, lay the birds on their side and roast for 12 minutes. Open the oven, turn the birds to the opposite side and roast for an additional 12 minutes. Now place the birds breast up and roast for 25 minutes longer.

Remove pan from oven, carefully remove pheasants and set them aside, loosely draped them in tin foil, to keep warm.

Pour off accumulated fat in the but reserve the brown bits in the bottom. Deglaze the roasting pan by placing it on the stove top over medium heat and pouring the rest of the white wine into the roasting pan and scraping with the edge of a spatula to remove the brown goodie. Pour the deglazing liquid into the sauce and whisk together.

Nest each pheasant on 2 slices of toasted bread and serve on a platter with a large glass dome cover. Spoon out the stuffing and carve the birds at table side. Serve the sauce in a gravy boat to add to the meat after it is carved. - Serves 4

BLINI WITH CAVIAR - Is it polite to belch on the high seas?

- 1/2 cup sour cream
- 2 Tbs. thinly sliced scallions
- 3 Tbs. milk
- 1 egg, beaten
- 2 tsp. lemon zest
- 1/4 cup flour
- 1/4 tsp. baking powder
- 1/4 tsp. sugar
- Salt
- 2 Tbs. butter
- 4 oz. black or red caviar

Stir together the sour cream and 1 Tbs. of sliced scallions.

Melt 1 Tbs. butter in a small bowl. Mix in milk, egg, and 1 tsp. lemon zest. Add flour, baking powder, sugar, and salt and mix until smooth.

Melt 1/2 Tbs. butter in a large nonstick skillet over medium-low heat.

Drop 6 individual tablespoon size scoops of batter into skillet and cook until undersides are golden brown, about 3 minutes.

Flip the 6 blinis and cook until golden and then cook about 2 minutes more. Repeat process and make 6 more blinis.

Top each of the blinis with the scallion sour cream and caviar. Sprinkle with lemon zest and scallions. - Serves 6

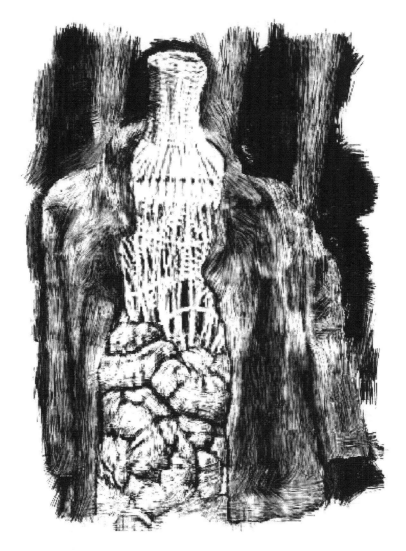

TRUFFLE PÂTÉ

- 2 oz. fresh black truffles*
- 1 cup Swanson's beef broth
- 2 lbs. chicken livers, cleaned and rinsed
- 1 white onion, chopped
- 1 large yellow apple, peeled, cored and coarsely chopped
- 1 shallots, minced
- 1/4 cup fresh lemon juice
- 1/4 cup warm water
- 2 envelopes unflavored gelatin
- 1 cup butter, cut into pieces
- 2 Tbs. cognac
- 1 tsp. salt
- 1 tsp. brown mustard
- Salt & pepper to taste

Butter a 6 cup terrine or enough small ramekins to hold 6 cups and line with a large enough sheet of plastic wrap to drape over the sides.

Clean the truffles carefully with a soft toothbrush and slice them into 1/4 inch pieces.

In a medium saucepan over medium-high heat, add the beef broth and bring it to a boil. Reduce the heat to medium and add the truffles**. Cook the truffles for exactly 45 seconds and remove the saucepan from the heat. Let the truffles steep for 1 minute and then pour the broth through a wire sieve into a bowl. Set both the broth and the truffles aside.

Stir the lemon juice, warm water and gelatin together in a mixing bowl and whisk until the gelatin has completely dissolved.

Combine chicken livers, onion, apple, reserved broth, and shallots in a medium saucepan. Bring to a boil over medium heat, then reduce the heat to a simmer and cook, covered for 5 minutes or until liver is just fully cooked. Pour lemon/gelatin mixture into the saucepan and simmer for another minute, stirring constantly. Remove from the heat and whisk in the butter, cognac, salt and brown mustard. Allow the mixture to cool 30 minutes.

Pour the mixture to a food processor and pulse until very smooth, and then let it rest 15 minutes. Adjust the seasoning with salt and pepper to taste. Layer 1/3 of the truffle pieces into the bottom of the prepared terrine or ramekins, then spoon 1/3 of the pate mixture on top. Add an additional layer of the truffles, then an additional 1/3 of the pate, then the last of the truffles and finish with the remaining pate.

Fold the plastic wrap back over the pate to seal and tap the terrine or ramekins several times on the work surface to settle the pate and truffles together. Place the pate in the refrigerator and chill for 24 hours.

Remove from refrigerator, peel back plastic wrap and invert it onto serving plate(s). Lift off the terrine or ramekins and pull away plastic wrap. Garnish with fresh parsley and serve with toast points. - Serves 6 to 10

> **coarsely chopped shiitake mushrooms and 3 Tbs. of black truffle paste can be substituted, although it will not be quite the same.

*http://www.gourmetfoodstore.com/truffles/Summer-Black-French-Truffles-Plantin-details-5893.asp

http://www.amazon.com/Urbani-Black-Truffles-Paste-Tube/dp/B000ORGO5O/ref=sr_1_1?s=grocery&ie=UTF8&qid=1399023179&sr=1-1&keywords=black+truffle+paste

CRÈME BRULEE

- 2 cups whipping cream
- 5 egg yolks
- 1/2 cup sugar
- 1 tsp. pure vanilla extract
- Brown sugar
- Boiling water
- 6 Tbs. brown sugar

Preheat oven to 325° F.

In a medium saucepan, add the cream, egg yolks and sugar. Whisk until completely blended and cook over medium heat, stirring constantly until the mixture is thick enough to coat the back of a spoon. Stir in the vanilla.

Divide the custard into 6 custard cups. Place the cups in a rimmed bake pan and pour about 1 inch of boiling water to pan.

Place the pan in the oven for 30 minutes. Remove the pan from oven and carefully lift the custard cups from water bath. Let the custard cool at room temperature for 15 minutes. Cover each custard cup with plastic wrap and refrigerate for at least 4 hours.

To serve, turn broiler to high and place custard cups on a baking sheet. Sprinkle the top of the crème brulee with brown sugar.

Broil until sugar is caramelized, about 5 minutes (watch very closely - so not to burn the sugar). - Serves 6

WATERCRESS SALAD - A private table, lights dimmed; the end of an elegant repast.

- 1 lb. fresh watercress, washed, stems removed
- 1/2 cup Farmer's cheese, grated
- 1/2 cup fresh strawberries
- 1/4 cup pecans, chopped and toasted
- 1 clove garlic
- 1/4 cup fresh lemon juice
- 1 Tbs. sour cream
- 1 Tbs. sugar
- 1/2 cup vegetable oil

Place garlic in a food processor and pulse until finely chopped. Add lemon juice, sour cream and sugar and blend.

While the blade is turning, slowly add oil to emulsify the dressing.

Arrange the watercress on plates and drizzle with dressing. Top with cheese, strawberries and pecans and drizzle with more dressing. - Serves 4

BUTTER SCONES WITH ORANGE/HONEY BUTTER - A snack before shopping on Regent Street?

Butter:

- 1 stick unsalted butter, softened
- 2 Tbs. honey
- 2 tsp. orange zest

In a small bowl, use an electric hand mixer to whip the butter until light and fluffy. Mix in honey and orange zest. Transfer butter mixture to a serving bowl and allow it to remain at room temperature.

Butter Scones:

- 1-3/4 cups all purpose flour
- 3 Tbs. sugar
- 1/2 Tbs. baking powder
- 1/2 tsp. salt
- 1 stick unsalted butter, chilled and cut into small cubes
- 2 eggs, beaten with 1/4 cup milk

Preheat oven to 450° F.

In a large mixing bowl combine the flour, sugar, the baking powder and salt.

Add the cubes of butter and toss them with your hands until they are all separate and coated with flour.

Cut the butter into the flour with a fork until the bits of butter are about the size of BB s.

Pour the egg/milk mixture into the flour mixture and stir until combined (but do not over mix or scones will be tough).

Place the dough on a greased cookie sheet and gently pat it into a 10 inch round. The dough should be about 1/2 inch thick. Using a sharp knife cut dough into 8 wedges.

Bake the round for 10 minutes then remove it from oven and cut through the wedges again. Separate the wedges by about 1 inch. Place the scones back in oven and continue baking until golden brown. Serve the scones warm with the orange honey butter. - Serves 8

EGGS BENEDICT FLORENTINE - Breakfast at 3 o'clock sharp, with Hojicha tea, fresh and hot.

- 1 Tbs. cornstarch
- 1/2 cup water
- 1/3 cup half & half
- 2 eggs, beaten
- 2 Tbs. clarified butter
- Salt and pepper, to taste
- 2 tsp. olive oil
- 1 bunch spinach, cleaned and stemmed
- 1/2 tsp. garlic, minced
- 4 large eggs, poached
- 2 English muffins, split and toasted
- Paprika

Sauce:

Place the corn starch in a heat proof bowl set over a medium saucepan of simmering water. In a small bowl, whisk together the water, half and half and eggs until completely blended. Add the egg mixture to the cornstarch and whisk until combined. Whisking constantly, cook the sauce until it thickens, about 8 minutes. Add in the clarified butter, whisking until incorporated. Season the sauce to taste with salt and pepper. Remove from the heat, cover and let stand in a warm place.

Spinach:

In an iron skillet, over medium heat, add olive oil and then add spinach. Cook until wilted, about 1 minute. Add minced garlic and stir for an additional 30 seconds.

Poached Eggs:

Bring the medium pot of water back to a gentle simmer. Tear a square of microwave safe plastic wrap off a roll and lay it out flat on a work surface. Dribble a few drops of olive oil on the plastic wrap and spread it with fingers. Drape wrap over a small bowl and press the wrap down into the bowl. Crack egg into bowl. Gather the plastic wrap above the egg and tie it closed with a twist tie. Repeat with each additional egg.

Lower the packets into the simmering water for exactly 3 minutes. Remove the packets with a slotted spoon. Cut the plastic wrap just below the twist tie with kitchen shears and remove poached egg.

Top each toasted English muffin with a quarter of the spinach/garlic mixture, create a divot in the spinach and gently add a poached egg to each. Drizzle the eggs with the butter sauce and garnish with paprika. - Serves 4

"At last he reached the center of the bridge. And there she was: Captain Mason, at the helm, calmly looking out at him."

CEMETERY DANCE

CHARCUTERIE PLATE

STEAK BÉARNAISE

POMME FRITES

CREAMED SPINACH

LOIN OF VENISON

CHOCOLATE FONDUE

MALODOROUS CHEESE PLATE

GENOISE W/ CALVADOS BUTTER CREAM

BREAKFAST SANDWICH

PASTRAMI ON RYE

DECONSTRUCTED B.L.T.

SADDLE OF LAMB

BLUEBERRY PANCAKES

JELL-O BRAIN MOLD

CROWN RACK OF LAMB

CHICKEN IN BRANDY SAUCE

CHARCUTERIE PLATE - West 67th Street would be a perfect place for a romantic meal, but it's probably a long way off.

- 1/2 head romaine lettuce
- 1/8 lb. thinly sliced prosciutto
- 1/8 lb. thinly sliced soppressatta
- 1/8 lb. thinly sliced smoked turkey
- 1/8 lb. provolone cheese
- 1/4 lb. Asiago cheese
- 1/4 lb. smoked Gouda cheese
- 1/4 cup pickled pearl onions
- 1/2 cup gherkin pickles
- 2 Tbs. Dijon mustard
- 1/4 cup fig preserves
- 1/4 lb. marinated artichoke hearts, drained and quartered
- 1 large baguette, sliced into rounds

Arrange prosciutto, soppressatta, turkey, cheeses, onions and gherkins on a large platter draped with lettuce. Serve with the artichoke hearts, mustard and fig preserves in small bowls. Place baguette slices around the outside ring of the plate. Charcuterie plate should be served at room temperature. - Serves 6 to 8

STEAK BÉARNAISE

- 2 (10 oz.) sirloin steaks
- Salt and pepper

- Olive oil

Béarnaise Sauce:

- 1/4 cup dry white wine
- 1/4 cup white wine vinegar
- 2 shallots, minced
- 1/4 cup chopped fresh tarragon leaves
- 1/4 cup parsley, finely chopped
- 3 egg yolks
- 1/4 cup cold water
- 1 stick butter, melted
- Salt and pepper
- 2 sprigs of tarragon

Preheat oven to 450° F.

Combine the wine, vinegar, shallots, tarragon and parsley in a saucepan and bring to a boil. Reduce the heat to low and simmer. Reduce the mixture by about two-thirds. Remove the vinegar reduction from the heat and whisk in cold water and then egg yolks. Replace the saucepan over low heat and continue to whisk until the mixture thickens. Remove the sauce from the heat and whisk in the butter a little bit at a time. Pour the sauce through a wire strainer and into a second saucepan. Salt and pepper the sauce to taste and keep sauce warm on the back of the stove.

Heat an iron skillet over medium-high heat until extremely hot. Rub the steaks generously with olive oil and season with salt and pepper. Sear steaks until they lift off the skillet easily without sticking, flip and brown the second side. Place the skillet in the oven for 8 minutes. Remove skillet from oven, place steaks on a platter, cover with tin foil and allow them to rest for 10 minutes.

Thinly slice the steaks and arrange them in a fan on a heated plate. Ladle the Béarnaise sauce over the sliced steaks and topped with a sprig of tarragon. - Serves 2 large or 4 small portions

POMMES FRITES

- 8 large baking potatoes, well-scrubbed
- 12 oz. peanut oil
- 11.2 oz. duck fat*
- Sea salt

Cut potatoes in half, lengthwise. Now cut each piece in half lengthwise. Cut each quarter into long 1/4 inch thick slices. Stack the slices and cut into 1/4 thick inch sticks.

Place potato sticks in a large bowl of cold water to soak. Change water 2 times over the next 30 minutes to remove the excess starch and then continue soaking for 1 hour longer. Drain potatoes, and spread them out on paper towel to air dry.

Place peanut oil and duck fat in a large, deep pot or fryer. Use kitchen thermometer and heat oil to exactly 320° F. Blanch the potatoes, in batches, for 5 minutes. Remove from oil with a slotted spoon and allow them to drain on paper towels. Heat the pot of oil to exactly 375° F. Fry potatoes in batches, for 5 minutes or until golden brown. Remove to a plate draped with paper towel and season with sea salt.

*http://www.williams-sonoma.com/products/duck-fat/

CREAMED SPINACH

- 2 packages fresh, stemmed or 3 packages frozen chopped spinach, thawed
- 4 Tbs. olive oil
- 1 cup white onion, finely chopped
- Cloves garlic, minced
- 1-1/2 cups plain Greek yogurt
- Salt and pepper to taste
- 1/2 cup goat cheese, crumbled
- 1/4 cup mint leaves, chopped
- A pinch of nutmeg

Rinse and dry fresh spinach or place thawed spinach in a large kitchen towel and squeeze out any excess liquid and then set spinach aside. Pour olive oil into an iron skillet over medium heat. Place the garlic and onions in the skillet and cook, stirring constantly for 5 minutes.

Add spinach and cook for 5 minutes more. Reduce the heat to low and add the Greek yogurt to the spinach. Gently fold to combine and continue to cook for 3 minutes longer. Season the creamed spinach to taste with salt and just a pinch of nutmeg. Sprinkle each serving with goat cheese and chopped mint. - Serves 4

LOIN OF VENISON

- 2 venison loin medallions, 2 inches thick
- 1/2 cup blackberries
- 1 cup dry red wine
- 1 cup Swanson's beef broth
- 1 Tbs. balsamic vinegar
- 1 Tbs. orange blossom honey
- Salt and pepper to taste
- Olive oil

Remove venison from refrigerator and allow the meat to reach room temperature, about 30 minutes.

Add the wine to an iron skillet over a high heat and cook for 2 minutes. Reduce the heat to low and add the blackberries, vinegar and broth. Simmer the sauce for about 10 minutes until blackberries have cooked down. Add the salt, pepper and honey to taste. Transfer to a small pot, cover and keep warm.

Salt and pepper both sides of the venison steaks and rub them with olive oil. Clean out and then heat the skillet until extremely hot and sear the steaks for 2 to 3 minutes on each side.

Remove the steaks and allow the meat to rest 5 minutes, then slice thin and arrange in a fan on a pool of blackberry sauce. - Serves 2

CHOCOLATE FONDUE

- 1 cup semi-sweet chocolate chips
- 2 Tbs. butter
- 1 (14 ounce can) sweetened condensed milk
- 2 Tbs. water
- 1 tsp. pure vanilla extract

In small saucepan, over medium heat, combine chocolate chips, butter, condensed milk and water. Cook and stir constantly until thickened, about 5 minutes. Remove from heat. Add vanilla.

Serve warm with pieces of fruit, pound cake and marshmallows. - Serves 2 to 4

MALODOROUS FRENCH CHEESE PLATE

- 1 bunch kale, rinsed
- 8 oz. Monte Enebro
- 8 oz. Quadrello di Bufala
- 8 oz. Epoisses
- 8 oz. Pecorino Foglie de Noce
- 8 oz. Caveman Blue
- 1 bunch white grapes
- 4 peaches, pitted and sliced
- 4 oz. fig preserves
- 12 oz. salted mixed nuts
- 1 baguette, slice into rounds

Spread the kale leaves out over a large platter. Arrange cheeses and fruit with a bowl of fig preserves to the center. Sprinkle platter with mixed nuts and place baguette rounds to the side. - Serves 4 to 8

PRALINE GENOISE WITH CALVADOS BUTTER CREAM - The corner Patisserie has nothing on you, big boy.

Sponge Cake:

- 1/4 cup unsalted butter, melted and warmed
- 1 cup cake flour, plus some for dusting pan
- 8 eggs, separated
- 1 cup sugar
- 2 tsp. pure vanilla extract
- 1/4 tsp. salt

Preheat the oven to 325° F.

Melt butter in a small bowl in the microwave, and then set it aside to cool.

Spray the bottom and sides of a 10 inch spring form pan with cooking spray and line the bottom with a round of parchment. Spray the paper and dust the inside of the pan with flour. Shake the flour around in the pan and then dump out any excess into the sink.

Sift the cake flour three times into a bowl using a wire strainer and set aside.

Using an electric hand mixer, whip the yolks, in a medium bowl, on medium speed 3 minutes until they thicken and turn a pale yellow. After the 3 minutes, gradually start adding 1/2 cup of the sugar, about 3 Tbs. at a time. Beat for 30 seconds, then add 3 more Tbs. and repeat. Once the sugar is added, beat at high speed for 5 minutes and then mix in the vanilla. Transfer the egg/sugar mixture into a second bowl and wash and dry the mixing bowl and the beaters.

Combine egg whites with the salt in the mixing bowl and mix on low for 1 minute. Increase the speed to medium-high for 5 minutes. With the mixer running, gradually add the remaining 1/2 cup of sugar. Continue beating medium-high speed for 2 minutes.

Gently fold 1/2 of the whites into the yolks. Sift 1/2 of the cake flour over the mixture and scoop the remaining whites over the flour. Fold together gently and then sift the remaining flour onto the batter and fold gently until the batter has no streaks and is an even color.

Drizzle half of the warm melted butter on top of the batter and fold 6 times. Add the remaining butter and fold 10 times, then pour the batter into the pan.

Bake about 35 minutes or until cake is golden brown and springy to the touch. Let the cake cool in the pan for 10 minutes, and then unclasp. Let cool completely before removing the bottom of the pan and the paper liner.

Praline Filling:

- 1-1/2 cups chopped pecans
- 3 Tbs. butter
- 1/2 cup light brown sugar
- 3 Tbs. whipping cream
- 1/2 cup powdered sugar
- 1/2 tsp. pure vanilla extract

Preheat oven to 350° F.

Bake pecans for 15 minutes or until golden brown.

Bring butter, brown sugar, and cream to a boil in a medium saucepan over medium heat. Allow to cook 1 minute, stirring constantly. Remove from heat; add the powdered sugar and vanilla. Whisk until smooth. Add pecans (1 cup reserved for garnish) and fold gently for 3 minutes.

Icing:

- 2/3 cup sugar
- 3 Tbs. water
- 6 egg yolks
- Pinch of salt
- 2 sticks butter, softened and cut into 8 pieces
- 1 tsp. pure vanilla extract
- 2 Tbs. Calvados (apple brandy)
- 1 store bought praline candy (optional)

Add the sugar and water to a small saucepan over medium heat with a kitchen thermometer attached. Place the egg yolks and salt to a mixing bowl and beat on high speed with an electric mixer until the eggs thicken.

When the thermometer in the sugar syrup reaches 238, remove it from heat. With the mixer on low speed, slowly drizzle the syrup into the yolks. Turn the mixer up to high speed and beat until the mixture has cooled, about 10 minutes. When the mixing bowl feels cool to the touch, begin adding the butter, one piece at a time. Mix well before adding another.

Now add the vanilla and Calvados and continue to beat until frosting is smooth.

Slice cake into 3 layers using a long length of dental floss. Spread the praline filling and reassemble the layers. Frost the cakes top first and then the side. Pat the reserved pecans into the frosting on the side of the cake. Use just enough pressure to ensure the pecan coating sticks to the frosting. Top the cake with the praline candy. - Serves 8 to 10

BREAKFAST SANDWICH WITH EGGS, GREEN PEPPERS, LETTUCE AND TOMATO - A police scanner crackling, this month's Vanity Fair and half your sandwich in your lap. Yeah, that's breakfast.

- 2 (10 inch) soft Italian rolls
- 4 Tbs. butter, melted
- 1 tsp. olive oil
- 1/2 cup green bell pepper, chopped
- 6 eggs
- 2 Tbs. milk
- 6 slices American cheese
- 6 slices ham or 8 slices cooked bacon
- 1 cup lettuce, finely shredded
- 6 slices tomato
- Salt and pepper
- Olive oil

Split Italian rolls lengthwise. Brush the inside of rolls with butter. Heat a large iron skillet over medium-high heat and brown the cut sides of roll and set aside.

Add olive oil to skillet still on medium-high and sauté green pepper until soft. Mix eggs and milk in a medium mixing bowl. Add egg mixture to the skillet, wait 30 seconds and stir once. Cover the skillet and allow eggs to set, about 3 minutes.

Remove skillet from heat and divide eggs in half. Using a spatula, transfer half the eggs to the bottom slice of each Italian roll. Top the eggs with ham or bacon, and then the cheese. Spread the shredded lettuce over the cheese and top with tomatoes. Salt and pepper to taste and drizzle with olive oil. - Serves 2 to 4

PASTRAMI ON RYE WITH WARM RUSSIAN DRESSING - Lean and warm, just the way you like it.

Warm Russian Dressing:

- 1/2 cup sour cream
- 2 Tbs. Heinz ketchup
- 1 Tbs. prepared horseradish
- 1 tsp. Worcestershire sauce
- 2 gherkin pickles, minced
- 2 Tbs. red onion, minced
- 1 tsp. fresh lemon juice
- Salt and pepper to taste

In a small saucepan over low heat, combine all ingredients and mix well. Set aside covered and keep warm.

- 1 lb. thin sliced pastrami
- 4 slices Swiss cheese
- 1/4 cup water
- 4 slices rye bread, lightly toasted
- Warm Russian dressing
- 4 garlic dill pickle spears

In a large iron skillet, over medium high, make 2 half-pound mounds of pastrami about the size of the bread. Place the mounds in the skillet and add 2 slices of cheese to each mound. Pour water in the pan and cover to steam the meat and melt cheese briefly.

Remove the lid and place the mounds of pastrami on the rye bread. Pour a liberal amount of warm Russian dressing over the meat and cheese and top with remaining bread slices. Cut sandwich on the diagonal and serve with pickle spears. - Serves 2

DECONSTRUCTED B L T – There's no need to deal with harassed waitresses when you make this at home.

- 10 slices bacon, diced into 1/2 inch slices
- 12 small plum tomatoes
- 3 cups iceberg lettuce, chopped
- 4 Tbs. ranch dressing
- 1/4 cup seasoned croutons, crushed
- Fresh cracked pepper

In an iron skillet over medium heat, cook the diced bacon until crisp; drain on paper towels.

Using a small sharp knife cut each tomato in half. Use a small spoon to remove the interior from each tomato half, thus creating cute little tomato bowls.

 In a bowl, toss lettuce and ranch dressing together. Next, fill tomato bowls with the lettuce mixture. Sprinkle with bacon and croutons. Season with black pepper.- Serves 12 to 24

CROWN RACK OF LAMB - Twelve ninety-nine would be an excellent price for a cut like this.

- 1 crown roast of lamb (ask butcher to prepare one)
- 1 Tbs. vegetable oil
- 1-1/2 tsp. salt, divided
- 1/2 tsp. pepper

- 2 cups cooked wild rice
- 1/2 lb. Portobello mushrooms, sliced
- 1/2 lb. white mushrooms, sliced
- 2 shallots, finely diced
- 1/4 tsp. chopped fresh parsley
- 2 Tbs. butter, melted

Preheat oven to 325° F.

Coat a roasting pan well with cooking spray and place roast in pan, standing upright.

In a small bowl, combine oil, 1 tsp. salt, and pepper. Mix well and rub it over the entire roast.

In a medium bowl, combine rice, mushrooms, shallots, parsley, butter, and remaining salt. Mix well, and then place rice mixture in center of the roast. Wrap ends of rib bones with tin foil to keep them from burning.

Roast for 1 to 1-1/2 hours or until a kitchen thermometer registers 160° F. Transfer the roast to a platter (be care the stuffing doesn't fall out the bottom) and allow it to rest for 15 minutes. Remove the tin foil caps before slicing between the bones. - Serves 6

CREAM CHEESE BLUEBERRY PANCAKES - Overworking and feeling guilty? This will fix things right up.

- 4 oz. cream cheese, softened
- 2 eggs, lightly beaten
- 1 cup all purpose flour
- 2-1/2 tsp. baking powder
- 1/2 tsp. salt
- 4 Tbs. sugar
- 1/2 cup light brown sugar
- 1 tsp. cinnamon
- 1 Tbs. lemon juice
- 1-1/4 cup milk
- 2 Tbs. butter, melted
- 2 tsp. pure vanilla extract
- 2 cup blueberries, fresh

Whip the cream cheese until smooth with an electric hand mixer. Add in eggs, lemon juice, milk, and melted butter; mix on low for 3 minutes.

Sift together the flour, baking powder, salt, sugar, brown sugar and cinnamon. Add half of the dry ingredients to the cream cheese mixture and fold to incorporate with a rubber spatula. Add in the last of the dry ingredients and fold again but try not to over mix.

Next, gently fold in the vanilla and fresh blueberries. Pour batter by the 1/2 cup full onto a hot, greased griddle. Let cook on one side until little bubbles start to form in the batter. Flip and cook until golden brown .Serve with pure Highland county maple syrup and butter. - Serves 4

JELL-O BRAIN MOLD - It's not a movie prop, it's dessert.

- Two (6 oz.) boxes peach Jell-O
- 1-3/4 cups boiling water
- 3/4 cup cold water
- 9 oz. fat-free evaporated milk, chilled
- 15 drops each of red, green and blue food coloring

Spray inside of the brain mold with a small amount of cooking spray and place the mold in a shallow bowl so it will sit level *.

Place Jell-O in a large bowl and add boiling water. Stir 2 minutes until mix is dissolved. Stir in 1 cup of cold water, evaporated milk and food coloring and stir well.

Pour the mixture into the brain mold and refrigerate until firm.

Shake the mold until the gelatin loosens, then place a flat plate upside down over the mold. Flip the mold and the plate together. Jiggle the mold off, leaving the brain on the plate.

*http://www.amazon.com/Human-Brain-Gelatin-Halloween-Party/dp/B000XEX8IE

MACADAMIA RACK OF LAMB – Wrapping a rack of lamb in bacon? Not a hard thing to get away with.

- 1-1/2 lb. rack of lamb – Frenched
- 1/3 cup macadamia nuts
- 1 Tbs. thyme
- 2 tsp. rosemary
- 1/3 cup dried pineapple
- 1/3 cup unsweetened coconut
- 1/4 cup coconut oil (olive oil if you can't find coconut)
- Salt and pepper
- 12 oz. package of thick cut bacon

Preheat the oven to 400° F.

Finely chop macadamia nuts with the thyme and rosemary in a food processor. Add the coconut oil, pineapple and coconut and pulse to a paste; season with salt and pepper.

Coat the lamb with half of the paste. Wrap the bacon slices around the lamb, between the bones and then spread the remaining macadamia paste over the bacon. Set the rack in a roasting pan.

Roast the rack for about 40 minutes for medium-rare. Transfer the lamb to a cutting board and let rest for 5 minutes before craving. - Serves 4

This recipe can be doubled and the lamb "crowned" if desired.

CHICKEN IN BRANDY SAUCE - So good, you'd be happy to ruin a brand new suit over it.

- 2 large boneless, skinless chicken breasts
- Salt and pepper
- 1/2 cup flour
- 1 cup chicken broth
- 1/4 cup brandy
- 1 Tbs. butter
- 1 tsp. lemon juice
- 3 Tbs. extra virgin olive oil
- 1/8 cup Italian parsley

Cut chicken breasts in half to create 4 equal portions.

Slip the breast portions in a 1 gallon Ziploc bag one at a time and pound flat with the edge of a fry pan until chicken pieces are 1/2 inch thick. Season chicken on both sides with salt and pepper to taste.

Heat an iron skillet over medium heat. Place the flour in a bowl and dredge each chicken portion. Place the olive oil to pan and allow it to come up to temperature.

Brown chicken 3 minutes per side or until golden brown. Remove chicken from the pan and cover with some tin foil to it keep warm.

Adjust heat to medium-high and whisk in the chicken broth to deglaze the skillet. Carefully add brandy (be careful for flare-ups), lemon juice and black pepper.

Simmer until sauce reduces by half. Reduce heat to low; add butter and whisk to combine. Place chicken cutlets on a platter and pour the sauce over top. Garnish with chopped parsley. - Serves 2 to 4

"...a Guillotine, blade down, a body sprawled on the platform; and in the tumbrel below, a fresh head."

BRIMSTONE

GRILLED CHORIZO

EGGS BENEDICT W/ TARRAGON SAUCE

BROILED DOVER SOLE

BEEF MEDALLIONS W/ BURGUNDY SAUCE

JULIENNE CARROTS

CAESAR SALAD

LEMON SHERBET

NEW YORK STYLE CHEESEBURGER

FUSSY SOUTH HAMPTON SANDWICH

COUNT FOSCO'S PICNIC

TOURNEDOS BORDELAISES

GREEN CHILI BEEF JERKY

PAUPIETTE OF SEA BASS

BRAISED PIGS FEET AND CHEEKS

HOMEMADE DOUGHNUTS

MADONNA'S FRENCH FRIES W/ KETCHUP

BETTY DAYE'S CHICKEN FRIED STEAK

DUCK MAGRET

SCALLOP A L'ETUVE'E

LINGUINI W/ WHITE TRUFFLE SAUCE

VINNIE'S CHEESEBURGER AND FRIES

TIRAMISU GELATO

CRÈME ANGLAISE GELATO

ITALIAN STYLE PANINI

CHICKEN BREAST W/ GRAVY

GREEN BEANS & CARROTS

GRILLED CHORIZO - We advocate a different grilling method than the one used on Mr. Jeremy.

- 2 chorizo sausage link
- 2 ciabatta roll
- 4 roasted piquillo peppers
- 6 arugula lettuce leaves
- Olive oil

Butterfly the chorizo links and grill or broil them along with the peppers, well charred.

Remove the sausages and allow them to rest for a few minutes.

Slice the ciabatta rolls and toast them to a light golden brown. Drizzle the rolls with olive oil; add the piquillo peppers then the arugula and the chorizo sausage. - Serves 2

EGGS BENEDICT WITH TARRAGON HOLLANDAISE SAUCE - Could be the best hollandaise this side of Paris, just don't tell the "beautiful people."

- 2 pieces of Canadian bacon
- 2 eggs
- 2 English muffins, split
- Butter, softened
- 2 Tbs. chopped parsley, for garnish

Sauce:

- 10 Tbs. butter, softened
- 3 egg yolks
- 1 Tbs. lemon juice
- 1/2 tsp. salt
- 2 tsp. dried tarragon

Bring a large saucepan, half way filled with water, to boil. Place a stainless steel bowl that will sit on top of the saucepan, but be sure it does not actually touch the water (or use a double boiler, if you have one). Whisk egg yolks in the bowl with lemon juice, water and salt. Put bowl of sauce ingredients above the rapidly boiling water and whisk until it becomes very thick. This will take about 2 minutes. Whisk in butter and tarragon. Set the sauce aside and keep it warm.

Lightly grill the Canadian bacon and set aside.

Fill 2 heavy coffee mugs half way with water. Gently crack an egg into the water of each cup. Make sure the eggs are completely submerged. Cover the cups with plastic wrap and microwave on high for 1 minute and 15 seconds or until the whites are set but the yolks are still runny.

Butter the toasted English muffin halves. Top with slice of Canadian bacon. Gently place a poached egg on top of meat, and then pour the warm tarragon hollandaise over the eggs. Garnish with some chopped parsley. - Serves 2

BROILED DOVER SOLE - Is there a Dr. Faustus on the guest list for this delectable feast?

- 2 Dover sole fillets
- 2 tsp. olive oil
- 1 Tbs. melted butter
- 2 Tbs. lemon juice
- 2 garlic cloves, minced
- 1/4 tsp. oregano
- Paprika for dusting

Set the oven rack to the broil position and turn oven to broil.

Lay fish fillets on a well greased iron skillet. Mix together olive oil, butter, lemon juice, garlic and oregano; brush fish with mixture. Lightly dust fish with paprika.

Broil the fish fillets approximately 4 to 6 minutes or until fish is opaque but not dried out. - Serves 2

BEEF MEDALLIONS WITH BURGUNDY SAUCE

Sauce:

- 1/2 cup onion, finely minced
- 1 cup good Burgundy
- 1/3 cup balsamic vinegar
- 1 bay leaf
- 1/2 tsp. black pepper
- 1 cup demi-glace *
- 2/3 cup button mushrooms, sliced
- 1/2 tsp. dried thyme

Add shallots, Burgundy, vinegar, bay leaves, thyme, and pepper to medium saucepan. Simmer the sauce over medium heat for about 20 minutes. Add the mushrooms and demi-glace and simmer for 10 more minutes. Reduce heat and cover the saucepan to keep sauce warm while cooking meat.

Beef:

- 6 (5oz.) beef tenderloin medallions
- 6 Tbs. butter
- Salt and pepper to taste

Heat butter in an iron skillet, over medium-high heat. Season the meat on both sides with salt and pepper. Sear for 4 minutes each side for rare. Let meat rest 5 minutes and serve with the Burgundy sauce. - Serves 2 to 6

*http://www.amazon.com/More-Than-Gourmet-Demi-glace-16-Ounce/dp/B0010OQQ2Q/ref=sr_1_3?s=grocery&ie=UTF8&qid=1372011524&sr=1-3&keywords=beef+demi+glace

JULIENNE CARROTS

To julienne a carrot, first cut both ends off the carrot and peel. Cut the carrot into 3-inch long chunks. Slice lengthwise along one side of the carrot so it will lay flat and won't roll around on you when cutting. Cut carrot into thin slices lengthwise. Stack a few slices on top of each other and slice again lengthwise so they are about the size of a wooden matchstick.

- 2 Tbs. butter
- 1/4 cup brown sugar
- 4 cups julienne carrots
- 1/4 tsp. salt
- 1/4 tsp. black pepper
- 1/4 cup chopped parsley

Melt butter in an iron skillet over medium heat; add sugar and stir. Add carrots, salt, and pepper and cook 10 minutes until carrots are tender, stirring occasionally. Top with the chopped parsley. - Serves 2 to 4

CAESAR SALAD

Dressing:

- 4 anchovy fillets
- 1 garlic clove, minced
- 1 cup Hellmann's mayonnaise
- 1/4 cup milk
- 1/2 cup grated Parmesan cheese
- 2 Tbs. lemon juice
- 1 Tbs. coarse brown prepared mustard
- Salt and pepper to taste

Place all ingredients in food processor and pulse until blended.

- 2 large heads romaine lettuce
- Fresh grated Parmesan cheese

Coarsely chop up the lettuce and toss in the dressing. Top with grated Parmesan cheese. - Serves 4

LEMON SHERBET

- 2 cups sugar
- 3 cups cold water
- Zest of 2 lemons
- 2 cup fresh squeezed lemon juice

Combine the sugar, water and lemon zest in a medium pot. Turn on the burner to high and bring to a boil. Allow mixture to boil for 5 minutes, stirring occasionally.

Remove the pot from the burner and allow syrup to cool.

Pour lemon juice into the cooled sugar syrup and refrigerate for 2 hours or until cold.

Pour the sorbet mixture into an ice cream maker* and freeze as recommended.

(This recipe works well with oranges or limes as well) - Serves 4

* http://www.amazon.com/Donvier-837409W-1-Quart-Cream-Maker/dp/B00006484E/ref=sr_1_22?s=kitchen&ie=UTF8&qid=1372033505&sr=1-22

NEW YORK STYLE CHEESEBURGER - Now here's a heart-warming thought.

New York Sauce:

- 1/2 cup Hellmann's mayonnaise

- 1 Tbs. Heinz ketchup
- 1 Tbs. yellow mustard
- 4 slices garlic dill pickle
- 1/4 tsp. garlic powder
- 1/4 tsp. paprika
- A dash of cayenne pepper

Combine all ingredients in a food processor until completely smooth.

New York Burger:

- 8 oz. ground sirloin
- 8 oz. ground chuck
- 3 Tbs. butter, melted
- 4 burger buns
- 8 lettuce leaves
- 8 thick slices of tomatoes
- 1/2 tsp. vegetable oil
- Salt and pepper
- 4 slices Velveeta cheese

Combine the ground meats in large bowl and blend by hand, but do not over mix. Gently form meat into four balls and season both sides with salt and pepper.

Open buns and brush lightly with butter, then place them under a broiler and toast until golden brown. Spread 1 Tbs. of sauce on top half of the buns. Lay 1 or 2 leaves of lettuce and 2 slices tomato on top half , over the sauce.

Coat the inside of a large iron skillet with vegetable oil. Place skillet over medium-high heat for about 5 minutes, so it gets nice and hot. Place burgers in the hot skillet.

Use the back of a metal spatula to press down hard on burgers, forming them into round patties. Allow the burgers cook for 1 to 2 minutes undisturbed.

Using the metal spatula, scrape the burgers from skillet and flip them over. Immediately top each burger with the cheese and cook about 1 to 2 minutes longer. Transfer patties to burger bun bottoms, close the buns and wrap them in sheets of paper towel for at least 1 minute before serving to steam them. - Serves 4

FUSSY SOUTHAMPTON SANDWICH - You'd pay, like, 15 bucks for a sandwich like this in The Hamptons.

- 12 oz. thinly sliced pancetta
- 2 thick slices (green zebra) heirloom tomato
- 1 avocado, pitted, sliced and peeled
- 1/4 cup fresh cilantro, coarsely chopped
- 2 Tbs. extra virgin olive oil
- 1 tsp. dried oregano
- Alderwood smoked salt
- Freshly ground black pepper
- 4 slices brioche, lightly toasted
- 4 oz. Camembert cheese, sliced
- 2 cups baby arugula

Cook pancetta in an iron skillet over medium heat until brown and crisp, about 5 minutes. Transfer to paper towels to drain.

Place tomato slices in small bowl and add basil, olive oil, oregano, and salt. Season with ground black pepper and gently toss to coat. Let the tomato slices marinade while you prepare the sauce.

Sauce:

- 1/2 cup Hellmann's mayonnaise
- 1/2 tsp. smoked paprika
- 1/4 tsp. ground cumin
- 1 Tbs. pancetta drippings
- Salt
- Pepper

Stir together mayonnaise, paprika, cumin and the drippings, add salt and pepper to taste.

Place 2 toasted bread slices on a clean work surface. Divide the cheese among bread slices. Top each with 3 slices avocado, 1 tomato slice and then pancetta, dividing equally. Top with arugula. Generously spread the sauce on remaining 2 toasted bread slices, and gently press on top on sandwich. Cut each sandwich in half and serve. - Serves 2

COUNT FOSCO'S PICNIC - All you'll need to find is a stone table and a copper beech to make it a perfect picnic.

- 1/2 lb. Grana Padano
- 1/2 lb. Robiola Bosina
- 1/2 lb. Asiago Pressato
- 1/2 lb. Pecorino Oro Antico
- 1/2 lb. Cacciota di Capra con Pepe
- 1/2 lb. Olli salami
- 1/2 lb. La Quercia prosciutto
- 8 oz. mixed olives
- 4 oz. tin paddlefish caviar**

- 4 oz. tin French Rougie Duck Foie Gras
- 3 loaves Pane con le Olive
- Italian Crostini
- 2 bottles Villa Calcinaia Chianti Classico Riserva Toscana

All items may be purchase online* or at specialty store. Wrap all the above items well and place in a wicker picnic basket with glasses, silverware and a white table cloth. - 6 to 8 (or just a snack for Fosco)

*http://www.murrayscheese.com/search?q=Cacciota+di+Capra+con+Pepe

**http://www.amazon.com/s/ref=nb_sb_noss?url=search-alias%3Daps&field-keywords=American-Paddlefish-Caviar-2-Ounce

***http://www.amazon.com/s/ref=nb_sb_noss?url=search-alias%3Daps&field-keywords=Rougie-Mousse-Duck-Truffle-11-2-Ounce&rh=i%3Aaps%2Ck%3ARougie-Mousse-Duck-Truffle-11-2-Ounce

TOURNEDOS BORDELAISE - Keep this waiting in the wings; along with a cold beer – just in case.

Beef:

- 4 beef tenderloin steaks (filet mignon), 2 inches thick
- 4 strips bacon
- Salt and freshly ground black pepper
- 2 Tbs. olive oil
- 1 Tbs. butter

Sauce:

- 1/4 stick butter
- 1/4 tsp. crushed black peppercorn
- 2 Tbs. olive oil
- 1/4 cup shallot, finely chopped
- 1/2 cup Madeira
- 1 to 2 cups demi-glace*
- 2 tsp. dried tarragon (2 Tbs. fresh)
- 1 tsp. dried thyme (1 Tbs. fresh)
- 1 Tbs. parsley, chopped

Croutons:

- 4 thick slices of any artisan bread
- 2 Tbs. softened butter
- 2 Tbs. prepared basil pesto

Mix together butter and pesto, toast the bread slices until golden brown and spread with butter mixture. Set the croutons aside.

Season the meat well with salt and pepper. Wrap the sides of meat with bacon and secure with toothpicks. Melt the butter and olive oil in a large iron skillet over medium-high heat until the mixture starts to brown slightly. Cook the tenderloins 4 minutes per side or until internal temperature is 130 for rare. Transfer the meat to a warmed plate, and cover with tin foil, allowing the meat to rest for 10 minutes.

In the same pan, and at the same heat, melt remaining butter and olive oil for the sauce. Add shallots and sauté for 2 minutes or until transparent. Add wine and simmer for 3 minutes. Add thyme, tarragon and peppercorns and reduce further for 3 minutes.

Add demi-glace to pan and simmer for about 5 minutes or until sauce thickens.

Place beef on serving plates on top of croutons, remove the toothpicks and drizzle the steaks with the wine sauce and garnish with chopped parsley.

Serve with sautéed mushrooms, Chateau potatoes and a cold Budweiser. - Serves 4

- For a demi-glace substitute, use a jar of beef gravy, a can of beef broth, a tablespoon of tomato paste and 1/2 cup of red wine, combine these and bring to the boil and simmer for 15 minutes stirring occasionally.

GREEN CHILI BEEF JERKY - Best enjoyed while pondering the London Times crosswords.

- 2 lbs. top round beef
- 1 cup green chili powder
- 1/4 cup kosher salt
- 1/4 cup black pepper, ground

Preheat oven to 150° F.

Place beef in freezer for 30 to 45 minutes in order to make it easier to slice.

Cut beef across the grain into 1/8 inch thick slices.

In a shallow dish, add chili powder, salt and pepper and mix well. Dredge the meat slices in this mixture.

Place the seasoned meat on wire racks place on a large roasting pan. Place the pan in an oven at 150 overnight or until dry and chewy.

PAUPIETTE OF SEA BASS - Paired with a nice Cakebread chardonnay, this is a deal at twice the price.

Fish:

- 4 skinless sea bass fillets, about 8 oz. each
- 4 Tbs. fresh thyme, chopped
- 2 very large baking potatoes, washed and peeled
- 4 Tbs. butter/olive oil mixture, melted
- Salt and white pepper

Sauce:

- 1 Tbs. olive oil
- 1/2 cup shallots, peeled and chopped
- 1/2 cup mushrooms, sliced
- 1 Tbs. fresh thyme
- 1 cup chicken stock
- 1 bottle dry red wine
- 2 Tbs. heavy cream
- 1/2 cup butter
- Salt and white pepper

Leek Bed:

- 2 Tbs. butter
- 2 leeks, cut into 1-inch strips and cleaned of all sand
- White pepper
- Sea salt

Trim each fillet a few inches from the edge, making them into rectangles about 2 x 5 inches. Salt and pepper the fillets and sprinkle with chopped thyme.

Using a mandolin slicer*, cut each potato along the long side into 20 very thin slices. Place a large sheet of plastic wrap on a work surface. Put 2 potato slices horizontally a bit below the center of the plastic wrap, overlapping their ends by about 1/4 of an inch. Keep overlapping the potato slices in pairs, building up vertically until you have a 5-row sheet of potato for the fillet.

Center the filet on the potato sheet and fold the edges of the potatoes over to enclose. Fold plastic wrap over the bundle and seal. Repeat with the other fillets. Refrigerate for 15 minutes or until ready to cook.

For the sauce, heat the oil in a saucepan over medium-high heat. Add shallots, mushrooms, and thyme. Cook for 8 to 10 minutes. Add the chicken stock and simmer until almost dry. Add the wine, bring to a boil and reduce until almost dry. Reduce heat to low and add the heavy cream. Whisk in the butter and add salt and pepper to taste. Pass the finished sauce through a strainer, reserving the mushrooms and shallots. Cover and keep the sauce warm.

To cook the fish, carefully remove bundles from the plastic wrap. Brush the entire bundle's surface with melted butter/olive oil mixture. Pour the remaining butter/olive oil mixture into a large nonstick pan over medium-high heat. Sauté the bundles until golden brown, about 2 to 3 minutes on each of the sides and the edges.

To make the leek bed, melt the butter in a pan over medium heat. Add the leeks and cook until soft, about 5 minutes. Add salt and pepper to taste. Keep warm.

To finish the dish, place a bed of leeks in the center of 4 plates and dribble the sauce around the leeks. Nest a sea bass bundle on top of the leeks. Spoon the reserved mushrooms and shallots on the fish. Sprinkle the top of the fish with a pinch of course sea salt and some fresh thyme. - Serves 4

http://www.amazon.com/The-Sharper-Image-Stainless-Adjustable/dp/B009V9CEGE/ref=sr_1_11?s=home-garden&ie=UTF8&qid=1400025288&sr=1-11&keywords=mandoline+slicer

BRAISED PIGS FEET AND CHEEKS - This appetizer is nothing to turn your nose up at, go on and give it a try.

- 5 lbs. split pig's feet
- 4 pig's cheeks
- Flour, seasoned with salt and pepper, for dusting
- 2 onions cut into chunks
- 3 large carrots cut into chunks
- 2 sticks celery cut into chunks
- 1 clove garlic, chopped
- 2 Tbs. tomato purée
- 1/2 bottle good red wine (the other half for the cook)
- 2 tsp. caraway seeds
- 1 bay leaf
- 1 chicken bouillon cube
- Water
- 3 Tbs. vegetable oil
- Salt and pepper to taste

Dust the cheeks and feet in seasoned flour. Pour vegetable oil into a 6 quart stock pot over medium-high heat. When the oil is hot, brown the meat on all sides, then remove them to a bowl and set aside.

Add all the veggies and bouillon to the pot and cook over medium high heat about 5 minutes. Place the meat back to the pot and add the red wine. Fill the pot with water until just covering the meat. Add caraway seeds and bay leaves.

Bring the pot to a boil and let it cook for 10 minutes. Cover, and reduce heat to medium-low.

Simmer for 2 hours, or until the meat is fork tender. To finish the dish, add the tomato purée and cook for 10 more minutes. - Serves 6

QUICK HOMEMADE FLAKEY DOUGHNUTS - (CROW - KNOTS)

- 2 cans flakey biscuits
- 2 tsp. ground cinnamon
- 1/2 cup sugar
- 4 Tbs. butter
- Vegetable oil, for frying

Blend the ground cinnamon and sugar together in a small bowl. In second bowl, melt the butter in a microwave.

Heat about 1/2 inch of vegetable oil, in an iron (even better, an electric skillet) so the oil reaches 350° F.

Spread out the biscuits on a clean surface and with a 1-inch biscuit cutter, empty shotgun shell or pill bottle, cut out a hole from the middle of each biscuit.

Fry in the oil, a few at a time, until lightly brown and then flip and fry the other side. Drain doughnuts on a brown paper bag. Dip in butter and toss in the cinnamon-sugar. - Makes 16 doughnuts

MADONNA'S FRENCH FRIES WITH HOUSE KETCHUP -
Take a moment between mouthfuls and......strike a pose.

- 2 lbs. potatoes
- Vegetable oil or duck fat* for frying
- Salt

Peel and cut the potatoes into sticks 1/2 inch thick. Soak the cut potatoes for several minutes in large bowls of cold water. Drain the potatoes and dry them on a towel.

Heat the oil to 325° F in an electric deep fat fryer. Deep fry the potatoes in batches. Drain the fries and place them in a brown paper bag.

When ready to serve, heat the oil to 375 and fry the potatoes a second time, until crisp and golden. Drain, add salt and serve while hot. - Serves 2 to 4

http://www.amazon.com/More-Than-Gourmet-Rendered-12-Ounce/dp/B009R8BI98/ref=pd_sim_sbs_gro_3?ie=UTF8&ref RID=0TGND27K835F14Q25B5M

House Ketchup:

- 2 (14.5 oz.) cans of whole, peeled tomatoes in juice
- 1 green pepper, finely diced
- 2 white onions, finely diced
- 3/4 cup brown sugar
- 1/2 cup vinegar
- 1 tsp. Dijon mustard
- 1/2 tsp. cinnamon
- 1/4 ground cloves
- 1/2 tsp. chili powder
- Salt to taste

Cook all ingredients in a medium saucepan for 30 minutes over medium heat until most the liquid has boiled away and the tomatoes have broken down (be sure not to burn the mixture). Pour half the mixture into a food processor and pulse until smooth and return it to the pot. Stir to incorporate and transfer to a non-metallic container. Refrigerate until serving.

BETTY DAYE'S CHICKEN FRIED STEAK - This is considered to be gourmet fare in Radium Hot Springs.

Ground Steaks:

- 1 egg
- 1/2 cup milk
- 3/4 cup self rising flour
- 1 tsp. Lawry's seasoned salt
- 1/2 tsp. ground black pepper
- 1/2 tsp. garlic powder
- 1 lb. lean ground beef
- Oil, for frying

Milk Gravy:

- 3 Tbs. excess seasoned dredging flour
- 3 Tbs. oil
- 1 cup milk, warm

Beat together egg and the 1/2 cup milk in a shallow dish and set aside.

Mix together 3/4 cup of flour, Lawry's season salt, pepper, and garlic powder in a 9 inch pie tin.

Divide ground beef into three equal parts and shape them into ovals about 1/4 inches thick.

Add each ground steak to the egg mixture, coating both sides. Then dredge them well in seasoned flour.

Heat oil in an iron skillet to 375° F and add the ground steaks to the hot oil. Cook and flip steaks until both sides are golden brown. Remove the fried steaks from the oil, drain on a paper towel lined plate and keep warm with tented tin foil.

Drain all but 3 Tbs. of the oil from the skillet. Add 3 Tbs. of the seasoned flour and stir into oil to form a paste or roux. Cook this mixture for about 5 minutes on medium heat, stirring constantly. Whisk in the warm milk a little at a time until desired thickness is reached. Pour the milk gravy over the steaks and serve hot. - Serves 3

DUCK MAGRET - You could definitely get use to this.

- 2 duck breasts with skin on
- 1/2 tsp. salt
- 1/4 tsp. ground black pepper
- 1/3 cup honey
- 1/4 cup balsamic vinegar
- Piment d'Espelette*

Cut shallow slits in the skin of the duck breast. Season the duck well on both sides with salt and pepper.

Preheat a large, lightly oiled iron skillet over medium-high heat and sear the duck breasts, skin side down, for 5 to 8 minutes, reducing the heat to medium-low after the 4-minute mark. Flip the duck breasts over and cook them for another 5 minutes. Transfer to a plate and cover to rest.

Remove most of the melted duck fat from the skillet and then turn the heat up to medium. Add the honey and balsamic vinegar, scraping up any of the browned bits as the sauce simmers. Cook the honey/vinegar sauce until it thickens. Season with salt to taste.

Return the duck breasts to the skillet, turning them to coat with the honey glaze. Remove them from the pan and carve them in slices, drizzle with extra glaze and dust with Piment d'Espelette. - Serves 2 to 4

*http://www.myspicesage.com/piment-despelette-p-700.html

SCALLOP A L'ETUVE'E - Have you tasted anything quite so good in your life?

- 1/2 lb. potato gnocchi

Shallot Beurre Blanc:

- 1 Tbs. butter
- 1 shallot, chopped
- 2 cups good white wine
- 1/2 cup heavy cream
- 2 sticks of butter, softened

Scallops:

- 2 Tbs. extra-virgin olive oil
- 1 cup pearl onions, peeled
- 12 jumbo sea scallops
- 1-1/2 tsp. minced garlic
- 1/4 cup good white wine
- 1/2 cup chicken stock
- Salt and black pepper to taste
- 1 cup frozen peas
- 3 Tbs. fresh basil, chopped
- 1 tsp. lemon zest
- 2 Tbs. parsley, chopped
- 1 Tbs. butter

Bring a large pot of water to a boil and add salt. Add the gnocchi and cook as directed on package.

In a small saucepan over medium-low heat, add 1 Tbs. butter and shallot. Cook for 5 minutes then add the wine. Add the cream and reduce the sauce by half. Add the 2 sticks of butter and stir until blended. Remove from stove and set in a warm place.

Heat the olive oil in an iron skillet over medium-high heat until hot. Add onions and cook for about 5 minutes or until light browned. Remove onions and set aside and add the scallops. Season the scallops with salt and pepper and cook undisturbed 1 minute. Turn and cook about 1 and 1/2 minutes longer. (Times vary depending on how big the scallops are). Remove the scallops to a plate and set aside.

Add the garlic to the pan and cook for 1 minute. Deglaze the pan with the wine. Add chicken stock and return the onions. Add the peas, basil, lemon zest, and butter. Simmer for 10 minutes. Return the scallops to the pan to warm.

To serve, place gnocchi in the center of plate. Using a slotted spoon; remove scallops and vegetables from the pan and top the gnocchi. Drizzle Beurre Blanc around the gnocchi and garnish with parsley. - Serves 2

LINGUINI WITH WHITE TRUFFLE SAUCE - Piazza Santo Spirito, 19 r, Florence, Italy - Phone +39 055 238 2383. Why bother, make it at home.

- 3 Tbs. extra virgin olive oil
- 3 Tbs. butter
- 4 cloves garlic, sliced

- 1-1/2 cups mushrooms, thinly sliced
- 1 lb. linguini
- 3/4 cup heavy cream
- 1/4 cup parsley, chopped
- Salt and white pepper to taste
- 1/2 cup fresh grated Romano cheese
- 6 Tbs. white truffle cream*

In a large pan combine olive oil and garlic and cook 2 minutes on medium heat. Remove garlic and add the mushrooms, cook until tender. Season mushrooms lightly with salt and pepper.

Boil the linguini al dente, drain and reserve l cup of the pasta water. Add the linguini to mushrooms and toss to combine. Add the heavy cream and continue to cook 2 minutes or until desired doneness. Add a bit of pasta water to thin if desired.

Add parsley and generous sprinkling of white pepper. Toss in the cheese and 3 Tbs. of the truffle cream. Transfer to warmed serving dish with tongs and drizzle with more truffle cream. - Serves 2 to 4

*http://www.amazon.com/s/ref=nb_sb_noss?url=search-alias%3Daps&field-keywords=Roland-White-Truffle-2-8-Ounce

VINNIE'S CHEESEBURGER AND FRIES - When in Florence.... just kidding.

Burger:

- 2 lbs. ground beef, chilled
- 1 Tbs. Worcestershire sauce
- 2 tsp. garlic powder
- 4 pieces of Velveeta cut into 2 x 2 x 1/2 inch squares
- Salt and pepper to taste
- 4 large buns, lightly toasted

Place beef, Worcestershire sauce, garlic salt, and pepper in a bowl and mix well. Portion the meat mixture into eight balls. Shape each ball into a thin round patty that's slightly larger than the bun.

Place the Velveeta pieces on 4 of the patties, cover cheese with remaining 4 patties.

Tightly pinch the edges of the patties together to form a tight seal.

Preheat a cast iron skillet over medium-high and cook the burgers about 3 minutes per side. After flipping, use a knife and poke top of burger to let some of the steam out. Remove patties from pan. Place them on the buns and add desired toppings. - Serves 4

Fries:

- 4 large baking potatoes cut into 1/4 inch-thick sticks
- 3 Tbs. vegetable oil
- Season salt
- Cooking spray

Preheat the oven to 450° F.

In a large bowl, toss the potatoes with the vegetable oil and season salt. Spread the potatoes in a single layer on a large bake sheet, sprayed with cooking spray. Bake about 15 minutes and flip them with a spatula. Bake 15 minutes longer or until golden and crisp. Remove and season to taste. - Serves 2 to 4

TIRAMISU GELATO - Something of a weakness for gelato?

- 3 cups whole milk
- 1 cup half & half cream
- 6 egg yolks
- 1 cup sugar
- 2 cups mascarpone cheese
- 2 tsp. pure vanilla extract
- 1 Tbs. instant coffee crystals
- 1/4 cup coffee liqueur
- 1/3 cup semi-sweet chocolate (shaved)
- 8 crumbled lady fingers

Combine milk and half & half in a medium pot. Bring up to just below a boil over medium heat. Whisk the eggs with the sugar until well blended in a large bowl. Slowly add the hot milk mixture into the beaten yolk/sugar mixture and whisking quickly to combine.

Return mixture to the saucepan on medium - low heat.

Using an electric hand mixer, combine the mascarpone cheese and vanilla in a large bowl; beat until very creamy.

Add the milk mixture to the bowl of mascarpone cheese and whip until combined.

Cover and chill until completely cold, at least 4 hours. Stir in the coffee crystals and pour mixture into ice cream maker and churn according to manufacturer's instructions.

While the gelato is soft but not quite set, pour in the coffee liqueur, chocolate shavings and crumbled lady fingers. Transfer gelato to a tightly sealed container and place in the freezer until firm. - Serve 4 to 6

CRÈME ANGLAISE GELATO - The Café Ricchi has nothing on this recipe.

- 6 egg yolks
- 1 cup sugar
- 2 tsp. cornstarch
- 3-1/2 cups scalded milk
- 2 tsp. pure vanilla extract
- 3 tsp. Cognac

Beat the egg yolks and sugar in a bowl with an electric mixer until very thick, about 5 minutes. Add the cornstarch and beat 3 minutes more.

Slowly pour the hot milk into the eggs and beat for 5 minutes. Pour the milk mixture into a medium saucepan and cook over low heat, stirring constantly, until thickened. To test the proper thickness, the custard should coat the back of a spoon when it is dipped in and lifted.

Remove from heat and add the vanilla extract and Cognac. Place the custard in a bowl, cover with plastic wrap, allow custard to cool to room temperature and then refrigerate at least 4 hours.
Place the mixture in an ice cream maker and churn as directed. Transfer the gelato to a container, cover and store in freezer until firm. - Serves 6

ITALIAN STYLE PANINI - Don't dread the long and frigid nights, take along a fine bottle of Chianti.

- 2 fresh ciabatta rolls
- Extra virgin olive oil
- 1/2 cup prepared basil pesto
- 4 thick slices fresh mozzarella cheese (in brine)
- 2 large tomatoes, cut into 8 thin slices
- Salt and pepper to taste

Heat a closed Panini press for about 5 minutes.

Split the rolls, brush outside of each half with oil. Spread the pesto on inside of both halves. Layer each sandwich with cheese and tomato. Sprinkle with salt and pepper.

When grill has heated, place sandwiches on grill. Close press and grill 5 minutes, until bread is toasted and cheese is melted. Slice sandwiches on diagonal and serve warm with a good bottle of Chianti. - Serves 2

CHICKEN BREAST WITH GRAVY - Sheer banality? Far from it.

- 4 chicken breasts, boneless, skin on
- 3 Tbs. butter
- 3 Tbs. olive oil
- 1/2 cup flour
- 1 quart Swanson's chicken broth, warmed
- Salt and pepper, to taste

- 1/4 cup chopped parsley

Season the chicken breasts generously with salt and pepper.

Place butter and olive oil in a large sauté pan over medium-high heat. Add the chicken, skin down to the pan. Cook 3 minutes or until well browned. Turn chicken over and cook an additional 3 minutes. Remove chicken from the pan and set aside on a tray.

Add flour to the drippings in the pan and stir to form a paste or roux. Cook the roux, stirring constantly for 2 minutes. Slowly add chicken broth to the roux and whisk to combine. Continue whisking until gravy comes to a full boil and thickens. Reduce heat to medium-low.

Return chicken breasts to the pan, skin side down, and baste gravy over the chicken with a spoon. Cover pan and continue cooking for 20 minutes. Adjust seasoning of gravy with salt and pepper to taste.

Serve gravy over the chicken breasts and garnish with chopped parsley. - Serves 4

GREEN BEANS & CARROTS

- 6 cups water
- 1/2 lb. fresh baby carrots
- 1/2 lb. fresh green beans, cleaned and trimmed
- A large bowl of ice water
- 2/3 cup chicken broth
- 2 Tbs. butter
- 1 tsp. sugar
- 1 Tbs. honey
- Salt and pepper to taste

In a large saucepan, bring water to a boil. Add carrots; cover and cook for 7 minutes. Add the green beans, cover and cook 2 minutes longer. Drain and immediately place vegetables in ice water. Drain through a colander and then place the vegetables in a large sauté pan over medium-high heat. Stir vegetable around pan for 45 seconds to remove excess water.

Add broth and butter to the pan and bring to a boil. Cook, uncovered, for about 5 minutes or until liquid is reduced to about 2 tsp. Add the sugar, honey, salt and pepper. Fold vegetables to coat and cook an additional 2 minutes. - Serves 4

LUMPY MASHED POTATOES

- 4-1/2 lbs. large baking potatoes, washed, peeled
- Water
- 2 tsp. salt
- 1-1/2 cup heavy cream

- 2 tsp. salt
- 1 tsp. black pepper
- 1 stick butter
- Salt and pepper to taste

Place potatoes in a medium stockpot and cover with cold water. Stir in salt and set over medium-high heat. Bring water to a boil and then lower the heat to medium. Partially cover the stockpot and cook until the potatoes are fork tender, about 25 minutes.

In a small saucepan, over medium heat, bring cream to a slight simmer. Stir in the butter, 2 tsp. of salt, and the black pepper. Remove saucepan from heat and cover to keep warm.

Keeping the burner on medium, remove the stockpot from the stove and carefully pour the water and potatoes into a colander in the sink. Place the potatoes back into the pot and return the pot to the stove. Continue to cook until all the water has evaporated from the stockpot, about 1 minute.

Mash the potatoes into small pieces. Adjust the heat to low and whisk in the warm cream mixture. Beat the potatoes with an electric mixer until they are light but still a bit lumpy. Adjust the seasoning with salt and pepper to taste. - Serves 6 to 8

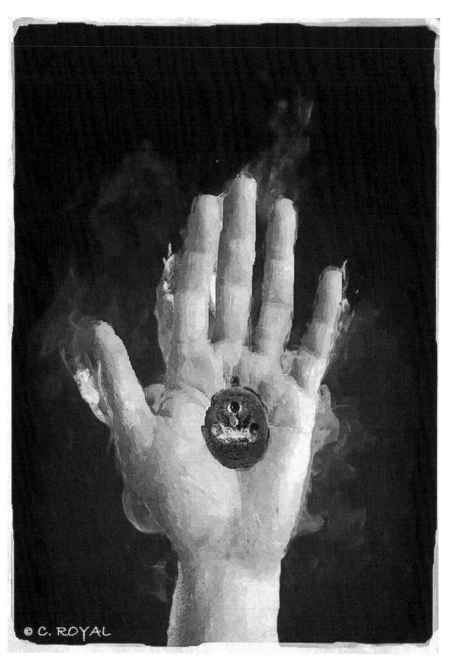

"...a pendent: a lidless eye over a phoenix, rising from fiery ashes, now pitted and partly melted."

DANCE OF DEATH

MEAT RAGU

LASAGNA NAPOLETANA

COEUR DE VEAU

STEAK TARTARE W/ CAPERS

LARGE FRUIT SALAD

ROMEO'S PEPPERONI PIZZA

PUB CHEESEBURGER

BANGERS AND MASH

BEEF & KIDNEY PIE

EGG WHITE OMELET

OVER WELL EGGS & RYE TOAST

CHICKEN CACCIATORE

EGGS IN ASPIC

BROOK TROUT

PLAICE A AL MORNAY

RACK OF SPRING LAMB

SALMON W/ COURT BULLION

PETIT FOURS

BLINI WITH CAVIAR

OYSTERS ON THE HALF SHELL

COLD LOBSTER TAIL

SMOKE STURGEON SPREAD

CRUDITÉS

FRENCH BAGUETTE

JUMBO COCKTAIL SHRIMP

SUCKLING PIG

MEAT RAGU - Now you know precisely what Nonnina's secret was.

- 1 lb. ground pork sausage
- 1 lb. country style pork ribs
- 1 lb. beef stew meat cut into 2 inch cubes
- 6 (12 oz.) cans diced tomatoes
- 4 Tbs. tomato paste
- 2 cups dry red wine
- 2 large yellow onions, very thinly sliced
- 3 cloves garlic, minced
- 8 to 10 fresh basil leaves, diced
- Extra virgin olive oil
- Salt and black pepper to taste

Heat olive oil in a large stockpot with a lid. Cook the meat (brown the meat in batches if necessary) in the oil over medium-high heat until nicely browned. Remove the meat and set aside in a large bowl.

Add the onions and garlic to the pot and cook them in the olive oil for about 5 minutes. Add the red wine to the onions and simmer for 15 minutes. Stir in the diced tomatoes and then the tomato paste. Season the sauce to taste with salt and pepper. Bring sauce to a slow boil, stirring every few minutes (do not let sauce burn).

Carefully add the meat and meat juices back to the pot. Add the basil and bring mixture back to a slow simmer and then reduce heat to low. Cover (leaving a crack to vent any steam) and cook for 4 hours, then season with salt and pepper to taste.

Remove any pork bones. Serve over pasta, rice or allow the sauce to cool to room temperature and use it to make lasagna. - Serves 6

LASAGNA NAPOLETANA - You've watched dozens of times, now it's your turn.

Meatballs:

- All the meats from the ragu
- 4 Tbs. chopped parsley
- 2 eggs
- 4 oz. Parmigiano-Reggiano, grated
- Salt and black pepper
- 4 slices of stale bread
- Olive oil for frying

Pour the ragu from the previous recipe through a colander, catching the sauce in a bowl and setting the tomato sauce aside. Place the colander of meat under the faucet and rinse with cool water. Shake and press as much water out and then place the meat on a clean kitchen towel to dry.

Place the dried ragu meat in a large food processor. Pulse the meat until it makes a coarse paste. Remove the paste and put it in a large bowl.

Cut the stale bread into 1-inch cubes and put in the food processor. Pulse several times to create coarse breadcrumbs. Add the breadcrumbs to the meat paste in the bowl and add the eggs, parsley and grated Parmigiano-Reggiano. Season the mixture well with salt and freshly ground black pepper. Mix well by hand.

Lightly oil hands and roll out small meatballs, about the size of a gumball. Once all the meatballs are assembled, heat 1/4 of an inch of olive oil in an iron skillet, over medium-high heat and fry the meatballs. Remove the meatballs from the pan and drain on paper towels.

Lasagna:

- 1 bowl of the sauce from the meat ragu

- 1 lb. browned Italian sausages, cut in 1/4-inch slices
- Meatballs (recipe above)
- 2 cups ricotta cheese
- 6 oz. mozzarella fior-di-latte, sliced
- 6 oz. smoked provolone, sliced
- 6 oz. block of Parmigiano-Reggiano, grated
- 1 – (9 oz.) box lasagna pasta sheets
- 1/4 stick of butter, softened

Preheat the oven to 350° F.

Boil the lasagna pasta sheets per instructions on the box.

Mix the ricotta with 1 cup of the reserved tomato sauce in a small bowl.

Butter a 12 x 16 inch lasagna dish, making sure to use the whole 1/4 stick.

Cover the bottom of the dish with 1/2 cup of tomato sauce. Place 3 or 4 sheets of pasta on the bottom of the pan (overlap them slightly). Then spread out 1/3 of the ricotta mixture on the pasta. Then add 1/3 of the sausage slices, 1/3 of the meatballs, 1/3 of the mozzarella and 1/3 of the smoked provolone. Top with 1/2 cup of the tomato sauce and sprinkle with some grated Parmigiano-Reggiano.

Repeat the process 2 more times. Spread the top with the remaining tomato sauce and grated Parmigiano-Reggiano.

Cover with tin foil and bake in the oven for 1 hour, then remove foil and continue baking until the top is golden brown. Let the lasagna rest for 10 minutes before serving. - Serves 6 to 8

COEUR DE VEAU (Braised Veal Heart with Carrots and Orange) - Not a dish found in Iowa, let alone Keokuk.

- 3 lb. veal hearts, cleaned and trimmed
- 2 onions, cut into 2 inch chunks
- 12 small carrots, peeled
- 1 cup dry white wine
- 2 large oranges, squeezed and peeled sliced into very thin strips
- 4 Tbs. butter
- Salt and pepper
- 2 Tbs. chopped cilantro

Place an iron skillet over medium-high heat. Add butter to skillet and sauté onions and veal hearts 7 to 10 minutes.

When meat is well browned, add carrots, white wine, orange juice and orange strips. Season the mixture with salt and pepper, to taste.

Cover skillet and cook for 2 hours over low heat. Transfer into a cutting board, cut the veal heart into thin slices. Return the sliced veal to the skillet and fold it back into the carrots. Serve in shallow bowls and garnish with chopped cilantro. - Serves 4 to 6

STEAK TARTARE WITH CAPERS AND DICED EGG - No, Monsieur.......Is no heat, no flambé. Is no cooked.

- 1 lb. beef tenderloin, finely minced by hand and chilled
- 1 Tbs. Dijon mustard
- 1 Tbs. extra virgin olive oil
- 2 egg yolks
- 1 tsp. finely chopped parsley
- Salt and fresh black pepper to taste
- 2 hard boiled eggs, finely chopped
- 1 onion, finely chopped
- 2 small finely chopped dill pickles
- 3 Tbs. capers
- 2 Tbs. chopped parsley
- 12 toast points

Place a large glass bowl in the freezer for 30 minutes. Into the chilled bowl, combine the minced tenderloin, mustard, olive oil, 1 egg yolk, parsley, and salt and pepper to taste. Blend by hand, form into a mound and place on a chilled serving plate.

Make a small indentation in the center of the mound with the back of spoon and carefully place the remaining egg yolk in it. Surround the mound with egg, onion, pickles and capers. Sprinkle all with chopped parsley. Serve immediately with toast points. - Serves 1 to 2 (if you share)

LARGE FRUIT SALAD - A staple for pasty faced, cliff dwelling New Yorkers, it would seem.

- 1/2 cup fresh lime juice
- 1/2 cup cold water
- 1/2 cup powdered sugar
- 3 medium nectarines, thinly sliced
- 2 cups watermelon balls
- 1 cup seedless grapes
- 1 kiwi fruit, peeled and sliced
- 2 large firm bananas, thinly sliced
- 1 pint fresh blueberries
- 1 pint fresh strawberries, stemmed and sliced

In a large glass bowl, combine the lime juice, water and sugar; stir until sugar is dissolved. Add fruit and toss gently. Cover and refrigerate for 1 hour before serving. - Serves 2 to 4

ROMEO'S PEPPERONI, GARLIC AND ONION PIZZA -
Be sure to share these with the SOC team.

- 1 package active dry yeast
- 1 tsp. sugar
- 1 cup warm water
- 3 cups bread flour
- 2 Tbs. olive oil
- 2 tsp. salt

In a medium bowl, stir yeast and sugar into the warm water. Let mixture proof for about 10 minutes. Stir in the bread flour, salt and oil. Mix until smooth and knead by hand for 10 minutes. Spray the bowl and dough ball with cooking spray. Cover and let dough rise for 30 minutes, in a warm space.

Turn dough out onto a lightly floured surface and roll the dough into a 19 inch round. Roll edges over to form a handle. Flip crust over and transfer to an 18 inch pizza screen.

- 3 Tbs. butter
- 1 yellow onion, diced
- 1 garlic clove, minced
- 12 oz. pepperoni, finely diced
- 1 tsp. red chili flakes
- 1 (14 oz.) can crushed tomatoes
- 1 beef bullion cube
- 1/2 tsp. red wine vinegar
- 2 tsp. oregano
- 3 tsp. basil

Heat butter in a large saucepan over medium heat. Add the onion and garlic and cook 5 minutes. Add the diced pepperoni, cook 5 more minutes. Add half the tomatoes, bullion cube, vinegar, oregano, basil and pepper flakes. Stir and remove from heat. Stir in second half of tomatoes.

- 40 slices pepperoni
- 1 yellow onion, sliced into thin rings
- 2 cloves garlic, minced
- 3 cups mozzarella cheese

Preheat oven to 500° F.

Sprinkle 2 cups of cheese and then add sauce by dribbling on top of cheese with a measuring cup. Using the bottom of the measuring cup, lightly blend sauce with the cheese (if desired). Add toppings and then the remaining cheese. Place pizza in oven and bake for 12 minutes or until golden brown. - Makes 1 large pizza

PUB CHEESEBURGER – RARE - Paired with a frothy Black & Tan, this is definitely not the usual burger.

Pub Cheese:

- 4 oz. cream cheese
- 4 oz. Cheddar cheese, grated
- 1/4 cup beer
- 1 tsp. spice brown mustard
- 1 Tbs. Worcestershire sauce
- 1/4 tsp. cayenne pepper
- 1 tsp. prepared horseradish
- 2 Tbs. dried chives

Put all ingredients in a food processor and pulse to combine.
Burger:

- 1 lbs. 75/25 ground beef
- 1 Tbs. Butter
- 1/2 medium red onion, finely chopped
- 1/4 cup beer
- 1 Tbs. rolled oats
- 1 tsp. thyme
- 1/2 tsp. salt
- 1 tsp. pepper
- 4 hamburger buns, lightly toasted
- Romaine lettuce
- 5 sliced tomatoes
- Salt and pepper to taste

Heat the butter in an iron skillet over a low heat, and cook the onion until browned. This may take a while, but it's worth it.

In a large bowl add ground beef, cooked onions, beer, oats and seasonings. Mix well by hand.

Divide the mixture into 4 equal balls, form the balls into patties a bit larger then the buns and put a small dimple in the center of each. Cover and refrigerate for 1 hour.

Cook the burgers on a medium-high, in the same iron skillet as the onions. Sear for 3 minutes, flip and cook 3 minutes more for rare. Serve on the bun, layered first with romaine lettuce, tomato slice, salt and pepper; then the burger and top with about 2 Tbs. of the Pub cheese placed in the dimple. Top the burger with the other half of the bun - Serves 4

BANGERS AND MASH - Served with a glass of milk, nothing stronger?

- 4 pork sausages
- 3 Tbs. vegetable oil
- 1 large yellow onion, thinly sliced
- 1 Tbs. flour
- 1 cup Swanson's beef broth
- 1/4 cup dry red wine
- Salt and pepper to taste
- 3 large potatoes, washed, peeled and chopped.
- 1 cup milk, warmed
- 6 Tbs. butter

Place 1 Tbs. of oil and 2 Tbs. of butter into an iron skillet. Turn heat to medium- low and add the sliced onions. Cook for 15 minutes, until golden brown. While the onions cook, bring a large pot of water to a boil and add the sausages and potatoes. Boil both together for 20 minutes.

Once the onions are browned, sprinkle in the flour, stir and cook for 1 minute. Add the red wine and cook 2 minutes. Add the beef broth and stir. Reduce heat to a simmer, and cook for 20 minutes. Season to taste with salt and pepper. Remove the onion gravy from the skillet and place a covered bowl.

Remove the sausages from the boiling water with tongs and pat dry with paper towel. Pour 2 Tbs. of oil into the skillet and cook sausages over medium heat until they are evenly browned.

Drain the potatoes and mash them in a large bowl. Add 4 Tbs. butter and the warm milk. Mix well and season with salt and pepper to taste.

Place an elongated mound of mashed potatoes to a plate, and put one sausage to each side of the potatoes. Cover well with the onion gravy. - Serves 2

BEEF & KIDNEY PIE - Back this one up with three fingers of Glen Grant.

- 1 lb. beef kidney, cut into 1-inch cubes
- 2 lbs. beef stew meat, cut into 1-inch cubes
- 1/2 cup flour generously seasoned with salt and pepper
- 4 Tbs. butter
- 3 Tbs. vegetable oil
- 1 yellow onion, finely chopped
- 8 oz. button mushrooms, sliced
- 2 cups beef broth
- 1 cup stout
- Salt and pepper
- 1 package frozen pie crust, thawed
- 1 egg, beaten

Place the half the seasoned flour in a large Ziploc bag. Drop the kidney cubes into the bag of flour. Seal bag and shake, coating all the meat well. Remove the coated kidney cubes and set aside on a plate. Add the remaining flour and the cubed stew meat, seal bag and shake well.

In a large iron skillet, over medium-high heat, add all the butter and 1 Tbs. vegetable oil. Once heated, add the floured kidney chunks and cook 10 minutes, browning on all sides.

Remove kidneys from skillet and set aside on a tray. Add an additional 1 Tbs. of oil to skillet and brown the floured beef in small batches. Cook for 10 minutes per batch. Remove beef from skillet and set aside.

Add the remaining oil to the hot skillet; add onions and cook for 5 minutes. Add sliced mushrooms and cook 5 minutes more.

Add beef and kidneys back to the skillet and fold into the mushrooms and onions mixture.

Sprinkle 2 Tbs. of the remaining seasoned flour over the mixture and incorporate. Pour in the beef broth and stout; stir until thickened. Re-season gravy with salt and pepper to taste. Transfer mixture to a large bowl and allow it to cool completely, about 45 minutes.

Preheat oven to 350° F.

Unroll pie crust and place one crust in a pie pan. Fill the pie shell with meat filling. Brush edges with some of the beaten egg, then place top crust on pie and seal the edges. Brush top crust with the rest of the beaten egg and poke 8 vent holes through the top crust. Place the pie in oven and bake 40 to 45 minutes, or until golden brown. - Serves 6

EGG WHITE OMELET - Just like at the Omeleteria only better.

- 5 large egg whites
- 2 tsp. milk
- 1 Tbs. unsalted butter
- Salt and pepper to taste

Whisk together the egg whites, milk, salt and pepper in a medium bowl until frothy and well combined.

Melt the butter in an omelet pan over medium heat. Swirl the pan to coat the surface with the butter. Add the egg mixture and stir constantly with wooden spoon, moving the eggs for about 2 minutes or until they just begin to set.

Now spread the eggs evenly across the pan with the back of the spoon and allow them to cook for about 2 minutes longer undisturbed.

Remove the pan from heat and slightly tilt the pan downward. Using the spoon flip a third of the omelet up and over itself. Now tilt the pan over a plate and roll the omelet, seam side down. Serve immediately. - Serves 1

OVER WELL EGGS & RYE TOAST - Make sure the yolks aren't runny, some people detest runny eggs.

- 2 slices rye bread
- 2 Tbs. butter
- 2 large eggs
- Salt and pepper to taste
- Chopped parsley

Cut a 2 inch round from the center of the rye bread with a juice glass. Melt butter in a medium nonstick skillet over medium heat. Place the slices of bread in skillet and grill 1 minute. Crack the eggs into the hole and cook until the bottom side of the bread browns.

Gently flip the rye toast with a spatula, and season with salt and pepper. Cook another 4 minutes or until the yolks are firm. Transfer to a plate and sprinkle with chopped parsley. - Serves 1

CHICKEN CACCIATORE WITH PLUM TOMATOES - After friends and family experience this, they'll let you into the kitchen more often.

- 3 lbs. boneless chicken thighs
- Salt
- Pepper
- 3 Tbs. olive oil
- 1 onion, coarsely chopped
- 2 cloves garlic, minced
- 8 whole plum tomatoes, stemmed
- 6 oz. tomato paste
- 1/2 cup Swanson's chicken broth
- 1 tsp. dried oregano
- 1 tsp. dried basil
- 3 cups sliced mushrooms
- 1 cup dry red wine
- 1 package angel hair pasta, cooked and set aside

Season the chicken thighs well with salt and pepper. Add oil to a large iron skillet and heat over medium-high heat. Carefully add chicken, skin side down and brown, undisturbed, for 3 to 4 minutes. Flip chicken and cook and additional 4 minutes. Remove chicken from the skillet and set aside.

In the same skillet add the onion and garlic and cook 1 minute. Add the tomato paste, chicken broth, oregano and basil and stir to combine. Return the browned chicken to the sauce and spoon the sauce over each piece. Reduce heat to low, cover and simmer for 45 minutes.

Add mushrooms, whole plum tomatoes and wine and simmer for another 20 minutes uncovered. Adjust seasoning with salt and pepper and serve chicken with sauce over angel hair pasta. - Serves 4

EGGS IN ASPIC - All the guests at River Oaks rave on and on about this offering.

- 1 stalk of celery, chopped
- 1 carrot, chopped
- 1 leek, chopped
- 2 Tbs. parsley, chopped
- 3 Tbs. fresh tarragon, chopped
- 2 Tbs. crushed peppercorns
- 4 egg whites
- 6 cups Swanson's chicken broth
- Unflavored powdered gelatin
- 1/2 cup good white wine
- Salt and pepper
- 8 eggs
- 24 red bell pepper strips, 1 inch long
- 24 asparagus tips, blanched

Pulse celery, carrot, leek, parsley, tarragon, peppercorns and egg whites in a food processor until well blended and pour mixture into a medium saucepan.

Add chicken broth and bring to a boil over medium heat, stirring constantly. When the egg whites start to firm up, stop stirring and reduce heat to low. Allow the mixture to simmer for 15 minutes.

Using a wire strainer and a cotton dish towel or cheesecloth, strain the broth mixture to obtain a clarified liquid. Add white wine and salt and pepper.

Measure the liquid and add the proper amount of gelatin according to the package instructions. Allow aspic to cool but not set.

Poach the eggs and drain on paper towels.

Pour a little of the aspic into 8 ramekins and place 3 asparagus tips and 3 red pepper strips on the aspic in an interesting design. Carefully place a poached egg in the center of each ramekin and fill with the aspic. Chill in the refrigerator until fully set.

Dip the ramekin into hot water to loosen and invert on to serving plates. - Serves 8

BROOK TROUT - This method is crazy simple...... "Fishing, with the arid plain behind me."

- 2 whole brook trout
- 2 lemons, divided
- 1/4 tsp. salt
- 1/2 tsp. lemon pepper
- 1/4 tsp. garlic powder
- 1/4 tsp. onion powder
- 4 pats of butter
- 1 bundle fresh dill weed
- Vegetable oil cooking spray
- Smoked paprika
- 1/2 cup dry white wine

Preheat oven to 475° F.

Line a shallow baking pan with tin foil and set a flat wire rack into the pan. Spray the rack with vegetable oil.

Rinse the trout in cold water and pat dry with a paper towel. Slice one of the lemons into thin disks with a sharp knife.

Lightly sprinkle the inside of the fish with salt, lemon pepper, garlic powder, and onion powder. Place 2 pats of butter and

3 sprigs of dill inside each trout as well, followed by half of the lemon slices.

Spray the entire skin of the fish with vegetable oil and set the fish on the wire rack. Spread dill sprigs over the skin, top with remaining lemon slices and dust with paprika. Pour the wine into the pan to form a pool under the rack. Place the fish in the oven and bake 25 to 30 minutes.

To serve, dust the fish lightly with a bit more paprika and garnish with lemon slices and some fresh dill. - Serves 2

PLAICE A AL MORNAY - If offered don't pass up this meal.

- 8 plaice fillets (flounder can be a good substitute)
- 4 Tbs. bacon fat
- 1-1/2 cups milk
- 1 medium onion, finely chopped
- 1 carrot, finely chopped
- 1 celery stalk, finely chopped
- 1 bouquet garni, (thyme, bay leaves, celery greens, and parsley bundle.)
- Salt and pepper
- 3 Tbs. butter
- 3 Tbs. all purpose flour
- 1/2 cup Gruyere cheese, grated
- 1/4 cup Parmesan cheese, grated
- 1/4 tsp. dry mustard powder
- Chervil or parsley sprigs, garnish

Grease a shallow ceramic baking dish with the bacon fat. Combine the milk, vegetables and bouquet garni in a medium saucepan and add salt and pepper to taste. Bring the seasoned milk to just under a boil, lower the heat and allow to simmer for 10 minutes. Remove from heat, cover and set aside to cool.

Fold the filets in thirds, end over end. Strain the seasoned milk into a deep pan, over medium heat, and bring to a simmer. Add the fish, folded side down and poach for 8 minutes or until the fish are firm and fully cooked.

Transfer the poached fish to the prepared baking dish, using a metal spatula. Cover with tin foil and keep warm.

Adjust oven rack to broiler position and turn broiler on to high.

Melt the butter in another saucepan, stir in the flour to create a roux and cook for 1 minute, stirring constantly. Slowly add the seasoned milk that was used to poach the fish and whisk constantly until a thick sauce is formed.

Now combine the 2 cheeses and then stir half the cheese mixture into the sauce, along with the mustard. Remove the tin foil from the baking dish, pour the sauce over the top of the fish and sprinkle with the remaining cheese mixture. Brown the fish briefly under the broiler. Garnish with chervil or parsley before serving. - Serves 4

RACK OF SPRING LAMB - Commodore Vanderbilt would be so proud.......

- 1-1/2 lb. rack of lamb
- 2/3 cup beef stock
- 1/3 cup dry white wine
- 1 clove garlic, minced
- 2 Tbs. Dijon mustard
- 1 Tbs. fresh tarragon, minced
- Olive oil
- Salt and pepper
- 2 Tbs. cold butter

Preheat oven to 425° F.

Make diagonal slashes on fatty side of lamb, almost but not quite all the way through to the meat. Rub the lamb with oil and season with salt and pepper.

In a large iron skillet, over medium-high heat, sear lamb, fat side down, until golden. Now turn the lamb fat side up. Place the skillet with the lamb in oven and cook until meat thermometer inserted in center reads 140, about 15 to 20 minutes. Remove from oven and transfer lamb to a cutting board.

Tent the roast with tin foil and let rest for 10 minutes before carving.

In the same skillet, bring stock, wine and garlic to boil and cook for 3 minutes. Whisk in the mustard. Remove from heat, add cold butter and whisk until butter has melted and sauce has slightly thickened. Whisk in tarragon. Pour sauce into a gravy boat and serve on the side with the carved lamb. - Serves 2

COMMODORE VANDERBILT - RIVER OAK ESTATE

POACHED SALMON WITH COURT BOUILLON, DILL, LEMON, CAPERS - You need a break, sip a nice Vermentino Di Sardegna.

Court Bouillon:

- 1 stalk of celery, chopped
- 1 onion, chopped
- 1 carrot, chopped
- 1 head of garlic, halved horizontally
- 2 sprigs parsley
- 2 sprigs thyme
- 1 bay leaf
- 6 peppercorns
- 2 tsp. fennel seed
- 1/2 tsp. coriander seed
- 1/2 cups dry white wine
- 2 tsp. salt
- 1 quarts water

Combine all the ingredients in a stockpot. Bring to a boil, and then lower to a simmer. Simmer uncovered for 30 minutes. Strain broth into a large container and set aside.

Salmon:

- 4-1/2 lb. salmon fillets
- 1 to 2 cups court bouillon
- 5 sprigs of fresh dill (reserve 1 for garnish)
- 4 sprig of fresh parsley
- Salt
- Freshly ground black pepper
- 8 slices lemon
- 3 Tbs. capers

Season the salmon fillets with salt and pepper. Put court bouillon, dill, and parsley in a pan large enough to hold all the fillets and bring to a simmer on medium heat.

Place salmon fillets, skin-side down in the pan. Cover and poach 5 to 7 minutes. Serve garnished with lemon, capers and dill springs. Great with wild rice and asparagus on the side - Serves 4

PETIT FOURS - These are just as elegant as the ones brought up from New Orleans but a whole lot easier to procure.

Frosting Glaze:

- 6 cups powdered sugar
- 1/2 cup water
- 2 Tbs. light corn syrup
- 1 tsp. almond extract
- Red food coloring
- Green food coloring

Combine water and corn syrup in saucepan over low heat. Add the powdered sugar and stir to mix. Remove from heat and divide into 3 small glass bowls. Stir in almond extract and food colorings (leaving 1 white).

Cakes:

- 1 Sara Lee pound cake
- 1/2 cup strawberry jam
- 8 oz. Junior Mints, melted
- 1/2 cup Nutella hazelnut spread

Remove pound cake from container and trim the crust to make rectangular block.

Slice the pound cake lengthwise into 1/2-inch slabs. Lay each slab on its side and slice them into equal strips about 2 inches wide. Divide the pound cake strips into 3 equal groups.

In the first group, spread a thin layer of strawberry jam on first 2 strips and layer 3 strips high.

For the second group, spread with the melted Junior Mints and stack 3 layers high.

Repeat with the third group, but add the Nutella and layer 3 high. Cut all the stacked strips into little square cakes.

Set each group of filled cakes on separate wire cake racks with a baking pan underneath to catch the excess glaze.

Carefully re-warm the pink frosting and pour over the strawberry cakes. Repeat process with the green frosting and pour over the mint cakes and then repeat with the plain white frosting and pour cover the Nutella cakes.

Collect the frosting run-off and place in small plastic sandwich bags. Carefully re-warm the frosting in the bags, poke a small hole in the bag's corner and pipe decorations, strips or designs on the petit fours (use a different color for the piping than what is on the cakes for contrast). Chill the petit fours to allow frosting to set.

BLINI WITH CAVIAR - Spread out a crisp white tablecloth, strike up Haydn's Emperor Quartet and have your own extravagant opening night.

- 1/2 cup sour cream
- 2 Tbs. thinly sliced scallions
- 1 Tbs. butter, melted
- 3 Tbs. milk
- 1 egg
- 2 tsp. grated lemon zest
- 1/4 cup flour
- 1/4 tsp. baking powder
- 1/4 tsp. sugar
- Salt
- 1/2 Tbs. butter
- 4 oz. black or red caviar

Stir together sour cream and 1 Tbs. of sliced scallions.

Place the 1 Tbs. melted butter into a medium bowl. Mix in the milk, egg, and 1 tsp. lemon zest. Add in the flour, baking powder, sugar, and salt and mix until smooth.

Melt 1/2 Tbs. butter in a large nonstick skillet over medium-low heat.

Drop 6 individual Tbs. size scoops of batter into skillet and cook until undersides are golden, about 3 minutes.

Flip the 6 blinis and cook until golden and cook 2 minutes more. Repeat process and make 6 more blinis.

Top each blinis with sour cream and caviar. Sprinkle with lemon zest and scallions. - Makes 12 blinis

BROILED OYSTERS ON THE HALF SHELL

- 2 dozen large fresh oysters in the shell
- 1 Tbs. butter
- 1 Tbs. olive oil
- 1-1/2 cups Italian breadcrumbs
- 1/4 cup grated Parmesan cheese
- 1/2 stick melted butter
- Rock salt

Shuck oysters and gently loosen oyster from shell, using your oyster knife.

Adjust oven rack to broiler position and preheat on broil.

Place butter and olive oil in a large skillet over low heat and stir in breadcrumbs. Remove from heat and add cheese.

Spread out enough rock salt in a shallow bake pan to hold oyster shells upright. Place oysters on the bed of rock salt. Spoon breadcrumb mixture on top of the oysters and drizzle with butter. Broil about 5 minutes or until top is crisp and nicely browned. - Serves 4

BROILED LOBSTER TAILS WITH BLOOD ORANGE BUTTER

- 1 cup salted butter
- Juice of 2 blood oranges
- Zest of 2 blood oranges
- 6 (6 oz.) lobster tails

Adjust oven rack to high position and preheat oven broiler to high.

Melt butter in a small saucepan over low heat and skim off the foam. Add blood orange zest, juice and a pinch of salt.

Pour half of the butter mixture into 2 small cups and set them aside for the dipping.

Using a very sharp knife split each tail in half lengthwise. Brush the lobster meat with the remaining butter.

Place lobster tails, meat side up, on a broiler pan and cook 8 to 10 minutes or until meat is a pale white and firm.

Remove the pan from the oven, transfer the lobster tails to 2 plates and serve warm with the cups of orange butter on the side. - Serves 2

SMOKED STURGEON SPREAD

- 2 cup smoked sturgeon, coarsely chopped
- 1 package cream cheese, softened
- 1/4 cup Hellmann's mayonnaise
- 1 Tbs. Parsley, chopped
- 2 Tbs. butter + some for toast
- 1/4 cup Vidalia onion, diced
- 1/4 cup celery, diced
- 3 Tbs. capers
- 1 loaf French bread, thinly sliced, buttered and toasted

Place butter in a medium saucepan over medium heat. Cook onions and celery for 3 minutes.

Place one half of the cooked onion, celery, cream cheese, mayonnaise and 1/2 of the sturgeon in a food processor and pulse until smooth.

Place the cream cheese mixture to a medium bowl. Fold in the remaining onion, celery, sturgeon along with the parsley and capers. Transfer sturgeon spread to a serving bowl and serve with buttered, toasted French bread slices. - Makes 30 canapés

CRUDITÉS

Vegetables:

- Asparagus, trimmed and blanched*
- Green beans, trimmed and blanched*
- Broccoli, blanched and cut into bite sized florets
- Celery, raw and cut into sticks
- Cucumbers, raw, peeled and cut in sticks
- Carrots, raw and cut in sticks
- Radishes, raw, trimmed
- Brussels sprouts, trimmed, split and roasted**
- Fennel, trimmed, split and roasted**

Dipping Sauce:

- 1 Tbs. vinegar
- 2 Tbs. olive oil
- 1 tsp. capers
- 2 anchovy fillets
- Salt and black pepper to taste
- 1 cup Hellmann's mayonnaise

- 1 clove garlic, peeled
- 1 bunch parsley

In a food processor, add vinegar, olive oil, garlic, salt, capers, pepper, anchovies, mayonnaise and parsley. Pulse the ingredients together until well blended and smooth.

Place a bowl of dipping sauce in the center of a large platter and arrange vegetables around the bowl.

*Blanching: Place vegetables in boiling water for 3 minutes, and then dip in ice water

**Roasting: Drizzle vegetables with olive oil, place on a cookie sheet and roast in a 400 oven for 40 minutes.

FRENCH BAGUETTE

Starter:

- 1/2 cup cool water
- 1/16 tsp. active dry yeast
- 1 cup bread flour

Dough:

- 1 tsp. active dry yeast
- 1-1/4 cups lukewarm water
- All of the starter
- 3-1/2 cups bread flour
- 2 tsp. salt or to taste

To make the starter, mix the yeast with the water, and then mix in the flour. Cover and let rest at room temperature overnight.

Mix everything (including the starter) together by hand until it forms soft, sticky dough. Knead for 5 minutes.

Place the dough in an oil coated medium bowl; cover the bowl with a dish towel. Let the dough rise for 1 hour, press the dough down and then let the dough rise 2 hours more.

Drop the dough onto a lightly greased work surface and divide the dough into three equal balls.

Shape each ball into a flat oval and drape each with plastic wrap. Let dough rest for 15 minutes.

Working with one loaf at a time, fold the dough in half lengthwise, sealing the edges. Lightly flatten the loaf, fold and seal again. Repeat with the other two loaves.

Gently roll the dough into a 16-inch log. Place the logs seam-side down onto a lightly greased bake pan.

Cover them with a dish towel and allow the loaves to rise about 1 to 2 hours, until loaves double in size.

Preheat oven to 450° F.

Make three shallow cuts lengthwise on each loaf with a sharp knife. Using a spray bottle, spray each loaf with warm water.

Bake for 30 minutes or until a deep golden brown. - Makes 3 loaves

JUMBO COCKTAIL SHRIMP

Cocktail Sauce:

- 1 cup Heinz ketchup
- 1/2 cup Heinz chili sauce
- 1 Tbs. horseradish
- Juice of 1/2 lemon
- 1 dash Worcestershire sauce
- Dashes of Tabasco to taste

Combine all the cocktail sauce ingredients together in a medium bowl and refrigerate until ready to serve.

Boiled Shrimp:

- 30 extra large shrimp, unpeeled
- 2 Tbs. Old Bay seasoning
- 1 lemon, halved
- 1 tsp. garlic powder
- 1 gallon water
- Lettuce leaves
- Lemon wedges

Fill a large bowl with ice water and set aside. In a large stockpot add the water, Old Bay seasoning, lemon halves and garlic powder. Bring mixture to a boil. Add the shrimp all at once to the pot and when the water returns to a boil, the shrimp should be fully cooked. Simple as that.

Remove the shrimp from the water using a wire strainer or slotted spoon. Place the shrimp into the ice water to stop the cooking process.

Peel the shrimp, leaving the tail-on and serve them on a bed of lettuce with cocktail sauce and lemon wedges. - Serves 6

SUCKLING PIG

- 1 whole suckling pig (about 10 lbs.)

Marinade:

- 2 cups chopped fresh cilantro
- 1/4 cup coarse black pepper
- 2 Tbs. garlic powder
- 2 Tbs. onion salt
- 2 cups margarita mix
- 3/4 cup fresh lime juice
- 3/4 cup fresh orange juice
- 1/2 cup tequila
- 1/2 cup triple sec
- 1/4 cup honey
- 3 cups olive oil

Place cilantro, pepper, garlic powder, and onion salt in a food processor. Puree mixture into a paste and transfer to a large stainless stain bowl. Pour in margarita mix, lime juice, orange juice, tequila, triple sec, and honey. Whisk to combine until smooth and well blended. Continue to whisk vigorously and slowly add the olive oil in a drizzle; blend until creamy and emulsified.

Transfer marinade to a large plastic container with a lid, (one that is large enough to accommodate the pig and the marinade). Place the pig, cavity side down, into the container. Using a coffee mug or ladle, coat the pig with the marinade and massage it in. Refrigerate in the container overnight. Turn the pig onto its back half way through the marinating process.

Preheat the oven to 275° F.

Remove the pig from the marinade and place it in a large roasting pan (belly down) supported by a heavy sheet pan. Cover the ears, snout, and tail with tin foil to retard burning. Place the suckling pig in the oven and slow roast for about 4 hours or 20 minutes per pound. Remove the foil for the last 45 minutes of roasting, if those areas seem undercooked.

Remove from oven and let rest for 15 minutes before carving. - Serves 8 to 10

'...she caught the cut edge of wallpaper and peeled it back,
revealing the smooth, cold expanse of steel."

BOOK OF THE DEAD

AESH BALADI (EGYPTIAN BREAD)

ROAST LAMB SHANK IN PAPYRUS

SALATAT FWAKI

KHALOTA (VEGETABLE STEW)

DATE CANDY

HERKMOOR MEATLOAF

HORS D'OEUVRES VARIES

CONSOMMÉ OLGA

KABOB EGYPTIEN

FILET MIGNON LILLI

VEGETABLE MARROW FARCIE

ROAST SQUAB AND CRESS

PÂTÉ DE FOIE GRAS EN CROUTE

BABA GHANOUSH

WALDORF PUDDING

PEACHES IN CHARTREUSE JELLY

PIZZA NEAPOLITAN

HAWAIIAN DOUBLE PINEAPPLE PIZZA

SHRIMP BISQUE

SMOKED STURGEON

SMOKED SALMON W/ CAVIAR PLATE

CRUSTY BREAD & PROSCIUTTO

SEVRUGA CAVIAR W/ CRAB TRUFFLE CUSTARD

BELUGA CAVIAR

CAVIAR & CRÈME FRAICHE CREPES

BROILED OYSTERS

FRENCH CHEESE

SHAVED PROSCIUTTO WITH MELON

GREEN TEA AND BUTTERED TOAST

POACHED EGGS

KIPPERS

RASHERS OF BACON

GRAPEFRUIT HALF

SCONES WITH JAM

RAW OYSTERS ON THE HALF SHELL

CROISSANTS

TRUFFLE SANDWICHES

COARSE BREAD, WILD BOAR SALAMI & OLIVES

AESH BALADI (EGYPTIAN BREAD) - These were not set aside for the Afterlife.....enjoy them now.

- 2 tsp. dry yeast
- 1 cup warm water
- 1 tsp. salt
- 3 cups flour

Dissolve the yeast in the warm water and then add the flour and salt. Work the mixture into a dough and knead for 5 minutes. Place dough in a well oiled bowl and cover with a damp cloth. Let the dough rise in a warm spot for 3 hours.

Preheat oven to 350° F.

Divide the dough into 6 equal portions and roll them into balls. Press the dough balls out into 5 inch circles about 1/2 inches thick.

Place the dough rounds onto an ungreased baking sheet and bake for about 10 minutes until a light golden brown. - Serves 2 to 6

ROASTED LAMB SHANK IN PAPYRUS

- 4 lbs. joint of lamb, goat or venison
- 12 cloves of garlic, peeled
- Olive oil
- Sea salt
- Freshly ground black pepper
- 3 sprigs fresh rosemary

- 3 sprigs fresh sage
- 3 sprigs fresh thyme
- 3 feet of parchment paper
- Water

Preheat oven to 425° F.

Rub the roast with olive oil and sprinkle generously with salt and pepper. Using a small knife, stab the roast viciously 12 times and insert a clove of garlic into each opening.

Spread out the parchment and lay the lamb 8 inches from one end. Drape the rosemary, sage and thyme sprigs over the roast. Fold the 8 inches of parchment paper up and over the meat. Roll the meat up in the paper tightly. Fold the sides under to make a bundle. Secure the bundle with kitchen twine.

Place the bundle, seam side down in a deep roasting pan. Pour water over the bundle until the pan fills to about 2 inches. Place roast in oven and cook for 2 hours.

Remove pan from the oven and let it rest 20 minutes. Carefully lift the sealed bundle onto a platter, and cut open at tableside to serve. - Serves 8

SALATAT FWAKI (FRESH FRUIT SALAD)

Fruit:

- 3 large oranges, peeled and segmented
- 3 large tangerines, peeled and segmented
- 3 large apples, cored and sliced
- 2 Tbs. lemon juice, to sprinkle on apples to prevent browning
- 1 cup green seedless grapes
- 1 cup red seedless grapes
- 3 large peaches, skinned, pitted and sliced
- Fresh mint sprigs

Wash and prepare fruit and arrange on a large platter, leaving the middle open for the dipping sauce. Garnish with fresh mint leaves.

Dipping Sauce:

- 1/4 cup fresh orange juice
- 1 cup plain yogurt
- 1/2 tsp. orange flower water*
- 3 Tbs. chopped pistachio nuts

Combine orange juice, yogurt and orange flower water. Stir until smooth. Place mixture in a small bowl and top with chopped pistachio nuts. *Orange flower water can be purchased in most Middle Eastern grocery stores. - Serves 4 to 6

KHALOTA (MIXED VEGETABLE STEW)

- 3 Tbs. olive oil
- 1 yellow onion, diced
- 3 tsp. Za'atar spice*
- 4 cloves garlic, minced
- 1/4 cup parsley, chopped (half reserved for garnish)
- 3 carrots, sliced

- 2 potatoes, diced
- 2 cups vegetable broth
- 2 zucchini, diced
- 1 eggplant, peeled and diced
- 8 oz. frozen lima beans
- 8 oz. frozen green beans
- Salt, pepper and cayenne to taste

Place oil in an iron skillet over medium-high heat. Add onions and cook 5 minutes. Add garlic, half the parsley, Za'atar spice, carrots, potatoes, and broth. Reduce heat to medium cover and simmer for 10 minutes.

Add zucchini, eggplant, green beans and lima beans. Reduce heat to low, cover and cook 30 minutes. Season the dish with salt, pepper and cayenne to taste. Transfer to a serving dish or 4 shallow bowls and garnish with remaining parsley.
- Serves 4

*Za'atar spice can be found at any Middle Eastern grocery store.

DATE CANDY

- 3 cups pitted dates
- Water
- 2 Tbs. cinnamon
- 1/2 tsp. cardamom
- 4 Tbs. chopped walnuts
- Honey
- 1/4 cup finely chopped almonds

Place the dates in a food processor. Pulse the dates and add just enough water to form a thick paste.

Empty the date paste into a bowl. Add cinnamon, cardamom and walnuts, blend together well.

Roll into cherry size balls. Coat in honey and roll in finely chopped almonds.

DUKKAH

- 1/2 cup hazelnuts
- 1/4 cup coriander seeds
- 3 Tbs. sesame seeds
- 2 Tbs. cumin seeds
- 1 Tbs. black peppercorns
- 1 tsp. fennel seeds
- 1 tsp. dried mint leaves
- 1 tsp. salt

Heat an iron skillet over medium-high heat, add the hazelnuts, and toast until lightly browned. Remove from the skillet and repeat the toasting with each of the seeds and the peppercorns individually. This will release the oils and enhance flavor.

Allow mixture to cool completely. Place all the ingredients in a food processor and pulse to a coarse consistency.

Serve with the aesh baladi or other flat bread and olive oil. Dip bread in oil and then dip in the dukkah.

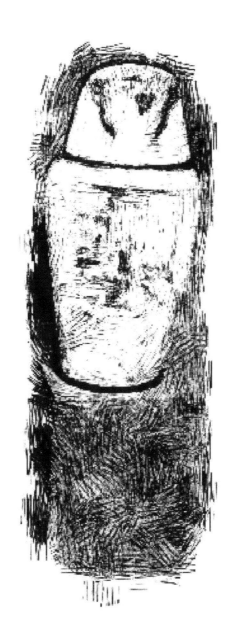

HERKMOOR TOMORROW'S MEATLOAF - Much better than Helmer's, you know with their by-products and all.

- Instant potatoes
- 2 lb. ground beef
- 1 egg, beaten
- 1/2 cup quick cooking oats
- 1/2 cup chopped green pepper
- 1/2 cup chopped red onion
- 1 tsp. pepper
- 1 tsp. salt
- 1/2 cup Heinz ketchup mixed with 1/4 cup brown sugar

Preheat oven to 350° F.

Prepare 4 servings of instant potatoes as directed on box and set aside.

In a bowl, combine ground beef, beaten egg, oats, green pepper, onion, salt and pepper and mix well by hand. On a large sheet of plastic wrap, pat ground beef into a 2-inch thick sheet.

Spoon potatoes lengthwise down center of the ground beef. Using the plastic wrap, bring the ground beef up and around the mashed potatoes and pat firmly to seal. Lift the wrapped meatloaf in a 13 x 9 baking dish and carefully remove the plastic wrap.

Place meatloaf in oven and bake uncovered for 30 minutes. Remove dish from oven and drain off fat.

Pour ketchup/brown sugar glaze over meatloaf. Place back in oven and bake 20 minutes longer.

Remove meatloaf from oven and let stand 10 minutes before serving. - Serves 8

HORS D'OEUVRES VARIES - Egyptian costumes are optional..............

Peanut Chicken Skewers with Chili Yogurt Sauce:

- 3/4 cup peanuts
- 1/3 cup panko
- 1/4 cup fresh cilantro
- Salt and black pepper
- 2 (8 oz.) boneless chicken breasts, cut into 24 strips
- 3 Tbs. vegetable oil
- 1/2 cup plain yogurt
- 2 tsp. Huy Fong chili-garlic sauce
- 24 wooden skewers soaked in water

Place peanuts, cilantro, and a dash of both salt and pepper in a food processor and pulse to medium crumbs. Transfer peanut mixture to a shallow pan, add the panko and mix together.

Stick the chicken onto the skewers and coat with the peanut mixture.

Heat the oil in a large iron skillet over medium heat and cook the chicken 2 to 3 minutes on each side.

In a small bowl, combine the chili-garlic sauce with the yogurt and blend.

Bacon-Wrapped Apricots with Sage:

- 24 fresh sage leaves
- 24 large dried apricots
- 8 slices bacon, each cut into 3 long strips
- 2 Tbs. pure Highland County VA maple syrup
- Toothpicks, for serving

Preheat oven to 375° F.

Stretch out a strip of bacon. Put a sage leaf at one end of the strip then an apricot on top of that. Roll the bacon up around the apricot and place on a baking sheet and repeat. Bake until the bacon is beginning to crisp, about 6 minutes. Flip the apricots and cook for about 5 minutes more.

Remove from oven and brush with the maple syrup. Serve on toothpicks.

FETA TURNOVERS

- 4 oz. crumbled garlic and herb feta cheese
- 2 Tbs. fresh dill
- 2 medium green onions, sliced
- 1/2 tsp. grated lemon peel
- Flour for dusting
- 1 sheet puff pastry, thawed

Preheat oven to 400° F.

In medium bowl, crumble cheese with fork. Stir in dill, onions and lemon peel blended.

On a floured surface, unfold pastry sheet and dust with flour. Roll pastry dough out into a 12 inch square with a rolling pin. Cut pastry dough into 16 equal squares. Spoon 2 rounded teaspoons of the cheese mixture onto center of each square.

Moisten edges with water. Fold square over, forming a triangle. Press edges of pastry together and crimp with a fork. Repeat with remaining turnovers and place on ungreased cookie sheet.

Bake 10 to 15 minutes or until puffy and golden brown. - Makes 16 pastries

CONSOMMÉ OLGA

- 1 carrot, finely chopped
- 1 leek, cleaned and finely chopped
- 1 celery stalk, finely chopped
- 1 small tomato chopped
- 1 Tbs. chopped parsley
- 1/4 lb. lean ground beef
- 1/4 tsp. salt
- 1/4 tsp. white pepper
- 3 egg white, beaten
- 8 cups Swanson's beef stock

Garnish:

- 1/4 cup port wine
- 6 sea scallops, raw and sliced into 18 discs
- 1 celery stalk, blanched and cut into fine strips
- 1 cucumber, seeded and cut into fine strips

In a large bowl, mix together vegetables, parsley and ground beef. Add salt and pepper and fold in egg whites.

Warm beef stock in a stockpot. Pour the warm stock into vegetable/egg mixture and then pour all contents back into the pot.

Turn heat up to medium-high and bring the soup to a slow boil, stirring constantly. When mixture begins to froth, stop stirring. Allow the egg mixture to solidify on the surface of the soup. Lower the heat to medium-low. Let the soup simmer for 30 minutes.

Line a wire strainer with cheesecloth or a clean muslin towel and carefully strain the soup into another pot to create the consommé. Heat the consommé to a rapid boil and add the port.

Place 3 scallops discs into bottom of each bowl. Ladle the boiling consommé over scallops (the hot liquid will quick-cook the scallops). Garnish with celery and cucumber strips. - Serves 6

KEBAB EGYPTIEN

- 2 boneless skinless chicken breasts
- 1 Tbs. plain Greek yogurt
- 1/4 tsp. salt
- 1/4 tsp. turmeric
- 1/8 tsp. dry mustard powder
- 1/2 tsp. curry powder
- 1/8 tsp. ground cardamom
- 1 tsp. lemon juice
- 8 wide onion chunks
- 4 small tomatoes, halved
- 8 bamboo skewers, soaked in water for 30 minutes.
- Lemon wedges, for garnish
- Fresh mint, for garnish

Cut the chicken breasts into 32 cubes.

In a large bowl, combine with the yogurt, salt, turmeric, mustard, curry powder and cardamom and lemon juice. Cover and refrigerate for 1 hour.

Thread 2 chicken pieces, 1 chunk of onion, 2 chicken pieces, 1/2 tomato.

Repeat with all 8 skewers and brush the assembled kebab generously with the marinade.

Cook 10 minutes, under the broiler. Turn skewers occasionally, reapplying the marinade.

Remove from oven and transfer to a platter, garnish with lemon wedges and fresh mint. - Serves 4 to 8

FILET MIGNON LILI

Beef:

- 4 petite filet mignon (6 oz. each)
- 1/2 tsp. salt
- 1/2 tsp. pepper
- 3 Tbs. black truffle butter
- Garlic cloves, minced
- 6 oz. foie gras or four 1/2 inch thick pate medallions
- Prepared artichoke hearts, cut in quarters
- 1 extra large potato, baked, peeled and sliced into four rounds

Sauce:

- 2 Tbs. butter
- 1/2 onion, minced
- 1 Tbs. tomato paste
- Bay leaf
- 1 sprig fresh rosemary
- 1/2 cup cognac
- 1 cup dry red wine
- 3 cups Swanson's beef broth
- Salt and pepper, to taste

To make the sauce, melt 1 Tbs. of the butter over medium heat; add onion and cook for 5 minutes. Add tomato paste, bay leaf and rosemary. Stir in cognac and red wine, bring to boil. Boil for 10 minutes. Add the beef broth and boil for 15 minutes.

Remove from heat and pour through a wire strainer into a saucepan and add 1 Tbs. butter. Salt and pepper sauce to taste and set aside over low heat.

Season meat with salt and pepper to taste.

In large iron skillet, melt truffle butter over medium heat. Add garlic and cook 2 minutes. Increase heat to medium-high, add filets mignons, sear 5 minutes, turn and cook 5 minutes more. Remove fillets from pan and let the meat rest for 5 minutes.

Meanwhile, add the foie gras or pate and cook for 30 seconds per side. Remove from pan and set aside. Add the artichokes to the pan and cook for 2 minutes.

Place a slice of potato on each plate; top with a filet mignon. Place a slice of foie gras or a medallion of pate on the meat. Ladle sauce around each steak and garnish with artichokes hearts. - Serves 4

VEGETABLE MARROW FARCIE

- 2 large zucchini
- 2 Tbs. olive oil
- 1 cup finely chopped onion
- 3 cloves garlic, minced
- 1/4 cup chopped fresh basil
- 1 tsp. dried oregano
- 1 Tbs. tomato paste
- 2 cups mushrooms, chopped
- 2 Tbs. red wine vinegar
- 6 cups cooked wild rice
- Salt and pepper
- 1/4 cup Parmesan cheese
- 1/4 cup fresh bread crumbs
- 2 Tbs. butter, melted
- Fresh basil, coarsely chopped

Slice the zucchini lengthwise; scoop out flesh with spoon leaving about a half inch of the flesh intact. Mince scooped out zucchini flesh and set aside.

Preheat oven to 375° F.

In an iron skillet, heat oil over medium heat. Add onion and garlic and cook 5 minutes. Add basil, oregano, zucchini flesh, and tomato paste. Cook mixture for 5 minutes. Add the mushrooms and cook for 5 minutes, then add the vinegar. Remove the skillet from heat and stir in cooked rice and 4 Tbs. of Parmesan cheese. Salt and pepper to taste.

Spoon the rice stuffing into hollowed out zucchini. Generously sprinkle top with bread crumbs and remaining Parmesan cheese; then drizzle with melted butter.

Place zucchini halves on a greased baking dish in oven for 30 minutes or until top is well browned.

Remove the pan and carefully slice in 4 inch slices. Garnish with fresh basil. - Serves 6 to 8

ROAST SQUAB AND CRESS

- 4 squab, partridges or Cornish hens
- 2 Tbs. olive oil
- 4 cloves garlic, minced
- 2 tsp. dried marjoram
- 1/2 tsp. salt
- 1/2 tsp. pepper
- 4 slices bacon
- 1 cup dry red wine
- 1 cup Swanson's chicken broth
- 12 oz. watercress

Preheat oven to 450° F.

Rinse birds inside and out and pat dry. In small bowl, mix oil, garlic, marjoram, salt and pepper. Massage the oil mixture inside and out of each bird. Secure a bacon slice over each bird's breast.

Place the birds in a roasting pan and roast in oven for 20 minutes (cook longer if using partridges or hens). Remove from oven. Remove the birds from the pan and let rest 10 minutes.

Place the roasting pan on the stove top, over medium-high heat. Stir in the red wine and chicken broth. Bring to boil, scraping to deglaze the pan. Cook 3 minutes, then pour through a wire strainer in a bowl containing the watercress. After 30 seconds, pour sauce back through the strainer into a gravy boat.

Make nests of wilted watercress and arrange the birds on top. Serve with sauce on side. - Serves 4

PÂTÉ DE FOIE GRAS EN CROUTE - Step up your next dinner party.

Dough:

- 2-2/3 cups flour
- 1/2 tsp. salt
- 2/3 cups cold butter, cubed
- 2 egg yolks
- 1/4 cup cream cheese
- 1/4 cup ice cold water

Combine flour, salt and butter in a food processor, pulse until ingredients form fine crumbs. Add egg yolks, cream cheese and water and pulse to form a dough ball. Remove dough and divide in half. On a floured surface, roll each piece into a rectangle slab. Wrap in plastic wrap and chill for an hour.

Filling:

- 12 oz. lean ground beef
- 12 oz. lean ground pork
- 1/2 tsp. paprika
- 1/4 tsp. ground clove
- 1/8 tsp. ground nutmeg
- 1/4 tsp. ground ginger
- 1 tsp. black pepper
- 2 tsp. salt
- 2 cloves garlic, minced
- 3 Tbs. onion, minced
- 2 tsp. dried thyme
- 1 Tbs. fresh parsley, chopped
- 2 Tbs. Amontillado sherry
- 2 eggs
- 1/4 cup Craisins (dried cranberries)
- 1/4 cup shaved smoked almonds

- 8 oz. foie gras *

Place all the filling ingredients in a large bowl and mix well with hands.

Preheat oven to 325° F.

Roll half the dough out to about 1/4 inch thick and trim it to a rectangle measuring 13 x 9 inches. Pile half the filling in the center of the dough. Add the foie gras to the middle of the filling. Cover the foie gras with remain filling and form into a loaf. Brush the edges of the dough with a wash made of 1 egg and 3 Tbs. water.

Roll out the other dough to about 1/4 inch and cut it into a rectangle 3 inches large than the first. Carefully lift the sheet of dough, center it and place over the loaf of filling. Gently mold the dough down around the filling. Trim any uneven edges and crimp them together with the back of a fork.

Cut some leaves shaped out of the dough scrapes to decorate the pastry, using some egg wash to adhere them. Cut 3 small holes in the top and insert small tin foil cones as vents. Brush the pastry well with the remaining egg wash.

Bake for 1 hour, checking after 45 minutes to be sure pastry isn't browning too quickly. If it is, cover the pastry loosely with a sheet of tin foil.

Remove from the oven and allow the pastry to cool completely, about 3 hours, before serving. - Serves 8

*http://www.amazon.com/Foie-Gras-Grade-Fresh-1-2/dp/B0036747GC/ref=sr_1_5?s=grocery&ie=UTF8&qid=1373852469&sr=1-5&keywords=foie+gras

BABA GHANOUSH

- 3 to 5 medium eggplants
- 5 Tbs. Tahini paste
- Juice of 1 lemon
- 3 cloves garlic, minced
- 1 Tbs. white vinegar
- Salt and white pepper to taste
- Olive oil
- Chopped parsley
- Chili powder
- Pickled vegetables
- Pita bread wedges

Preheat oven to 350° F.

Roast the eggplants in the oven for 30 minutes.

Remove the eggplants from the oven. Peel and discard the seeds. Strain the liquid from the eggplant flesh by placing them in a wire strain for 20 minutes over the sink.

Add eggplants, Tahini paste, lemon juice and vinegar to a food processor and pulse into a paste. Adjust to taste with salt and white pepper.

Spoon the paste onto a serving plate, make a well in the paste with the back of a spoon and pour in some olive oil.

Garnish with chopped parsley and chili powder. Serve by surrounding the mound with pickled vegetables and pita bread.

WALDORF PUDDING WITH RUM SAUCE

Sauce:

- 1 cup raisins
- 2/3 cup butter
- 1 cup sugar
- 1 cup heavy cream
- 1/4 cup Myers's dark rum
- 1 quart of boiling water

In a large saucepan, combine raisins, butter and sugar. Stir over medium heat, until the butter is melted and the sugar is dissolved. Continue to cook, stirring, until the sauce begins to caramelize and becomes a light brown. Stir in cream and continue cooking until the sauce thickens. Remove from heat and place on a low heat to keep warm.

- 1/4 cup sugar
- 1/4 cup butter, softened
- 1/2 cup flour, sifted
- 2 eggs
- 1 Tbs. baking powder
- 1/4 cup apples, chopped
- 1 tsp. pure vanilla extract
- 1/4 cup dates, minced
- 1/4 cup walnuts, chopped

Preheat the oven to 350° F.

Heavily butter 4 ramekins. In a medium bowl, using an electric hand mixer, whip butter and sugar together until creamy and then beat in eggs until well blended.

Add flour and baking powder into the egg mixture and beat 1 minute. Add in dates, apples, walnuts and vanilla extract and blend gently with a wooden spoon.

Fill the buttered ramekins 3/4 full and place them on a baking pan. Pour enough boiling water into the roasting pan to come halfway up sides of ramekins creating a water bath. Place pan in oven and bake for 30 minutes.

Remove pan from oven and let pudding cool down to room temperature.

Flip puddings onto individual dessert plates, add the 1/4 cup rum to the sauce and stir. Pour the rum sauce over the puddings, dim the lights and light the sauce with a long wooden match. - Serves 4

PEACHES IN CHARTREUSE JELLY

Jelly:

- 5 tsp. unflavored powdered gelatin
- 2 cups water
- 1/2 cup sugar
- 1 cup yellow Chartreuse

Start by dissolving gelatin in a bowl with 1 cup of water. In a small pot, bring the rest of water to a boil. Add sugar and stir until sugar is dissolved. Remove from heat and allow cooling for about 30 minutes. Add Chartreuse and the bowl of gelatin water. Stir until completely blended.

Pour into mixture into a 13 x 9 Pyrex baking dish lined with plastic wrap. Refrigerate until completely set.

Peaches:

- 1 quart boiling water
- 1 large bowl ice water

- 4 large ripe peaches
- 4 cups water
- 2 cups sugar
- 1/4 cup lemon juice
- 1 cinnamon stick
- 3 whole cloves
- Fresh mint leaves

Dip the peaches in boiling water for about 30 seconds; then immediately transfer them to ice water bath. Carefully slip off the peach skins by hand. Cut the peaches in half and remove pits.

In a medium pot, over medium heat, combine the 4 cups of water and sugar. Stir continuously until sugar is completely dissolved and water is clear. Turn heat to high, bring to a boil and cook for 1 minute.

Add the lemon juice, cinnamon stick and cloves. Add the peach halves and reduce heat to medium-low; continue cooking for 5 minutes.

Remove pot from heat and allow the peaches and syrup to cool to room temperature.

Place the pot of peaches in the refrigerator for at least 8 hours or better yet, overnight.

To serve, flip the jelly onto a baking sheet and carefully remove plastic wrap. Using small, decorative cookie cutters, cut jelly into attractive shapes.

Using two table knives lift the jelly pieces and arrange on plate. Slice peaches in crescents and fan it out over the jelly. Garnish with mint leaves and drizzle with syrup. - Serves 4

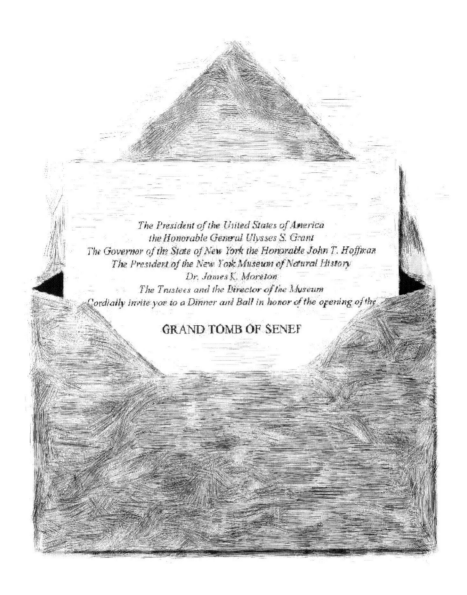

PIZZA NEAPOLITAN - Serve this one up with a large iced tea and admire your handiwork.

Dough:

- 4 cups bread flour plus some for dusting

- 2 tsp. salt
- 2 tsp. dry yeast
- 1 cup room temperature bottled water
- 1/3 cup room temperature soda water

Sift the flour, salt, and yeast together into a large mixing bowl. Add bottled water and mix into flour by hand until no dry flour can be felt. Pour in soda water and mix by hand until a smooth dough is formed.

Lightly flour a work surface and scoop out the dough. Divide the dough into four equal parts. Gently form each piece of dough into a ball and coat with olive oil. Place each in a Ziploc bag and refrigerate 12 hours.

Remove dough from Ziploc bags, shape them into balls, and allow them to rest at room temperature for about 2 hours.

- 1 Tbs. dried oregano
- 2 cups Heinz tomato sauce
- 1 lb. fresh mozzarella, cut into 1 inch cubes
- 24 fresh basil leaves

Preheat oven to 475° F.

Again on a lightly floured surface, gently form dough balls into 12 inch ovals, place ovals on pizza screens that have been generously sprayed with cooking spray. Using a 1/2 measuring cup, ladle the tomato sauce on each crust.

Sprinkle sauce with oregano and sparsely place mozzarella cubes over the surface of the pizza. Place the basil leaves on the sauce, in between the cheese. Bake pizzas for 10 to 12 minutes or until the crust is golden brown. - Serves 4 to 6

HAWAIIAN DOUBLE - PINEAPPLE WITH HONEY GLAZED HAM, EXTRA GARLIC PIZZA - A freaking monster of a good pie.

Dough:

- 4-1/2 cups bread flour plus some for dusting
- 1-1/2 Tbs. sugar
- 1 Tbs. salt
- 2 Tbs. dry yeast
- 3 Tbs. olive oil
- 2 cups warm water

Combine flour, sugar, salt, and yeast in food processor using the dough blade. Pulse 3 to 4 times until combined. Add olive oil and water. Run food processor until mixture forms ball that jumps around in the bowl above the blade, about 30 seconds. Continue to let the dough dance around for 15 seconds longer. Mixing may also be done by hand, in a large bowl (but it's not as much fun for the dough ball).

Transfer dough ball to lightly floured work surface and knead for 10 minutes until a smooth ball is formed. Divide dough in half and place each one in a separate, lightly oiled bowl. Cover tightly with plastic wrap and allow rising in a warm spot until they have doubled in volume (about 1 hour).

Turn single dough ball out onto lightly flour surface. Gently press out dough into an 8 inch circle, leaving outer edge about 1 inch thicker than the rest. Gently stretch dough by draping over knuckles into a 16-inch circle about 1/4 inches thick. Transfer dough to a baking sheet, pizza pan or pizza screen. Repeat with the second dough ball.

Ham & Pineapple Topping:

- 4 Tbs. brown sugar
- 2 Tbs. white vinegar

- 4 Tbs. vegetable oil, divided
- 1 tsp. brown mustard
- 1/2 lb. ham steak, cut into 1 inch cubes
- 1 (15 oz.) can pineapple chunks, drained
- 6 cloves garlic, chopped

Place 2 Tbs. of oil and garlic in a large iron skillet over medium heat. Mix together brown sugar, vinegar, remaining vegetable oil, and mustard in a medium glass bowl. Add cubed ham and pineapple to mixture and toss until well coated. Using a slotted spoon remove ham and pineapple from mixture; transfer to the hot skillet. Allow to cook undisturbed for 4 minutes, flip with a metal scapula, and cook 4 minutes longer or until lightly caramelized. Remove ham and pineapple from skillet and set aside to cool.

- 2 cup prepared marinara sauce
- 4 cups shredded mozzarella cheese
- 1/2 tsp. crushed red pepper

Preheat oven to 450° F.

With the pizza crusts now on baking sheets, pizza pans or pizza screens, sprinkle half the cheese evenly over the pizza crusts, leaving a 1/2-inch border. Top with ham/pineapple mixture; sprinkle with red pepper. Dribble marinara sauce on the pizza and top with the remaining cheese. Bake pizza for 12 minutes or until the crust is crisp and lightly browned. - Serves 4 to 6

SHRIMP BISQUE – Surprisingly, cafeteria dining at its finest.

- 1/2 stick butter, divided
- 2 lbs. medium head-on shrimp
- 1 bay leaf
- 8 cups water
- 3 carrots, peeled, chopped
- 2 celery stalks, chopped
- 1/2 white onion, chopped
- 1/2 cup cognac
- 1/4 cup white rice
- 3 Tbs. tomato paste
- 3 sprigs fresh parsley & 3 sprigs fresh thyme tied in a bundle
- 1/4 tsp. cayenne pepper
- Salt and white pepper
- 1/2 cup heavy cream
- 1 to 2 Tbs. fresh lemon juice
- Chives, coarsely chopped, for garnish

Peel and remove heads of shrimp (reserving shells and heads in a bowl). De-vein and chop each shrimp into three pieces, place them in a lidded container and set aside in the refrigerator.

Place a stockpot over medium-high heat and add 1 Tbs. of butter. Add the shrimp shells and heads and cook for 3 minutes. Add the bay leaf and 8 cups water to the pot and simmer for 30 minutes, uncovered. Place a wire strainer over a large bowl and carefully strain the shrimp stock. Set the stock aside and allow it to cool.

Rinse the stockpot and return it to the stove top on medium-high heat. Melt 1 Tbs. butter and allow it to bubble slightly. Add shrimp meat and cook for 3 to 5 minutes, stirring occasionally. Transfer cooked shrimp to a plate and set aside. Add remaining 2 Tbs. butter to the pot along with carrots, celery, and onion and cook for 20 minutes.

Carefully add the cognac to the pot. Stir vegetables until most of the cognac has evaporated. Add the rice and stir for 2 minutes. Add shrimp stock, tomato paste, parsley/thyme bundle and cayenne pepper. Simmer uncovered for 25 minutes or until rice is fully cooked. Season the mixture to taste with salt and white pepper. Remove pot from heat and remove the parsley/thyme bundle. Add the cooked shrimp to the pot.

Purée in a blender or food processor, in batches, until smooth, and return to the pot. Stir in heavy cream and return bisque to stove over medium-low heat. Add lemon juice a little at a time and taste. Readjust with more lemon juice, salt and white pepper to taste. Garnish with chopped chives. - Serves 4 to 6

SMOKED STURGEON CROQUETTES - Dispense with the decorum and take a double heap of each.

- 6 to 8 red potatoes, (about 3/4 of a lb.)
- 1/2 stick butter
- Milk
- 2 eggs, beaten
- 1 lb. smoked sturgeon, flaked and deboned
- 1/4 cup minced chives
- 1/4 cup chopped parsley
- Black pepper
- 1/2 cup panko bread crumbs
- 1/2 cup Parmesan cheese
- Vegetable oil, for frying

Garnish:

- 1 cup sour cream
- 1/4 cup minced chives
- Paprika
- Caviar

Combine panko and Parmesan cheese in a shallow dish or pie pan.

Boil potatoes in a stockpot of salted water about 25 minutes or until fork tender. Drain potatoes and transfer them to a large bowl. Using a wooden spoon combine the potatoes, butter and just enough milk to moisten. Use an electric mixer to whip the potato mixture until smooth. Mix in the eggs.

Fold in the sturgeon, chives, parsley, and pepper to the potato mixture. Once blended form mixture into small 2-inch patties about 1/2 inch thick, and dredge in the Panko/cheese coating.

Heat vegetable oil in a large iron skillet, over medium-high. Fry the sturgeon patties about 3 minutes on each side or until browned. The sturgeon croquettes can be held in a warm oven until all the cakes are done.

Mix the sour cream and chives together. Serve sturgeon croquettes topped with a spoonful of sour cream, sprinkled with paprika and caviar. - Serves 6 to 8

SMOKED SALMON WITH CAVIAR

- 2 eggs
- 1 Tbs. balsamic vinegar
- Kosher salt
- Cracked black pepper
- 4 romaine lettuce leaves, torn into pieces
- 1/2 lb. smoked salmon, thinly sliced
- 4 Tbs. whipped cream cheese
- 1 small jar Sevruga or Beluga caviar
- 1/4 cup pickled pearl onions
- 12 dill pickle chips
- 4 slices rye bread, toasted and cut into points
- 1 Tbs. Savor brand Vegetable & Dill Seasoning *

Place the eggs a small saucepan and cover them with cool water. Bring water to a boil and simmer for 3 minutes. Transfer the eggs to a bowl of ice water to cool. Carefully peel the eggs and halve them lengthwise.

In a medium bowl, whisk together vinegar and 3 Tbs. olive oil and season with salt and pepper to taste. Toss the lettuce leaves in the dressing.

Make a nest of lettuce to one side of a plate and top with the smoked salmon slices. Surround the salad with the halved eggs.

Make a small mound of cream cheese to the opposite side of the plate and create a dimple in top of the cream cheese. Top the cream cheese with caviar. Arrange the pearl onions, pickles and rye toast point around the plate.

Sprinkle the plate with vegetable dill seasoning. - Serves 2 to 4

* http://www.amazon.com/Vegetable-and-Dill-Dip-Mix/dp/B00EO516H8/ref=sr_1_17?s=grocery&ie=UTF8&qid=1398997499&sr=1-17&keywords=bagel+seasoning

CRUSTY BREAD & SAN DANIELE PROSCIUTTO

- 3 cups bread flour
- 1 tsp. active dry yeast
- 1 tsp. salt
- 1-1/2 cup water, warmed

- 18 oz. Prosciutto Di San Daniele, thinly sliced*
- 8 oz. Ambrosi Italian Butter**

Mix together flour, yeast and salt in a large bowl. Add warm water and stir until the dough is mixed well. Cover the bowl with plastic wrap and set aside in a warm place overnight.

Place a Dutch oven along with its lid in place, into the oven while preheating it to 450° F and heat the pot and lid for 20 minutes.

Meanwhile, dust a work surface with flour fairly heavy. Turn the dough out onto the work surface and very gently, form the dough into a round dome shape (do not knead or deflate the dough). Let the loaf rest while the pot and lid finish heating up.

Remove the Dutch oven from the oven with mitts and remove the lid. Very gently lift the dough and place it in the pot. Place the lid back on and return the Dutch oven to the oven.

Bake bread for 30 minutes. Open the oven, remove the lid, and bake for an additional 10 minutes. Remove the pot and let cool 5 minutes before inverting the pot to remove the loaf.

Serve with butter and slices of Prosciutto Di San Daniele. - Serves 6 to 8

*http://www.igourmet.com/shoppe/Prosciutto-di-San-Daniele-by-Principe---Sliced-.asp

**http://www.amazon.com/Ambrosi-Italian-Butter-8-45-oz/dp/B00BPN9TH6/ref=sr_1_1?s=grocery&ie=UTF8&qid=1398998342&sr=1-1&keywords=italian+butter

SEVRUGA CAVIAR WITH CRAB TRUFFLE CUSTARD

- 2 eggs + 1 egg yolk
- 1/2 tsp. white truffle butter, melted
- 1 cup whipping cream
- 1 Tbs. tamari
- 1/2 lb. cooked jumbo lump crab meat
- 3 Tbs. sour cream

- 1 Tbs. finely chopped chives
- 2 tsp. lemon juice
- Salt and fresh ground black pepper, to taste
- 1 oz. Sevruga caviar

Preheat the oven to 350° F.

Arrange 6 small ramekins or 6 crème brulee dishes in a deep baking pan. Bring a medium saucepan of water to a low simmer for what's called a water bath.

Beat together the eggs, egg yolk, and melted truffle butter in a medium bowl and set aside.

In another small saucepan over medium heat, combine the cream and tamari. Bring to a simmer, stirring constantly; remove from the heat and let cool 3 minutes. Slowly whisk about 1/4 cup of the hot cream mixture into the beaten eggs to temper. Whisking constantly and briskly, slowly pour the tempered eggs into the hot cream mixture. Once well combined, transfer the mixture into a large container with some sort of pouring spout.

Now carefully pour the mixture into the ramekins or crème brulee dishes, just about 3/4 full.

Carefully pour enough hot water from the medium saucepan into the baking pan to reach halfway up the containers to create a water bath.

Cover the deep baking pan with tin foil and bake 10 minutes or until a toothpick poked in the center of the custards comes out clean.

Carefully remove the baking pan from the oven and remove the ramekins. Allow custards to cool to room temperature on the counter.

In a small bowl, gently fold together the crab, sour cream, chives, and lemon juice. Season the crab mixture with salt and pepper.

To serve, spoon a small amount of the crab mixture on top of the custards, then top with a small heap of Sevruga caviar. - Serves 6

CAVIAR & CRÈME FRAICHE CREPES

- 1-1/4 cups buckwheat flour
- 4 eggs
- 1/4 cup vegetable oil
- 1 cup milk
- 1 cup water
- 1/4 tsp. salt
- 2 cups crème fraîche
- 4 oz. favorite caviar
- Zest of one lemon
- 1/4 cup chopped parsley

Combine flour, eggs, oil, milk, water, and salt in a food processor. Pulse until well blended and refrigerate, covered, for 1 hour.

Apply cooking spray to a 10 inch nonstick pan and place over medium-high heat. Add 1/4 cupful of batter to pan and swirl to coat bottom. Cook crepe 45 seconds or until golden on bottom. Use a spatula to flip the crepe and cook 30 seconds longer.

Transfer to a plate and repeat with the remaining batter. Spread each crepe with 1/8 cup crème fraiche to one side and roll up loosely. Top with a dab more of the crème fraiche, caviar, lemon zest and garnish with chopped parsley. - Serves 2

OYSTERS ROCKEFELLER

- 18 fresh oysters on the half shell
- 3/4 stick butter
- 2 cups fresh spinach leaves
- 1/4 cup unseasoned prepared bread crumbs
- 2 Tbs. chives
- 2 Tbs. fresh celery leaves
- 2 Tbs. tarragon leaves
- 3 Tbs. parsley
- 1/8 tsp. anise seeds
- Tabasco Sauce to taste
- 1/4 tsp. salt
- Rock salt
- Lemon wedges and parsley sprigs for garnish

Using an oyster knife, pry open the oyster shells from the back hinge. Remove oysters and place them in a bowl with any oyster juice (liquor). Pick 18 of the shells that are in the best shape and throw away the rest.

Melt the butter in a large saucepan over medium heat. Add spinach, bread crumbs, chives, celery leaves, tarragon, parsley, anise seeds, Tabasco Sauce and salt. Cook for 15 minutes, stirring constantly. Remove spinach mixture from heat, pour into a food processor and puree. Allow the mixture cool to room temperature.

Adjust the oven rack to the broiler position and preheat the broiler. Spread a layer of rock salt about 1/2-inches deep on an oven proof platter. Set oysters shells in the rock salt, and push them down to make them level.

Place an oyster and some of the oyster juice in each shell. Add a spoonful of the spinach mixture over each oyster and spread to the rim of the shell. Broil (watching carefully so it doesn't burn) until spinach starts to bubble and brown slightly, about 5 minutes. Garnish the platter with the parsley and lemon wedges. - Serves 4

FRENCH CHEESE BOARD

- 1 bundle red or rainbow chard
- 7 oz. Saucisson Sec dried sausage, sliced
- 8 oz. Gruyere
- 8 oz. Delice de Bourgogne
- 4 oz. Roquefort
- 4 oz. Ossau Iraty
- 4 oz. Selles Sur Cher
- 4 oz. Tomme de Savoie
- 4 oz. Brie de Bourgogne
- 2 pears, cut in wedges and cored
- 2 apples, cut in rings, cored and rinsed in lemon juice
- 1/2 lb. grapes, washed and cut into clusters
- 4 figs cut in half
- 8 strawberries cut in half
- 1/2 cup walnuts
- 1 large baguette, slices

Lay a bed of red, rainbow chard or other greenery on a cutting board or a piece for clean slate. Place sausage in the center and arrange cheese around the meat.

Make labels for each cheese by cutting a groove in wine corks and slipping in a piece of white paper with the name of the cheese written or printed on it. If possible stick a small knife in the top of each cheese.

Place the fruit to the outer edge of the arrangement and scatter the walnuts over the board. Place the bread in a linen lined basket beside the cheese board. - Serves 8 to 10

PAPER THIN PROSCIUTTO WITH MELON

- 1/4 lb. thinly sliced Prosciutto
- 1 honeydew melon
- 1 lemon
- 1 (8 oz.) container of fresh mozzarella cheese, cut into 1/2 inch cubes
- 1 bundle fresh basil
- Cracked black pepper

Cut the melon in half and remove the seeds. Using a melon-baller, scoop the melon into small balls. Place melon balls in a bowl, sprinkle with lemon juice and toss.

Take a small strip of prosciutto and wrap it around a melon ball. Pierce through with a toothpick; add a mozzarella cube and top with a basil leaf. Repeat for all melon balls and arrange on a platter. Sprinkle platter generously with fresh cracked pepper. - Serves 4 to 6

GREEN TEA AND BUTTERED TOAST - Not the usual breakfast thank you...........

- Quality loose green tea leaves
- Distilled or natural spring water
- 1 loaf sliced country white bread
- Butter, room temperature

Green tea is at its best when the leaves are loose in the water while steeping. Also, the tea should be steeped in a glass or ceramic vessel. Use 1 tsp. of loose green tea leaves per 6 ounce cup.

Use only distilled or natural spring water. Allow the water to come to a full boil over high heat. When the water comes to a boil, remove from the heat and pour it into your favorite ceramic teapot. This will heat the pot, while cooling the water a bit. After 1 minute, pour the water into the cups. Discard any extra water from the teapot.

While the tea cups are warming, measure 1 tsp. of tea leaves per tea cup into the tea pot. Pour the water from the tea cups back into the tea pot and cover. Allow tea to steep for no more than 3 minutes to avoid bitterness.

Gently pour the tea back into the cups from the teapot using a strainer.

For decaffeinated green tea, let the tea steep for only 30 seconds in the teapot, and then pour off all the water. The water poured off will contain most of the caffeine. Add more hot water to the teapot and allow tea to steep for no more then 2-1/2 minutes. This method will remove about 75% of the caffeine.

For Perfect Toast:

Place a loaf of sliced country white bread in the refrigerator for at least 4 hours. Remove 2 to 4 slices of bread from the bag.

Place the toast in the toaster and press down the toaster lever. Immediately after pressing the lever, place a small plate up side down over the toasters slots (this will warm up the serving plate). Remove the plate after exactly 3 minutes 30 seconds (be careful, it's hot).

Count 5 seconds more and unplug the toaster. This will cause the toast to magically pop up. Immediately spread each slice of toast with 1/2 Tbs. of room temperature butter. Cut toast on the diagonal and transfer to the warmed plate.

POACHED EGGS - A late breakfast that should fully satisfy the senses.

- 1 egg
- Water
- Olive oil

Bring a small saucepan of water to a gentle simmer. Tear a square of microwave safe plastic wrap off a roll and lay it out on the counter top. Dribble a few drops of olive oil on the plastic wrap and spread it around with your fingertip. Drape the wrap over a small bowl and press the wrap down into the bowl. Crack an egg into bowl. Gather the plastic wrap above the egg and tie it closed with a twist tie.

Lower the packet into the simmering water for exactly 3 minutes. Remove packet with a slotted spoon. Cut the plastic wrap just below the twist tie with some kitchen shears and remove poached egg. - Serves 1

JUGGED KIPPERS

- 2 pair of kippers (2 dried, smoked herring - split and flattened)
- Water
- 1 stick of butter, frozen
- 2 Tbs. sour cream mixed with 1 tsp. prepared horseradish
- 2 Tbs. chopped chives

Bring a medium pot of water to a boil. Put the kippers in a heat proof pitcher or "jug" (the container should be tall and fairly narrow). Pour enough boiling water into the pitcher to cover the kippers.

Cover the top of the jug with a sheet of tin foil and seal. Allow kippers to steep for 7 minutes, and then discard the water from the jug. Place the jugged kippers on a warmed plate and grate 3 swipes of the frozen butter over top of the kippers with a cheese grater. Garnish with a dollop of horseradish sauce and sprinkle with chives. - Serves 1

RASHERS OF BACON

- 8 to 12 rashers of bacon, back bacon or Canadian bacon

Preheat oven to 400° F.

Arrange rashers* in a single layer on a shallow rimmed bake sheet lined with tin foil or parchment paper. Bake rashers for 10 to15 minutes (turning once during cooking) or until it has reached desired crispness.

*http://www.britishbacon.com/home/29-irish-style-bacon-rashers.html

GRAPEFRUIT HALF

- 1 grapefruit
- 2 Tbs. white or brown sugar
- 2 maraschino cherries

Cut the grapefruit in half, (between the two dimples, not along them), with a large, sharp knife. Using a special grapefruit knife, (this is a double edged, serrated knife with a bent tip). Run the edge of the knife along the inside of each segment side. Then make a full circle of the outside perimeter between the edge of the segments and the peel.

Place the grapefruit half in a bowl a bit larger than the fruit. Sprinkle the surface of the grapefruit with white or brown sugar and garnish with a maraschino cherry in the center. - Serves 2

SCONES AND JAM

Strawberry Banana Jam:

- 4 cups strawberries, cleaned and stemmed
- 2 cups bananas, peeled
- 4 cups sugar
- 1/4 cups fresh lemon juice

Place strawberries, bananas, sugar and lemon juice in a large saucepan. Mash ingredients together by hand (leave mixture a bit chunky). Place saucepan on stove over low heat and stir until the sugar is dissolved.

Increase heat to medium, and bring the mixture to a boil, stirring often, for about 15 minutes. Let the jam cool to room temperature, then transfer to a lidded container and refrigerate over night.

Buttered Scones:

- 1-3/4 all purpose flour
- 5 Tbs. sugar
- 2-1/2 tsp. baking powder
- 1/2 tsp. salt
- 1/3 cup cold butter
- 1 egg, beaten
- 1/2 tsp. pure vanilla extract
- 6 Tbs. heavy cream
- 1 stick butter, room temperature
- Strawberry Banana Jam (or other prepared fruit jam)

Preheat the oven to 400° F.

In a large mixing bowl combined flour, 3 Tbs. sugar, baking powder and salt and stir until well combined. Using a fork, press the butter into the flour mixture until it looks like fine crumbs. Add egg, vanilla and 5 Tbs. of cream.

Using your fork, blend together until the mixture forms soft dough (but try not to over mix).

Place dough on a lightly floured work surface and gently roll in the flour to coat. Slightly flatten the dough and fold it in half and press down. Repeat this kneading process 6 more times.

Place the dough on cookie sheet. Roll or press the dough into about an 8 inch disk then sliced the dough into 8 wedges with a sharp knife. Using a pastry brush, moisten the top of the dough with the rest of the heavy cream and sprinkle with the left over sugar.

Bake 14 to 16 minutes or until light golden brown. Remove from oven, separate wedges and serve warm with butter and jam. - Serves 4 to 8

RAW OYSTERS ON THE HALF SHELL - Tip the shell back, suck it down, smack your lips and repeat.

- 1/2 cup prepared horseradish
- 1 Tbs. dark brown sugar
- 1/2 tsp. fresh lemon juice
- 1-3/4 cups Heinz ketchup

In a small bowl combine horseradish, brown sugar, lemon juice and ketchup and mix well. Chill in refrigerator.

(SHUCKING AN OYSTER)

Fold a clean heavy towel in half and then half again and place it on a work surface. Place the oyster, hinge side facing out, in the fold of the towel. Place the tip of an oyster knife in the seam of the hinge. Push the knife into the hinge (a heavy work glove may be use for protection). Wiggle the knife from side to side a bit in order to pry the shell open. Once the blade has pried open the hinge, open the shell wide enough to slide the tip of the knife inside the oyster. Keep the tip of the blade slanted upwards and scrape it along the inside top of the oyster shell.

Slide the blade along the roof until it reaches the muscle that connects the two shells. Sever the muscle from the top shell. Lift off the top shell to reveal the raw oyster. Slip the tip of the oyster knife underneath the flesh of the oyster and into the spot where the muscle connects to the bottom shell. Clean any grit, loose shell or mud from oysters. The oyster should be plump and floating in its liquor.

- 2 dozen oysters in the shell, shucked
- Crushed ice
- Tabasco Sauce
- Lemon wedges

Place a small bowl of cocktail sauce, with a small spoon on bed of crushed ice in a tray and surround with the oysters. Add few drops of Tabasco sauce to each oyster and serve with lemon wedges. - Serves 4

CROISSANTS - A light snack while catching up on your newly acquired thriller, perhaps?

Dough:

- 2 eggs
- Warm water
- 1/4 cup sugar
- 5-1/2 to 6 cups bread flour
- 2-1/4 tsp. instant active yeast
- 1/2 cup nonfat dry milk
- 1 Tbs. salt
- 2 Tbs. butter, melted
- 1 egg + 1 Tbs. water, beaten for egg wash

Butter Slab:

- 2 cups unsalted butter, cold
- 3/4 tsp. Salt
- 1/2 cup all purpose flour

To make your "starter" crack the eggs into a Pyrex measuring cup. Add just enough warm water to equal 2 cups. Beat until completely blended and transfer to a large mixing bowl. Add 1 Tbs. of the sugar, 2 cups of the bread flour, and the yeast. Mix the starter with a wooden spoon until smooth. Cover bowl with plastic wrap and set aside.

While the starter rises, make your butter stab. Mix the butter and 1/2 cup all purpose flour in a food processor until the mixture is very smooth. Scoop the butter mixture out onto a floured sheet of plastic wrap and mold it into a square about 8 x 8 inches. Wrap the butter in the plastic wrap and set it in the refrigerator for an hour to chill.

To finish up the dough, stir the melted butter into the starter. Sift together the remaining 3 and 1/2 cups of the bread flour, the rest of the sugar, dry milk, and salt. Add the flour mixture to your starter and mix, with your hands, to form a soft dough.

Once the dough is smooth, pat it into a square shape and wrap it in plastic wrap that has been lightly sprayed with vegetable oil and set it in the refrigerator for about 30 minutes.

Remove the dough from the refrigerator, unwrap it and place on a lightly floured work surface. With a floured rolling pin, very gently roll the dough into a 12-inch square. Place the butter slab (unwrapped of course) in the center of the dough, so it resembles a diamond of butter on a square of dough.

Pull the 4 dough flaps up and over the edges of the butter until they meet in the middle. Seal the edges of the dough together by pinching and tucking the seams.

Lightly dust the top of the dough bundle with flour, then flip the dough over and whack it gently with a rolling pin, until it forms rectangle. Now - rolling from the center out, form a rectangle about 20 x 10 inches. Fold the bottom third of the dough up to the center, and the top third down over that. Wrap the dough in the oiled plastic wrap again and this time place it in the freezer for 15 minutes.

Repeat the rolling, folding, freezing process 2 more times.

Remove the dough from the freezer one last time. Unwrap the dough and place it on a lightly floured work surface. Dust the top of the dough, lightly with flour. Using your rolling pin, roll the dough into a long and narrow strip, 8 x 30 inches. Lift the dough a bit off the table so it can relax and shrink back a bit. Roll the dough out one last time so you have a long strip about 8 x 40 inches.

Use a household ruler to mark along one long sides of the dough every 5 inches with a knife. Position the ruler's edge half way between the knife marks and lightly press down. Slice the dough into wedges, starting from the knife mark to the center line on the opposite end with a pizza cutter.

Stretch the wedge to about 10 inches in length and roll it up from wide end to point. Curl the points around to form the classic crescent shape. Shape the rest of the croissants in the same way and arrange them on two parchment lined baking sheets. Be sure to leave as much space as possible between them. Brush the croissants with the egg wash and place the baking sheets in a warm spot for about 2 hours or until they are about doubled in size.

Preheat oven to 425° F.

Bake the croissants for 18 to 20 minutes or until they turn a rich brown color. Serve warm with softened butter. - Serves 8 to 16

AUTHENTIC PROCACCI'S PANINI TARTUFATI - This is a close second to the Panini Tartufati at Procacci's.

- 4 cups bread flour
- 6 Tbs. warm water
- 2 Tbs. sugar
- 1 Tbs. yeast
- 1 cup warm water
- 1 tsp. salt
- 3 Tbs. cold butter, cubed

Add the yeast, sugar and 6 Tbs. warm water in a bowl. Mix and set aside for 10 minutes or until the yeast blooms. Add in the flour and 1 cup water and mix for 5 minutes. Add in the salt and mix for 5-6 minutes more. Add in the butter and mix for 3 minutes longer. Remove the dough, grease the bowl and the dough ball and transfer the dough back to the bowl. Covered the bowl with plastic wrap and place it in a warm spot until doubled in size.

Divide the dough into 16 pieces and shape into logs. Transfer to a sprayed, parchment lined tray and cover. Allow loaves to rise 45 minutes. Preheat oven to 375° F and bake for 15 to 20 minutes or until lightly golden brown.

Allow rolls to cool slightly before splitting and applying a generous amount of Urbani white truffle butter.* - Serves 8 to 16

*http://urbani.com/white-truffle-butter.html

"TRUFFLE" SANDWICHES

- 12 oz. portabella mushrooms, cleaned and sliced
- 2 Tbs. butter
- 1 cup shredded Fontina cheese
- 1/2 cup fresh grated Parmesan cheese
- 2 Tbs. chopped fresh Italian parsley
- 4 thick slices crusty bread
- 2 Tbs. white truffle butter*
- Salt

Preheat a Panini press or griddle. Meanwhile melt butter in an iron skillet over medium high heat. Add mushrooms and cook 5 minutes. Remove the skillet from the heat and let cool. Drain any liquid from the skillet and then stir in parsley, Fontina, and Parmesan cheese.

Brush the side of two slices of bread that will be facing out with truffle butter and sprinkle with salt. Add filling and place the two remaining slices of bread on top and brush with the remaining truffle butter.

Press sandwiches on Panini grill or place on griddle until golden brown (if using a griddle, flip and brown the other side) and all the cheese has melted. Serve immediately. - Serves 2

*http://urbani.com/white-truffle-butter.html

COARSE BREAD WITH WILD BOAR SALAMI AND OLIVES - The scent of lemon flowers and salt air would add to this repast, but you'll have to draw a line somewhere.

- 3 tsp. dry yeast
- 2 cup lukewarm water
- 1/3 cup molasses
- 1/2 Tbs. salt
- 1/4 cup shortening
- 3 cups white bread flour
- 1 cup whole wheat bread flour
- 1/4 cup sugar
- 4 Tbs. melted butter

Dissolve yeast in water, stir and let mixture bloom for 5 minutes. Add molasses, salt, sugar, shortening and 1 cup of white flour. Stir until well blended, about 5 minutes. Add rest of flours and knead with greased hands 10 minutes.

Place dough in a greased bowl and cover. Set in a warm place until dough doubles in size. Knead dough again, cover and let rise once more until doubled.

Divide in half and shape into loaves. Loosely cover and let loaves rise one hour.

Preheat oven to 350° F and bake the bread for about 45 minutes. Remove the loaves from oven and brush with melted butter. Serve with wild boar salami, olive oil and Gaeta olives - Serves 4 to 6

* http://www.amazon.com/Wild-Boar-Salami-Creminelli-pack/dp/B00FPNN964/ref=sr_1_1?ie=UTF8&qid=139125103 3&sr=8-1&keywords=Creminelli-Wild-Boar-Salami-salami

"And yet these were not lovers – these were enemies, joined in a mortal struggle..."

FEVER DREAM

SALAMI & CHIPATI BREAD

SANDWICHES

ROAST KUDU

HAM

TURKEY

CUCUMBER

SUCCOTASH

FIELD PEAS

HAM STEAK WITH RED EYE GRAVY

LOBSTER CLAWS

BEER BATTER FISH

PUMPKIN SPICE DOUGHNUT

BACON, EGGS & GRITS

OLD FASHIONED EGG CREAM

CRAW FISH PO'BOY

CATFISH FRIED

CATFISH OVEN FRIED

CATFISH BAKED

CATFISH BROILED

PINE BARK STEW

HUSH PUPPIES

RICE BEANS SPAM

SARDINES

SMOKED SALMON

STONE CRAB CLAWS

TRUFFLE & FOIE GRAS SANDWICH

DOUBLE CHOCOLATE FAT ONES

CHOCOLATE BANANA CREAM FAT ONES

ALLIGATOR ETOUFFEE

ROAST SADDLE OF LAMB

RIBS

PICKLED EGGS

PIG'S TROTTERS

BEER PICKLES

SALAMI & CHAPATI BREAD - This recipe is a walk in the park, just remember where we parked.

- 1-1/2 cups whole wheat flour
- 1/2 cup all purpose flour
- 1 tsp. salt
- 1 Tbs. vegetable oil
- 3/4 cup warm water

- 1 lb. thick slices hard salami

In mixing bowl, combine flours, salt, olive oil, and water. Stir together to form a soft dough. Knead the dough ten times, then cover bowl tightly with plastic wrap. Let dough stand at room temperature for 1 hour.

Form 10 equal sized balls from the dough. Roll out each ball on a lightly floured surface into 6-inch rounds.

Heat an ungreased iron skillet over medium high heat. Lay the rounds on the hot skillet. Cook until the dough starts to puff slightly, then turn and cook until light golden brown spots form. Remove chapati to a kitchen - Serves 4

SANDWICHES - How about a "light" lunch for the heat of the day?

Capri Sandwich:

- 2 slices Italian bread
- 1 fresh ripe tomato, sliced
- 1 ball fresh mozzarella, sliced
- 1 handful fresh basil leaves
- 1 Tbs. basil pesto

- 1 splash balsamic vinegar

Assemble sandwich and grill if desired. - Serves 1

Turkey & Ham Sandwich:

- 1 onion roll, sliced in half
- 1 Tbs. Hellman's mayonnaise
- 1 tsp. Dijon mustard
- 1 Tbs. cranberry sauce
- 2 slices roast turkey breast
- 2 slices Swiss cheese
- 2 slices smoked ham
- 2 slices dill pickle

Assemble the sandwich and brush the outside with a bit of oil. Grill over medium heat until golden brown on both sides. - Serves 1

KUDU POT ROAST

- 1 cup dry red wine
- 1 cup water
- 3 tsp. salt
- 3 large bay leaves
- 10 whole cloves
- 1/2 tsp. ground allspice
- 1 large onion, sliced
- 1 (4 to 5 lb.) kudu, venison or beef rump roast*
- 3 Tbs. bacon drippings or oil
- 1 (10 oz.) bar dark chocolate
- 1/4 cup port

- 1 (12 oz.) jar pear preserves**
- salt and pepper, to taste

Combine wine, water, salt, bay leaf, cloves, allspice and onions for the marinade. Put meat in a deep plastic container and pour marinade over meat. Cover and refrigerate for 1 to 2 days.

Drain the marinade and set aside. Dry the surface of the meat with paper towels.

Add bacon grease to a Dutch oven over medium heat. Brown all sides of roast well and then add 1 cup of the reserved marinade. Cover, reduce heat to medium-low and simmer for 3 hours or until meat is tender. Check the liquid level often and add more marinade as needed.

Remove roast and wrap in tin foil to keep it warm.

To make the gravy: Strain the meat juices into a medium saucepan pot. Add the chocolate bar and whisk until melted. Add the port and pear preserves. Reduce the sauce until thick enough to coat the back of a spoon. Adjust the seasoning with salt and pepper.

Transfer the kudu roast to serving platter and slice thin. Serve roast with gravy on the side. - Serves 8

*https://www.osgrow.com/
** http://www.amazon.com/Braswells-   Pure-Pear-Preserves-10-
5oz/dp/B0043JD9DE/ref=sr_1_1?s=grocery&ie=UTF8&qid=
1398766301&sr=1-1&keywords=pear+preserves

BAKED HAM

- 8 lb. whole cooked ham
- 2 Tbs. whole cloves
- 1/2 cup orange marmalade
- 1/3 cup pure Highland County VA maple syrup
- 1/4 cup freshly squeezed orange juice
- 12 celery stalks

Place oven rack in the lowest position, and then preheat it to 350° F.

Using a sharp knife, remove any rind, and then score fat diagonally at 2-inch intervals to form a diamond pattern. Stud the center of each diamond with a whole clove.

Place marmalade, maple syrup and orange juice in a small saucepan over medium heat. Stir until marmalade has melted and mixture is well combined. Place ham on a bed of celery placed in a roasting pan. Brush ham with half the marmalade mixture. Bake ham, basting with remaining marmalade mixture every 10 minutes, for 1 hour or until glaze is golden. Slice and serve warm or cold.

APRICOT GLAZED HAM

- 2 packaged pre-cooked ham steaks
- 3 Tbs. dark brown sugar
- 3 Tbs. Smucker's apricot preserves
- 2 tsp. ground mustard
- Dash ground cloves

Preheat oven to 350° F.

Place ham steak in a baking dish coated with cooking spray. Combine the remaining ingredients; spoon over ham. Bake ham for 15 minutes or until completely heated through. - Serves 2

HAM SALAD

- 2 cups ham, diced
- 1/4 cup celery
- 1/4 cup onion
- 8 Tbs. Hellmann's mayonnaise
- 2 Tbs. sweet pickle relish
- Black pepper to taste
- 1 hard boil egg, chopped
- 1 Tbs. parsley

Mince the ham, celery and onion together in the food processor. Mix in mayonnaise and fold in diced egg, relish and parsley. Add pepper to taste. Serve on lettuce leaves or as sandwiches. - Serves 4

BUNGALOW TURKEY BREASTS

- 6 boneless, skinless turkey breasts
- 2 Tbs. olive oil
- 2 Tbs. dried basil
- 1 envelope Lipton onion soup mix

Rinse the breasts under cold water and pat dry with a paper towel. Coat them with olive oil. Rub the Lipton soup mix and basil onto each breast. Place seasoned turkey breast in a crock pot. Cover, and cook on low for 5 to 6 hours. - Serves 6

ROAST TURKEY BREAST

- 1 (5 lb.) turkey breast, skin on
- 2 Tbs. melted butter
- salt and pepper
- 1 stick butter and a muslin towel for basting
- 2 cups Swanson's chicken broth
- 1/4 cup dry white wine

Preheat oven to 450° F.

Place the turkey breast on a wire rack in a roasting pan. Massage in the 2 Tbs. of butter over the breast. Generously season the turkey with salt and black pepper. Melt the butter in a large bowl, and soak the muslin towel in it until it's well saturated. Cover the turkey completely with the buttered towel and place roasting pan in the preheated oven. Pour the chicken stock and white wine into the roasting pan, around turkey breast.

Roast for 45 minutes then remove towel and roast 15 minutes more. When internal temperature reaches 155° F or when juices run clear after turkey is pierced, remove the turkey from the oven. Cover and allow meat to rest 10 minutes. – Serves 8

CUCUMBER SALAD

- 1 lb. English cucumber, peeled, sliced 1/8 inch thick
- 3/4 tsp. salt
- 1/2 cup sour cream
- 2 Tbs. fresh dill, finely chopped
- 1 Tbs. white wine vinegar
- 1/4 tsp. freshly ground black pepper

Place a wire strainer over a large bowl. Add the cucumbers and 1/2 tsp. of the salt and toss to combine. Let sliced cucumbers sit in strainer at room temperature for 1 hour.

Gently press down on the cucumbers to remove excess moisture. Discard the cucumber juice from the bowl and add sour cream, dill, vinegar, pepper, and remaining 1/4 tsp. of salt in the bowl. Add the cucumbers and toss by hand to evenly coat. Refrigerate for 30 minutes before serving. - Serves 2 to 4

SUCCOTASH - Take pleasure in the nightfall, the bird songs and the gravy.

- 2 Tbs. butter
- 2 Tbs. vegetable oil
- 1 onion, finely chopped
- 1green pepper, finely chopped
- 3 cloves garlic, minced
- 4 cups corn kernels
- 1 cup sliced okra
- 2 tomatoes, chopped
- 1/2 tsp. Cajun seasoning
- 1 cup Swanson's chicken broth

Melt butter and oil in an iron skillet over medium heat. Add onion, bell pepper and garlic, sauté until onion has softened. Add in corn, okra and Cajun seasoning, cook 5 minutes, stirring occasionally. Add broth and bring to a boil, reduce heat to low and cook, uncovered for 45 minutes, stirring occasionally. Add the tomatoes and stir just before serving. - Serves 4

FIELD PEAS

- 2 slices bacon, diced
- 1 onion, chopped
- 2 cups chicken broth
- 3 cups shelled fresh field peas
- 2 cups cold water
- 1/4 cup okra, sliced

- 1 fresh chili pepper
- Salt and pepper

In a large iron skillet, fry the bacon over medium-high heat until it begins to brown. Add the onion and cook, until soft. Add the broth, stir, and remove from the heat.

Rinse field peas and place in a large saucepan. Add water, okra, chili pepper, and the broth mixture. Bring to a simmer over medium heat, and cook for about 15 minutes, until the peas are tender. Season with salt and pepper to taste. - Serves 4

HAM STEAK WITH RED EYE GRAVY

- 1 lb. cooked ham steak
- 3 Tbs. butter
- 1 cup strong coffee
- 1/2 cup heavy cream
- 2 Tbs. brown sugar

Melt butter in an iron skillet over medium heat. Add steak and cook until lightly browned, about 3 minutes per side. Remove ham and set aside, covered to keep warm.

Add coffee, cream and sugar to the skillet and simmer for 5 minutes. Transfer ham to a plate and pour gravy on top. - Serves 1 to 2

LOBSTER CLAW COCKTAIL - Not your usual dive bar fare but hey, we'll take it.

- 1 lb. lobster meat, cooked (2 large lobster tails)
- 1/4 cup Heinz ketchup
- 2 Tbs. VOS Amontillado (or any good sherry)
- 1 Tbs. grated horseradish
- 4 Tbs. celery, chopped
- 1/4 tsp. cayenne pepper
- 1 Tbs. lemon juice
- 2 tsp. chives, chopped
- 2 tsp. capers, chopped
- 4 green leaf lettuce leaves
- 4 lobster claws, shelled with meat intact
- 4 lemon wedges

With a sharp knife, medium dice the lobster tail meat. In a mixing bowl blend ketchup, sherry, horseradish, celery, cayenne, lemon juice, chives and capers. Add diced lobster tail meat and toss. Cover and chill for 3 hours.

Drape the lettuce leaves in 4 over sized martini glasses. Add the lobster salad and garnish with intact lobster claw meat and lemon wedges. - Serves 4

BEER BATTER FISH - A waterfront dive just wouldn't be a dive without this one.

- Vegetable oil, for frying
- 1-2/3 cups flour
- 2 Tbs. cornstarch
- 1/4 tsp. baking soda

- 1/4 tsp. baking powder
- 1/4 tsp. salt
- 1 cup of cold Abita Turbo Dog beer
- 1/2 cup of cold water
- 8 small, boneless Halibut filets

Sift together all dry ingredients in a medium bowl. Use a whisk to mix in the beer and the cold water. Set batter aside for 10 minutes to rest.

Place the oil in a large, deep saucepan and heat to 350° F or use a deep fat fryer. Dip each filet into the batter and slowly lower them, one at a time into the hot oil. Fry each one, turning occasionally, for about 5 minutes or until cooked through. Transfer the fish to a tray lined with newspaper. - Serves 2 to 4

PUMPKIN SPICE DOUGHNUT - Two of these and a regular coffee will really hit the spot.

- 2 doughnut pans or muffin tin*

- 1/2 cup vegetable oil
- 3 eggs
- 1-1/2 cups sugar
- 1-1/2 cups canned pumpkin
- 1-1/2 tsp. pumpkin pie spice
- 1-1/2 tsp. salt
- 1-1/2 tsp. baking powder
- 1-3/4 cups all purpose flour

- 3 Tbs. cinnamon
- 3 Tbs. sugar

Preheat the oven to 350° F.

Lightly grease pan with cooking spray. With an electric mixer, beat together the oil, eggs, sugar, pumpkin, spices, salt, and baking powder until smooth. Add the flour and stirring with a wooden spoon until smooth (do not over mix).

Fill doughnut pans or muffin tin about 3/4 full (the batter will make 2 batches).

Bake for about 15 minutes, or until a toothpick inserted into the center comes out clean. If you're making muffins, bake for 23 to 25 minutes.

Remove the doughnuts from the oven, let cool slightly before transferring them to a rack to cool. Place doughnuts in a bag of cinnamon sugar and gently shake.

For muffins, butter and sprinkle tops with cinnamon-sugar

*http://www.wilton.com/store/site/product.cfm?id=95C582A0-1E0B-C910-EA77273CAA507790

BACON, EGGS & GRITS - Score big with this southern breakfast classic.

- 8 cups milk
- 1 Tbs. salt
- 2 cups uncooked white grits
- 1 cup butter
- 4 eggs, beaten
- 2 tsp. dried sage
- 2 cups shredded Cheddar cheese
- 8 slices cooked bacon, crumbled

Preheat oven to 350° F.

Place 6 cups of milk and the salt in a large saucepan and cook over medium-high heat until milk begins to simmer. Slowly whisk in the grits and butter. Reduce heat to medium and cook uncovered, stirring often, for about 20 minutes or until thick.

Remove grits from heat and stir in remaining 2 cups milk. Stir in eggs, sage, and 1 cup of cheese. Pour grits mixture into a lightly greased 13 x 9 baking dish. Top with remaining 1 cup cheese. Bake the grits for 45 minutes. Remove the bake dish from oven and sprinkle with crumbled bacon. - Serves 8

HELEN'S OLD FASHION EGG-CREAM - You'll seldom find one of these outside New York, so take advantage.

- Fox's U-Bet chocolate, vanilla, strawberry or coffee syrup*
- Whole milk or heavy cream
- Seltzer water (a siphon style soda spritzer works best - bottled seltzer works, but you won't get as foamy a head)

Take any tall 8oz. glass and place in the freezer for 5 minutes.

Squeeze in 1 inch of U-Bet syrup into the bottom of the glass. Add 1 inch whole milk or heavy cream.

Tilt the glass and spray or pour the seltzer off a spoon, to make a large, foamy head (a pressurized cylinder works best). Stir only right before drinking.

*http://www.webstaurantstore.com/foxs-u-bet-chocolate-syrup-22-oz-squeeze-bottle/711SQCHOC.html

CRAW FISH PO'BOY DRESSED - This should taste familiar, and somewhat Creole.

Remoulade Sauce:

- 1 cup Hellmann's mayonnaise
- 3 Tbs. dill relish
- 2 Tbs. parsley, chopped
- 2 Tbs. chives, chopped
- 2 Tbs. capers, minced
- 2 tsp. Creole mustard
- 1-1/2 tsp. garlic, chopped
- 1 tsp. Tabasco sauce

In a small bowl, combine all ingredients, stirring well.

Po'Boy:

- Vegetable oil for frying
- 1 cup cornmeal
- 1/2 cup all purpose flour
- 2 tsp. Tony Chachere's Creole seasoning
- 1 tsp. salt
- 1 tsp. ground black pepper
- 1 cup milk
- 2 tsp. Tabasco sauce
- 1 (16 oz.) package craw fish tail meat, drained
- 4 eight inch sub rolls, sliced and lightly toasted
- Shredded iceberg lettuce
- 1 large tomato, sliced

Heat about 3 inches of vegetable oil to 350° F in the bottom of a Dutch oven (or use a deep fryer). Combine cornmeal, flour, Creole seasoning, salt, and pepper in a medium bowl.

In a separate bowl, combine milk and Tabasco sauce. Soak crawfish tails in milk mixture for 15 minutes, and then dredge the crawfish in the flour mixture.

Fry crawfish tails a handful at a time until golden brown, about 3 minutes. Drain on paper towels. Serve on hoagie rolls "dressed" with shredded lettuce, tomato and remoulade sauce. - Serves 4

CATFISH FRIED - Any way you cook it, the catfish is an excellent choice.

- 6 skinless catfish fillets
- Vegetable oil for frying
- 2 cups cornmeal
- 2 Tbs. baking powder
- 2 Tbs. salt
- 1 tsp. cayenne pepper
- 1/2 tsp. apple pie spice
- 1 tsp. black pepper
- 1 tsp. paprika
- 1 tsp. garlic powder

Whisk together the cornmeal with all the other dry ingredients. Pour about 3 inches of vegetable oil into a Dutch oven or large iron skillet. Heat the oil over medium-high heat to 350° F.

Dredge the catfish into the seasoned cornmeal and carefully place in hot oil. Fry for about 2 minutes and then turn heat down to medium. Continue frying the catfish for 3 minutes. Carefully flip fillets and cook for 4 minutes more. Gently remove the catfish with a slotted spatula and let them drain on paper towel. - Serves 3 to 6

CATFISH OVEN FRIED

- 6 catfish fillets
- 2 cups milk
- 3 cups all purpose flour
- 3 cups cornmeal
- 1 tsp. salt
- 1 tsp. cayenne pepper
- 1 tsp. black pepper
- 3 Tbs. garlic powder
- 4 Tbs. dried thyme
- 1/4 cup melted butter

Soak catfish in milk, in the refrigerator, for 1 hour.

Preheat oven to 400° F.

In a bowl, mix together flour and cornmeal. Season the cornmeal mixture with salt, cayenne and black pepper, garlic powder and thyme.

Take the fish from the milk bath and dredge in cornmeal mixture. Put the fillets on a greased cookie sheet and drizzle the melted butter over the fish. Bake catfish for 10 to 12 minutes. Fish should be crisp and golden brown. - Serves 3 to 6

CATFISH BAKED

- 4 catfish fillets
- 1 tsp. green Tabasco sauce
- 2 Tbs. butter, melted
- 2 tsp. garlic salt
- 2 tsp. dried thyme
- 2 tsp. smoked paprika
- 1/2 tsp. red pepper
- 1/4 tsp. black pepper

Preheat oven to 450° F.

Combine all dry ingredients in a small bowl. Brush both sides of fish with Tabasco sauce, and then brush again with melted butter. Generously sprinkle catfish with spice mix on both sides.

Place fish in a 13 x 9 baking dish, sprayed with butter flavored cooking spray. Bake for about 10 minutes or until fish flakes easily with a fork. Serves 2 to 4

CATFISH BROILED

- 8 catfish fillets
- 1 egg
- 1/4 cup milk
- 1/3 cup course yellow cornmeal
- 1-1/2 tsp. fresh lemon zest
- 1/2 tsp. celery salt
- 1/2 tsp. dried thyme
- Course black pepper

Adjust oven rack to broiler position and preheat to broil.

Spray a baking pan with cooking spray. Beat the egg and milk together in a pie tin, until well combined.

In a separate pie tin, combine cornmeal, lemon zest, celery salt, thyme and a good amount of ground pepper and mix well.

Dip catfish fillet in egg mixture and then dip in cornmeal mixture until well coated.

Arrange catfish in the baking pan and broil for about 5 minutes per side. Be careful not to over-cook. The fish should be moist and flakey. - Serves 4 to 8

PINE BARK STEW - A favorite in Sunflower - ask for it by name, just don't go askin' 'bout no Doanes.

- 6 strips bacon, diced
- 1 lb. any fish, cut in 2 inch chunks
- 2 cups potatoes, medium diced
- 1 cup white onions, diced
- 1 tsp. salt
- 1/2 tsp. black pepper
- 1/4 tsp. cayenne pepper
- 1/2 Tbs. fresh thyme
- 5 cups hot water
- 1-1/2 cups diced tomatoes

In a Dutch oven, over medium heat, fry bacon until crisp. Remove the bacon and set aside.

Pour off half of the grease and add the diced potatoes and onions. Cook until potatoes and onions are soft and lightly browned, about 10 minutes. Season the potatoes with salt, pepper, cayenne, and thyme.

Place fish chunks on the top of potato mixture and cover with hot water. Adjust heat to a simmer. Cover pot and cook for 25 minutes.

Add tomatoes and continue to simmer, uncovered for 10 minutes more. Carefully fold everything together and top with the bacon before serving. - Serves 6

HUSH PUPPIES - And who could go without these deep fried gems?

Fried:

- Oil for frying
- 2 cups yellow cornmeal
- 1 cup all purpose flour
- 1 tsp. Lowery's seasoned salt
- 1/2 tsp. pepper
- 1 tsp. baking powder
- 1 tsp. baking soda
- 1 tsp. sugar
- 2 eggs, beaten
- 1 cup buttermilk
- 1/8 cup bacon drippings

Heat the oil to 350° F in a Dutch oven or deep fryer.

Mix all of the dry ingredients in a large mixing bowl. Add eggs, bacon drippings and buttermilk. Whisk to combine and let stand 5 minutes. Carefully drop hush puppies in the oil, using two table spoons (one for scooping and one for scraping. Cook until they just float and are lightly brown.

Baked:

- 1 cup yellow corn meal
- 1 cup all purpose flour
- 3 tsp. baking powder
- 1 tsp. salt
- 1 tsp. sugar
- 1/4 tsp. cayenne pepper
- 1/2 cup onion, finely diced
- 2 eggs, beaten
- 2/3 cup milk

- 4 Tbs. vegetable oil
- bacon drippings

Preheat oven to 425° F.

 Lightly coat a mini muffin tin with bacon drippings (or spray with cooking spray).

Blend cornmeal, flour, baking powder, salt, sugar and cayenne in mixing bowl. Stir in onion, eggs, milk and vegetable oil.

Pour batter into the muffin tin just about 1/2 full. Bake 14 to 17 minutes, or until a toothpick inserted into center comes out clean. Repeat a second batch if there is any more batter.

RICE BEANS SPAM - These next two are "novel" indeed...

- 1 lb. dry kidney beans
- 1/4 cup olive oil
- 1 large onion, chopped
- 1 green pepper, chopped
- 2 Tbs. garlic, minced
- 4 celery stalks, chopped
- 6 cups water
- 2 bay leaves
- 1 tsp. dried thyme
- 1/4 tsp. dried sage
- 1 Tbs. dried parsley
- 1 tsp. Cajun seasoning
- 2 tins Spam, cubed

- 4 cups water
- pinch of salt
- 2 cups long grain white rice

· Rinse beans, and soak in a large pot of water overnight.

In an iron skillet, heat the oil over medium heat. Cook the onion, green pepper, garlic, and celery for 5 minutes.

Drain beans and transfer to a large stock pot with 6 cups water. Stir the cooked vegetables into beans. Season with bay leaves, thyme, sage, parsley, and Cajun seasoning. Bring the pot to a boil, and then reduce heat to medium-low. Simmer for 2 and 1/2 hours, covered. Add Spam into beans, and continue to simmer for 30 minutes.

Meanwhile, in a separate pot, bring the 4 cups of water and salt to a boil. Add rice, stir and reduce heat. Cover, and simmer for 20 minutes.

Serve a scoop of rice over the prepared beans. - Serves 8

SARDINES TOAST ....and a bit eccentric to boot.

- 2 tins sardines in mustard
- 1 Tbs. fresh dill, chopped
- 1 Tbs. Heinz malt vinegar
- 1/2 tsp. lemon pepper
- 8 slices Italian bread (cut diagonally)
- 3 Tbs. melted butter
- 1 ripe avocado
- 1 small tomato, diced
- Lemon juice
- Salt
- Cilantro, finely chopped

Place the sardines in a small mixing bowl and stir in the dill, malt vinegar and lemon pepper. Fold to combine (but don't make a mush) and set aside.

Adjust the oven rack to broiler position and preheat to broil.

Brush each slice of bread, generously, on one side with the melted butter. Place the bread slices on a wire cooling rack and place under the broiler until golden brown and crisp (watch carefully so tops don't burn).

Halve the avocado and remove the pit. Scoop out the avocado and place it in a small bowl. Mash into a paste, fold in the diced tomato, and add a dash of lemon juice and season with salt to taste.

Spread avocado spread onto the toasted bread, top with sardine mixture and garnish with cilantro. - Serves 2 to 8

http://www.amazon.com/Heinz-Malt-Vinegar/dp/B00ID9PFN2/ref=sr_1_2?s=grocery&ie=UTF8&qid=1398505206&sr=1-2&keywords=english+malt+vinegar

SMOKE SALMON PUFF PASTRIES - This is first class and something you could get use to.

- 1 package puff pastry, thawed
- 1 beaten egg
- 1 Tbs. milk
- 4 Tbs. fresh dill, minced
- 2 packages cream cheese, softened
- 4 Tbs. capers, minced
- 2 Tbs. caper juice
- 1 Tbs. lemon pepper
- 12 oz. sliced smoked salmon

Mix together the cream cheese, half the dill, and lemon pepper in a medium bowl.

Coarsely dice up about 1/2 of the smoked salmon along with the capers and fold into cream cheese mixture. Slowly add the caper juice, a bit at a time and stir. Add just enough caper juice to smooth out the spread. Transfer the spread to a Ziploc bag and place in refrigerator.

Set out 2 baking sheets, one with parchment paper and one without.

Lightly flour a work surface and roll out 1 sheet of puff pastry to flatten any creases. Pinch together any cracks as well.

Beat together the egg, milk and the rest of the dill, and then apply this wash to the puff pastry sheet with a brush.

Using a pizza cutter cut the puff pastry sheet into 10 equal rectangles. Place the cut puff pastry on parchment papered bake sheet and place the second bake sheet right on top of the dough.

Bake the puff pastry 15 minutes, remove from oven and remove the top bake sheet. Transfer puff pastries to a cooling rack. Repeat this process with the other puff pastry sheet. Remove the salmon spread from the refrigerator and snip off corner of the Ziploc bag, with some kitchen shears, to make about a 1/2 inch opening. Line up 6 of the puff pastries and squeeze the spread on the pastries. Lay some of the sliced salmon in the center of the spread and press down gently. Place a second pasty over the spread. Repeat to make another layer and top with a third pastry. Repeat the process, making 6 three layer pastries (you'll have 2 extra pastries to nibble on). Cover and refrigerate, Serve cold. - Makes 18 pastries

STONE CRAB CLAWS WITH MUSTARD SAUCE -
Excellent with some icy vodka to wash it down..... and at this point, you should be in need of a drink.

- 4 lbs. Florida stone crab claws*
- 1/2 cup sour cream
- 1-1/2 Tbs. prepared mustard (yellow or brown)
- 2 tsp. butter
- 1/2 tsp. parsley flakes

Thaw crab claws if frozen and keep chilled.

Combine sour cream, mustard, butter, and parsley in a small bowl. Cover with plastic wrap and microwave on high for 30 seconds. Stir and serve warm with the chilled crab claws. - Serves 2 to 4

*http://www.incrediblestonecrab.com/stonecrabs

TRUFFLE & FOIE GRAS SANDWICH — EASY - Eat this one slowly, in between sips of hot tea with milk and sugar perhaps.

- 1 half fresh baguette
- 2 Tbs. butter, softened
- 1 Tbs. Dijon mustard
- 3 thick medallions of Duck Foie-Gras-with-Black-Truffles*
- 3 leaves of leaf lettuce

Place the baguette on a cutting board and slice it in half lengthwise. Spread the inside of one half with 1 Tbs. of butter and then spread the other half with mustard. Lay out the slices of pate and then pile on the lettuce leaves. Place one half of baguette on top of the other half and cut in half, if desired. - Serves 1

*http://www.zabars.com/d-artagnan-medallion-duck-foie-gras-with-truffles/422L005.html?cgid=PF_Starters

TRUFFLE & FOIE GRAS SANDWICH – HARD

- 1 whole fresh baguette
- 4 Tbs. fig preserves
- 2 Tbs. black truffle butter
- 1 lb. grade A foie gras cubes*
- 1 cup micro greens

Preheat oven to 400° F.

Use a thin, sharp knife, slice the foie into 2 inch sections, run the blade under warm water after each slice. Using an oven proof, non stick sauté pan, preheated over high heat until the pan's surface is very hot. Sear the foie briefly, about 15 to 20 seconds a side. Transfer pan to the oven for 1 to 2 minutes. Remove from oven and salt and pepper to taste.

Slice the baguette in half lengthwise. Spread the inside of each half with truffle butter and then spread the bottom half with fig preserves. Add the slices of foie gras and place micro-greens on next, then the top half of baguette. Cut sandwich in quarters. - Serves 1 to 2

DOUBLE CHOCOLATE FAT ONES - Buckle a few of these around your waist.

Dough:

- 1 package yeast
- 1/8 cup warm water
- 3/4 cup warm milk
- 1/4 cup sugar
- 1/2 tsp. salt
- 1 egg
- 3 Tbs. vegetable oil
- 2-1/2 cups all purpose flour

In mixing bowl, dissolve yeast in warm water. Add milk, sugar, salt, egg, shortening and 1 cup of flour. Using a wooden spoon, mix ingredients for 2 minutes. Add remaining flour and stir until smooth.

Cover bowl with plastic wrap and let rise in warm place for 1 hour. Turn dough out onto floured surface. Roll dough out into a 1/2 inch thickness. Cut with round cookie cutter or the rim of a large drinking glass. Place rounds on a floured bake sheet and cover. Let dough rise for 30 minutes.

In deep fryer or Dutch oven heat vegetable oil to 350° F. Slide doughnuts into hot oil, 2 at a time. Fry doughnuts about one minute on each side until a light golden color. Carefully remove from oil, drain and cool completely.

Using a sharp, narrow knife, make a small incision and then carefully move the blade back and forth, and make a large cavity inside of the doughnut to hold the filling.

Filling:

- 4 egg yolks
- 1/3 cup sugar
- 2 Tbs. cornstarch

- 3 Tbs. cocoa powder
- 1/4 tsp. salt
- 1 cup milk
- 3 oz. semi-sweet chocolate
- 2 Tbs. butter
- 1 tsp. pure vanilla extract

Whisk together egg yolks, sugar, cornstarch, cocoa powder, and salt in a cool medium saucepan. The mixture will be fairly thick. Slowly whisk in the milk. Place pan over medium-low heat and stir constantly. When mixture just comes to a boil, remove from heat. Add chocolate chunks, butter, and vanilla to the hot mixture and stir until incorporated. Transfer filling to a small bowl and drape a sheet of plastic wrap on the surface of the cream to keep the filling from creating a "skin." Chill for at least 2 hours.

Glaze:

- 1/2 cup butter
- 1/4 cup milk
- 1 Tbs. light corn syrup
- 2 tsp. pure vanilla extract
- 4 oz. semi-sweet chocolate chips
- 2 cups powdered sugar

Combine butter, milk, corn syrup and vanilla extract in a saucepan over medium-low heat until the butter melts. Add chocolate chips and whisk until smooth.

Remove pan from the heat and whisk in the powdered sugar. Set saucepan in a larger pot of hot water to keep glaze from firming up.

Assemble:

Place filling in a pastry bag and generously fill the doughnut. Dip one flat side of the filled doughnut in glaze. Allow glaze to firm up before serving. - Makes 18 pastries

CHOCOLATE BANANA DOUBLE CREAM FAT ONES -
Turn the lock and put up the closed sign. You won't want to
be disturbed while wolfing these down.

Dough:

- 1 package yeast
- 1/8 cup warm water
- 3/4 cup warm milk
- 1/4 cup sugar
- 1/2 tsp. salt
- 1 egg
- 3 Tbs. vegetable oil
- 2-1/2 cups all purpose flour

In mixing bowl, dissolve yeast in warm water. Add milk,
sugar, salt, egg, shortening and 1 cup of flour. Using a

wooden spoon, mix ingredients for 2 minutes. Add remaining flour and stir until smooth.

Cover bowl with plastic wrap and let rise in warm place for 1 hour. Turn dough out onto floured surface. Roll dough into a 1/2 inch thickness. Cut with round cookie cutter or the rim of a large drinking glass. Place rounds on a floured bake sheet and cover. Let dough rise for 30 minutes.

In deep fryer or Dutch oven heat vegetable oil to 350° F. Slide doughnuts into hot oil, 2 at a time. Fry doughnuts about one minute on each side until a light golden color. Carefully remove from oil, drain and cool completely.

Using a sharp narrow knife make a small incision and then carefully move the blade back and forth, making a large cavity inside of the doughnut to hold the filling.

Filling:

- 1/2 quart heavy cream
- 1 cups sugar
- 2 tsp. pure vanilla extract
- 4 egg yolks
- Pinch of salt
- 3 bananas
- 1/4 cup cornstarch

In a medium saucepan over medium-high heat, bring cream, salt and sugar to a slow boil. In a separate bowl whisk the egg yolks and corn starch. When the cream comes to a boil, add a few tablespoons of the cream to the egg and whisk, a few more and then add the remaining cream. Pour cream/egg mixture back into saucepan and return to a boil, remove from heat and place in a food processor, add the bananas, puree then strain through a metal strainer. Cover and refrigerate for at least 2 hours.

Glaze:

- 1/2 cup butter
- 1/4 cup milk
- 1 Tbs. light corn syrup
- 2 tsp. pure vanilla extract
- 4 oz. milk chocolate chips
- 2 cups powdered sugar

Combine butter, milk, corn syrup and vanilla extract in a saucepan over medium-low heat until the butter melts. Add chocolate chips and whisk until smooth.

Remove pan from heat and whisk in the powdered sugar. Set saucepan in a larger pot of hot water to keep glaze from firming up.

Assemble:

Place filling in a pastry bag and generously fill the doughnut. Dip one flat side of the filled doughnut in glaze and set, glaze side up until set. - Makes 18 pastries

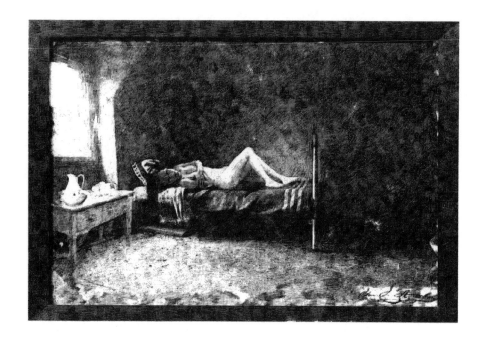

ALLIGATOR ETOUFFEE - Straight from the Atchafalaya Basin and an old family recipe.

- 1 lb. alligator meat; cut in thin strips*
- 1 stick butter
- 1/2 cup onions, chopped
- 4 celery stalks, chopped
- 1/2 cup green peppers, chopped
- 2 garlic cloves, minced
- 1 (14 oz.) can tomatoes, with juice
- Salt and pepper to taste
- Cayenne pepper
- Fresh parsley, chopped

In a Dutch oven, over medium heat, sauté onions, celery, green pepper and garlic in butter until soft, about 5 minutes. Sprinkle in the flour and stir. Cook an additional 3 minutes. Add tomatoes and simmer, covered for 20 minutes. Lower heat, add alligator meat and cover. Allow to simmer 1 hour or until tender. Add salt, pepper and cayenne to taste. Serve with rice and garnish with chopped parsley. - Serves 4

*http://www.lintonseafood.com/alligator_meat_s/29.htm

ROAST SADDLE OF LAMB - Stop and take note. This roast is perfection.

- 6 garlic cloves
- 1 tin anchovies
- 1 Tbs. fresh rosemary
- 1 Tbs. fresh thyme
- 1 Tbs. fresh mint
- Olive oil
- 6 lb. boneless saddle of lamb
- Salt and pepper
- 1/4 cup water mixed with 2 tsp. cornstarch
- 2 tsp. balsamic vinegar

Preheat the oven to 350° F.

Place garlic, anchovies, rosemary, thyme and 2 Tbs. of the olive oil in a food processor and pulse into a paste.

Spread the saddle of lamb out on a clean work surface with the out side facing up. With a sharp knife, slice the fat in a crosshatch pattern. Season both sides of the lamb generously with salt and pepper. Rub the garlic paste over the inside of the lamb. Roll up the roast to form a tight cylinder. Wrap and secure the roast about every 2 inches with kitchen twine. Season the outside of the roast again with salt and pepper.

In a large iron skillet over medium-high heat, add 2 Tbs. of the olive oil. Once oil is hot, add the lamb roast and sear it. Rotate the meat until browned all over. Transfer the skillet to the oven and roast the lamb for 1 hour or until the internal temperature reads 120° F.

Remove roast from the oven and transfer to a cutting board. Loosely cover with tin foil and let meat rest for 15 minutes. - Serves 6

Skim off the fat from the juices in the skillet. Place the skillet on a burner set to medium-high heat. Add the water/cornstarch and bring liquid to a simmer. Whisk in 2 tsp. of olive oil and balsamic vinegar. Season the gravy with salt and pepper to taste.

Cut and discard the kitchen twine from the roast and slice the roast crosswise. Serve with the skillet gravy.

B-B-Q RIBS - Why would you settle for coffee and a sandwich?

- 1 cup brown sugar
- 1/3 cup apple cider vinegar
- 3 Tbs. salt
- 2 Tbs. garlic powder
- 2 Tbs. onion powder
- 2 Tbs. smoked paprika
- 1 Tbs. black pepper
- 2 racks pork ribs, trimmed of fat

Place the brown sugar, vinegar, salt, garlic powder, onion powder, paprika and pepper in a medium bowl and whisk into a paste.

Line a roasting pan with tin foil. Place the ribs in the pan bone side up and coat with half of the marinade. Flip the ribs over and coat with the remaining half. Cover with another sheet of tin foil and refrigerate for 4 to 6 hours.

Preheat oven to 325° F.

Remove the ribs from the fridge and let stand at room temperature while the oven is preheating (do not remove the tin foil).

Bake ribs, covered, for 1 hour. Remove top sheet of foil and continue baking for 45 minutes or until the ribs are tender. - Serves 4 to 6

PICKLED EGGS - These traditional dive bar snacks all erupt in explosions of flavor.

- 6 hard boiled eggs, peeled
- 3/4 cup cider vinegar
- 3/4 cup water
- 1/2 cup sugar
- 6 whole cloves
- 2 jalapeno peppers, sliced in half lengthwise and seeds removed
- 1 tsp. cumin
- 1 bay leaf
- 1/2 tsp. dry oregano
- 1/4 onion, sliced
- 1 garlic clove, peeled

Peel the hard boiled eggs and place them in the bottom of a clean glass jar. In a medium saucepan add vinegar, water, the onion, jalapeno, sugar, and spices. Bring the mixture to a boil and cook until onions are translucent, about 5 minutes. Remove from heat and let cool 15 minutes.

Pour the vinegar mixture over the eggs, covering the eggs completely. If you want to make pickled beet eggs place some canned beets and beet juice in with the eggs in the jar. Secure the jar lid and refrigerate for at least 6 days. Eggs will last up to one month and get better over time.

PIG'S TROTTERS

- 4 pig's feet, split in half lengthwise
- 2 yellow onions, chopped
- 2 stalks celery, chopped
- 2 garlic clove, chopped
- 1 bay leaf
- 1 tsp. salt
- 1 cup cider vinegar
- 1 tsp. black pepper
- 2 tsp. crushed red pepper
- 1 cup barbecue sauce
- Water, to cover

Wash the pig's feet in a basin of cold, salted water. Using a disposable razor, shave any noticeable hairs off the skin.

Place all the ingredients in a 4 quart Dutch oven and cover with water. Bring water to a boil over medium-high heat and then reduce heat to a simmer.

Cover the pot with lid and allow pigs feet to cook 3 hours or until tender (check water ever hour and adjust level). Serves 4

BEER PICKLES

- 24 oz. Abita Turbo Dog beer
- 1/2 cup water
- 4 cups white vinegar
- 2 cups sugar
- 2 Tbs. salt
- 4 tsp. mustard seeds
- 4 tsp. peppercorns
- 8 garlic gloves
- 8 whole banana peppers
- 4 tsp. dill
- 20 medium cucumbers

- 4 (1 quart) mason jars

Wash Mason jars in hot water then dip them in boiling water and set aside to dry.

Place beer, water, vinegar, sugar and salt into a large saucepan, over medium high heat, and bring to a boil.

Line up prepared mason jars and adding the spice ingredients divided equally among the jars.

Cut cucumbers into wedges and stuff as many as possible into each jar. Add the hot pickling liquid into each jar until almost full. Secure lids and make sure they are tight. Carefully place each sealed jar in boiling water, for 5 minutes, to ensure the seals are airtight and then allow the jars to cool on the counter overnight.

Once jars have cooled, place them in a refrigerator. Pickles should be ready in about 3 to 5 days. - Makes 4 jars

"She tried to scream, her mouth filling with stagnant water..."

COLD VENGEANCE

BACON AND ONION BURGER

HAGGIS STUFFED CHICKEN

HUEVOS RANCHEROS

LAMB STEW AND CRUSTY BREAD

CRAYFISH CRAW FISH

GRITS

JALAPENO HUSH PUPPIES

MOON PIE

STEAK & KIDNEY PUDDING

CRAW FISH PO'BOY

MEATBALL PARMESAN SUB

CHICKEN AND DUMPLINGS

CORNBREAD

GREEN JELL-O

RED JELL-O

MEATLOAF

BBQ

ROAST CHICKEN

ITALIAN SPECIALTY

MOTHER SAUCES

RACK OF LAMB PERSILLADE

EPINARDS A LA CRÈME

ROTISSERIE CHICKEN

CUCUMBER SANDWICHES

PASTRAMI SANDWICH

NEW YORK CHEESECAKE

TRUFFLE TORTE CHEESECAKE

BLT

DOVER SOLE WITH TRUFFLE BUTTER

MOUSSE OF ROASTED ROOT VEGETABLES

BIALY WITH LOX SPREAD

VEGGIE LASAGNA

BACON AND ONION BURGER - You'll call this burger "ideal."

- 2 lbs. fresh ground beef (80/20)
- 1 clove garlic, minced
- Salt and black pepper
- 4 strips bacon, diced
- 1/2 onion, chopped
- 1 cup grated sharp Cheddar cheese
- 4 burger buns or onion rolls, toasted
- Lettuce, shredded
- Tomato, slices thick

Preheat oven to 400° F.

In a bowl combine beef, garlic, salt and pepper. Form the beef mixture into 8 patties, about a 1/2 inch thick and set aside.

In an iron skillet over medium heat, fry bacon until crisp. Remove bacon and drain on a paper towel. Keep the skillet and bacon drippings over the stove and sauté onions until tender. Place bacon, onion and cheese in a bowl and combine by hand.

Form cheese mixture into 4 balls and place them in the center of 4 of the patties. Top each with another patty, flatten and seal the edges.

Grill the burgers in the same skillet, over medium-high heat for approximately 2 minutes per side. Place skillet in oven for about 5 minutes to finish cooking the burgers. Serve on toasted buns with lettuce, tomato and your favorite condiments. - Serves 4

HAGGIS STUFFED CHICKEN BREAST - Things will never be the same after preparing this twist on a classic dish.

- 1/2 lb. beef heart, cut into 2 inch wide strips
- 1/2 lb. beef liver, cut into 2 inch chunks
- 1/4 lb. lambs stew meat, cut in 1 inch cubes
- 1 cup yellow onion, finely chopped
- 2 tsp. Scottish whiskey
- 1 cup oatmeal, toasted in a 375° F oven for 10 minutes
- 1 tsp. salt
- 1/2 tsp. black pepper
- 1 tsp. dried thyme
- 1/2 tsp. dried rosemary
- 1/8 tsp. freshly grated nutmeg

Place the beef heart in a 4 quart Dutch oven and pour in just enough cold water to cover the meat. Place a lid on the Dutch oven and simmer for 1 hour or until fork tender.

After the hour is up, add the beef liver, lamb stew meat and onions. Cover and simmer for 20 minutes more.

Remove the meat mixture to a cutting board with a slotted spoon and allow to cool. Mince the meat fairly fine and place in a mixing bowl with 1 cup of the cooked stock. Add all of the remaining ingredients mix well and set aside.

- 4 large boneless skinless chicken breasts
- Salt and pepper to taste

Preheat oven to 375° F.

Make a slice lengthwise into each chicken breast (being careful not cut through) to form a pocket.

Stuff the pocket in each of the chicken breasts with 1/4 of haggis mixture. Secure each chicken breast with 2 toothpicks. Season the chicken with salt and pepper to taste. Brown the chicken breasts on one side in a large, well oiled iron skillet, over medium-high heat.

Place skillet in the oven, brown side up and cook for 30 minutes or until chicken is cooked through and juices run clear. - Serves 4

HUEVOS RANCHEROS WITH SOUR CREAM & JALAPENO SALSA - This is the perfect late morning breakfast, especially when enjoyed outdoors.

Jalapeno Salsa:

- 1/4 cup onion, coarsely chopped
- 1 jalapeno pepper, seeded and coarsely chopped
- 1/4 cup cilantro
- 1 (14 oz.) can diced tomatoes, drained
- 1/2 tsp. salt
- 1/2 tsp. pepper
- 1 tsp. oregano

Combine onion, jalapeno peppers, and cilantro in a food processor and pulse 3 times.

Add tomatoes, salt, pepper and oregano. Pulse until salsa reaches desired consistency.

- 1 (14 oz.) can black beans, drained
- 1 Tbs. fresh lime juice
- 1/2 tsp. ground cumin
- 3 Tbs. melted butter

- 4 small corn tortillas
- 4 eggs
- 1/4 cup sour cream
- 4 oz. queso fresco
- 1/4 cup cilantro, finely chopped

Preheat oven to 400° F.

Combine beans, lime juice, cumin, and 1 Tbs. butter in a microwave safe bowl and cover with plastic wrap. Heat the bean mixture in microwave until hot, about 1 to 2 minutes.

Lightly brush tortillas, on both sides, with butter and place on cookie sheet. Bake tortilla until crisp.

Heat the remaining butter in an iron skillet over medium heat. Add the eggs and cook 1 minute. Pour 1/4 cup hot tap water into the skillet and cover. Steam the eggs to a desired doneness.

Serve on warm plates. Assemble by placing the eggs on the tortillas and top with the beans, sour cream, salsa, queso fresco, and cilantro. - Serves 2 to 4

LAMB STEW AND CRUSTY BREAD - Just eat.

- 2 lbs. lamb, stewing chunks
- 1-1/2 cup potatoes, chopped
- 1/2 cup onions, chopped
- 1/4 cup celery, chopped
- 1/4 cup carrots, chopped
- 5 Tbs. flour
- 5 Tbs. vegetable oil

- 3 tsp. salt
- 1 can tomatoes, with juice
- 1/2 tsp. sugar
- 1 Tbs. Worcestershire sauce
- 4 cloves garlic, chopped
- 1/2 cup beef broth
- Salt and pepper

Heat the oil in a Dutch oven, over medium-high heat.

Place the flour in a bowl and dredge the meat. Add the floured meat to the hot oil in small batches. When one batch has browned on both sides, push them to one side and add a bit more of the meat. Once all the meat has browned, sprinkle 3 tsp. of salt over the meat and stir. Add all the vegetables and fold together to mix. Add the tomatoes with the juice, sugar, Worcestershire sauce and garlic. Stir thoroughly to combine. Add beef broth (or red wine if you like). Turn heat down to low and allow the stew to simmer for 1 hour covered. Remove the lid and continue to simmer for about 45 minutes. Season to taste with salt and pepper. Serve the stew with a loaf of the crusty bread recipe. - Serves 6 to 8

CRUSTY BREAD

- 3 cup bread flour
- 1 tsp. active dry yeast
- 1 tsp. salt
- 1-1/2 cup water, warmed

Mix together the 3 dry ingredients in a large bowl. Add the warm water and stir with a wooden spoon until the dough is mixed well. The dough should be smooth but sticky. Cover the bowl with plastic wrap and set aside in a warm place overnight.

Place a Dutch oven with its lid into the oven set to 450° F and heat for 20 minutes.

While the Dutch oven is preheating, dust a work surface fairly heavily with flour. Scrape the dough from the bowl onto the work surface. With floured hands, gently shape the dough into a round loaf. Let the loaf rest for 10 minutes.

Remove the hot pot from the oven and remove the lid. Ever so gently, lift the dough and place it in the pot. Put the lid back on and return the pot to the oven. Bake the bread for 30 minutes. Open the oven, remove the lid and bake an additional 10 minutes. Remove the Dutch oven and let it cool about 5 minutes before inverting the pot to get the loaf out. - Serves 4 to 6

CRAYFISH CRAW FISH - A crayfish by any other name still tastes amazing.

- 2 heads garlic, unpeeled and cut in half
- 8 bay leaves
- 1/2 cup Old Bay seasoning
- 2 Tbs. Zatarain's liquid crab boil seasoning
- Salt and pepper to taste
- 4 large oranges, halved
- 4 large lemons, halved
- 4 large whole artichokes
- 12 red potatoes, washed
- 12 ears corn, shucked and cut in sections
- 2 large onions, sliced
- 2 (16 oz.) packages whole button mushrooms, cleaned
- 1/2 lb. fresh green beans, trimmed
- 1 lb. smoked sausage, cut into 1/2 inch slices
- 6 lbs. live craw fish, rinsed

Use one of those gas turkey fryers, fitted with a large pot with the strainer insert. Fill the pot half way with water. Add the garlic, bay leaves; Old Bay and liquid crab boil seasonings, salt, pepper, oranges, lemons, artichokes, and the potatoes. Bring the water to a boil over high heat, then reduce to a simmer, and cook for 20 minutes. Stir in the corn, onions, mushrooms, and green beans; cook 15 minutes more. Stir in the sausage and cook for another 5 minutes. Turn the heat up and add the craw fish. Continue to simmer until the craw fish shells turn a bright red, about 5 minutes.

Remove strainer basket from the pot and drain. Serve crayfish-craw fish by dumping the basket on a picnic table covered with newspapers. - Serves 10 to 12

GRITS - Grits is groceries.

- 2 cups water
- 2 cups whole milk
- 1 cup old fashioned grits (not instant)
- Salt to taste
- 1/4 cup heavy cream
- 4 Tsp. butter

In a heavy saucepan, heat water and milk until simmering. Stir the grits into the simmering mixture. Cook until the grits are tender and have thickened to the consistency of oatmeal, stirring often to keep them from sticking or scorching, about 20 minutes. Season the grits generously with salt and stir in the cream and butter. Remove from heat and let the grits rest for 5 minutes. Serve hot with butter. - Serves 4

JALAPENO HUSH PUPPIES - A true delicacy, as well as a local favorite.

- Vegetable oil, for frying
- 2 cups Martha White corn muffin mix
- 2 eggs
- 1/4 cup onions, fine chopped
- 1/4 cup sharp Cheddar cheese, shredded
- 1/4 cup jalapeño peppers, seeded and fine chopped
- 1/4 tsp. salt
- Pineapple juice

In a Dutch oven or deep fryer, heat oil to 350° F.

In a medium bowl mix all ingredients (except juice) until well blended.

Add just enough pineapple juice to make a stiff batter.

Drop batter, using 2 table spoons, one for scooping and one for scraping, into oil and fry until hush puppies begin to float and are golden brown. Drain on paper towels and serve hot. - Serves 6 to 8

MOON PIE - It is what it is......not really a pie.

Filling:

- 1 envelope unflavored gelatin
- 1/3 cup ice cold water
- 1/3 cup warm water
- 1 cup sugar
- 2/3 cup light corn syrup
- 1/8 tsp. salt

To make the cream filling add the gelatin to 1/3 cup cold water to a large mixing bowl and set aside. Combine the sugar, corn syrup, salt and the 1/3 cup of warm water in a medium saucepan set over medium heat. Heat until the mixture reaches 234 on a kitchen thermometer. Using an electric mixer on low speed, carefully add the hot sugar into the bowl of gelatin. Once well blended turn speed up to high and beat until mixture becomes fluffy, about 10 minutes.

Cookies:

- 2 sticks butter, at room temperature
- 1/2 cup powered sugar
- 1 cup all purpose flour
- 1 cup whole wheat flour
- 1/4 tsp. salt
- 1/2 tsp. baking powder
- 1 tsp. pure vanilla extract

Preheat oven to 350° F.

Line a large baking sheet with parchment paper. Whip the butter and sugar together with an electric mixer on medium speed. Add the all purpose and wheat flour; salt, baking powder and vanilla and combine with a wooden spoon. Form the dough into a ball, wrap in plastic wrap and flatten it into a disk. Refrigerate for 20 minutes to firm up the dough. Transfer the dough to a lightly floured work surface and roll it out to about 1/4 inch thick. Use a 3 inch round cookie cutter or a drinking glass, cut out 12 cookies. Transfer the cookies to the prepared baking sheet. Bake until the cookies are golden brown, about 10 minutes. Remove from oven and allow them to cool.

Spoon the filling onto 6 of cookies. Place the other cookie on top and press gently until filling comes to the outer edge of the cookie.

Chocolate Shell:

- 8 oz. dark chocolate chips
- 1 Tbs. Crisco shortening

Add the chocolate and shortening to a Pyrex bowl and microwave at 30 second intervals, until melted and stir until smooth. Dip the moon pies to coat.

Allow excess chocolate to drip off back into the bowl and transfer the moon pies to a wire rack resting on a plate. Place the 6 moon pies to the refrigerator to set, about 15 minutes. - Serves 6

STEAK & KIDNEY PUDDING - Pull up a bar stool and tuck into this Half Moon classic.

- 2 Tbs. vegetable oil
- 1-1/2 lbs. beef top round, cut into 1 inch cubes
- 1 lb. beef kidney, cut into 1 inch cubes
- 1 onion, coarsely chopped
- 2 carrots, sliced
- 2 Tbs. all purpose flour
- 1-1/4 cups Swanson's beef broth
- 2/3 cup good red wine
- 1 bay leaf
- 1/4 cup fresh parsley, finely chopped
- 1 Tbs. tomato puree
- 1-1/4 self rising flour
- 1/2 tsp. baking powder
- Pinch salt
- 3/4 cup vegetable shortening
- 2 to 3 Tsp. cold water
- Butter for greasing bowl
- Salt and pepper to taste

Preheat the oven to 350° F.

Place a Dutch oven over medium-high, add vegetable oil and allow it to heat up. Add the beef and kidney cubes and cook until well browned. Add the onion, carrots and fold to combine. Sprinkle flour over the meat mixture and stir thoroughly. Add the broth, red wine, bay leaf, parsley and the tomato paste. Bring everything to a boil, cover with the lid and place in the oven. Cook for 1 hour. Remove Dutch oven from the oven, season with salt and pepper to taste, and allow to cool completely.

To make the crust: Place the self rising flour, baking powder, and salt into a mixing bowl. Cut the shortening into the flour using a fork until it resembles course corn meal. Add just enough cold water to form a stiff dough. Allow dough to rest for 30 minutes.

Grease a medium sized heatproof bowl with butter. Take 2/3 of the dough and roll into a circle large enough to line the bowl and hang over the outside edge about 1/2 inch. Carefully press the dough into the bowl, making sure there are no cracks. Add the cooled meat filling. Roll the remaining dough in to a circle large enough to cover the entire top of the pudding. Wet the 1/2 inch of overhanging dough with water, lay the dough on top. Press the dough firmly and crimp around the edge with the back of a fork to seal.

Completely encase the entire bowl and crust with 2 layers of heavy tin foil and seal tightly. Lightly scrunch up a large sheet of tin foil so it forms a disc.

Place the tin foil disk into the bottom of a large stockpot. Rest the tin foiled wrapped, sealed bowl on disk. Make sure the bottom of the bowl is not in direct contact with the bottom of the pot. Add enough water to reach halfway up the sides of the sealed bowl.

Cover the pot with its lid and turn the burn up to medium-high. Steam the pudding in the rapidly boiling water for 2 hours, checking the water level every 30 minutes. Have a second pot of boiling water on the stove to add to the stockpot if the water level becomes too low.

Carefully remove the pudding from the stockpot, remove foil, invert on a large rimmed plate to serve. - Serves 4

CRAW FISH PO'BOY WITH SPICY REMOULADE (HOLD THE LETTUCE) - Wrapped in butcher paper, just like you ordered.

Remoulade Sauce:

- 1 cup Hellmann's mayonnaise
- 3 Tbs. dill relish
- 2 Tbs. fresh parsley, chopped
- 2 Tbs. fresh chives, chopped
- 2 Tbs. capers, chopped
- 2 tsp. Creole mustard
- 2 tsp. shallots, chopped
- 1/2 tsp. prepared horseradish
- 1 tsp. Tabasco sauce

In a small bowl, combine all ingredients, stirring well. Cover and chill.

Po'Boy:

- Vegetable oil, for frying
- 1 cup cornmeal
- 1/2 cup all purpose flour
- 2 tsp. Creole seasoning
- 1 tsp. salt
- 1 tsp. black pepper
- 1 cup buttermilk
- 2 tsp. Tabasco sauce
- 1 (16 oz.) package craw fish tail meat, thawed, rinsed and drained
- 4 Hoagie rolls, split

Place vegetable oil in a Dutch oven to about 2 inches in depth, or in a deep fryer fill as directed. Heat the oil to 350° F.

In a medium bowl, combine cornmeal, flour, Creole seasoning, salt, and pepper.

In a separate bowl, combine buttermilk and Tabasco sauce. Soak craw fish tails in milk mixture for about 10 minutes while the oil heats up. Dredge the soaked craw fish tails in the flour mixture and shake off any excess.

Fry the craw fish, in small batches, for approximately 3 minutes, or until golden brown. Remove with a slotted spoon and drain on paper towels.

Serve on hoagie rolls with remoulade and wrapped in butcher paper. - Serves 4

MEATBALL PARMESAN SUB - Go on; talk with your mouth full. You can't help it!

Meatballs:

- 2 cups stale bread, torn into large pieces
- 3/4 cup milk
- 3 tsp. salt
- 1/2 tsp. black pepper
- 1-1/2 lbs. ground beef
- 1-1/2 lbs. ground pork
- 1/2 yellow onion, finely minced
- 3 eggs, beaten
- cloves garlic, minced

- 1 tsp. ground fennel seeds
- 6 Tbs. dried parsley
- 2 Tbs. dried oregano
- 6 Tbs. grated Parmesan cheese
- 8 cups tomato sauce

Place torn bread in a small bowl, cover with milk, salt and pepper and let soak 20 minutes.

Place ground beef and ground pork in a large bowl and mix, by hand, until well combined.

Squeeze out excess milk from bread and add bread to the meat mixture. Fold until fully incorporated. Add onion, eggs, garlic, fennel, parsley, oregano, and grated cheese and mix until combined.

Pinch out and roll enough of the meat mixture to create a ball about the size of a golf ball and then flatten slightly. Place meatball on a dish and repeat until you have used up all the meat mixture.

Heat a large iron skillet over medium-low heat. Place half the meatballs in the skillet and by turning every few minutes, let each meatball brown on all sides, about 20 minutes total. Repeat browning process with the second batch of meatballs.

Transfer browned meatballs to a Dutch oven, cover with tomato sauce, and bring to a low simmer. Cook covered, gently stirring occasionally, for about 30 minutes. Turn off heat and let meatballs rest in the sauce for 30 minutes before serving.

Sandwiches:

- 4 (8 inch) sub rolls
- Parmesan cheese, grated
- 8 slices mozzarella cheese

Preheat the oven to 350° F.

Cut a wedge out of the top of each roll and create a "boat." Ladle some sauce into each roll, then add three meatballs and sprinkle each sub with Parmesan cheese and top with mozzarella.

Place the subs on a tin foil covered baking sheet and bake until the cheese melts and browned a bit. Remove from oven and serve whole. - Serves 4

CHICKEN AND DUMPLINGS - For these next ones, just remember you're on a "Mission."

- 1 whole chicken, cut up
- 2 stalks celery, medium chopped
- 1 carrot, sliced
- 1 onion, sliced
- 2 Tbs. fresh parsley, chopped

- 1 tsp. salt
- 1/4 tsp. pepper
- 5 cups water
- 2-1/2 cups Bisquick mix
- 2/3 cup milk

Place chicken in a Dutch oven over medium-high heat. Add celery, carrot, onion, parsley, salt, pepper and water. Cover and bring to boiling. Reduce heat and simmer for 2 hours.

Remove the chicken and vegetables from Dutch oven using a slotted spoon. Skim off about 1/2 cup of the fat from broth and reserve. Carefully transfer the broth into large bowl and reserve 4 cups.

Return the reserved chicken fat to the Dutch oven and place over low heat. Add in 1/2 cup of the Bisquick and stir until mixture is smooth and bubbling. Slowly whisk in the reserved 4 cups of the broth creating a nice roux and increase heat to medium-high. Allow to boil 1 minute, stirring constantly.

Debone the cooled chicken with your fingers and throw all the bones away.

Carefully return the chicken meat and the vegetables to thickened stock. Reduce heat to low and simmer 20 minutes.

In a medium mixing bowl, combine the remaining Bisquick and milk; make a soft dough.

Carefully drop dough in by the spoonful on to the surface of the hot chicken mixture. Cook uncovered for 10 minutes, then cover the Dutch oven and cook 10 minutes longer. Season the tops of the dumplings with black pepper before serving. - Serves 4 to 6

CORNBREAD

- 1/4 cup bacon drippings
- 1-1/2 cups yellow cornmeal
- 3 Tbs. all purpose flour
- 1 tsp. baking soda
- 1 tsp. baking powder
- 1 tsp. salt
- 2 cups of buttermilk
- 1 egg, beaten
- Butter, softened

Preheat oven to 450° F.

Add the bacon drippings to an iron skillet and place the skillet into the oven for 15 minutes (don't worry if it smokes).

In a mixing bowl, combine cornmeal, flour, baking soda, baking powder and salt. Carefully remove skillet from the oven and swirl hot fat around to coat skillet.

Pour the fat from the skillet into the cornmeal mixture and stir. Now add the buttermilk and beaten egg. Gently fold until ingredients are just combined (do not over mix).

Pour the cornbread batter into the hot skillet. Carefully place the skillet back into the oven and bake for 20 to 25 minutes.

Remove cornbread from oven and allow it to cool for 5 minutes. Carefully invert the skillet onto a plate and slice. Serve with softened butter. - Serves 6

GREEN JELL-O SALAD

- 1 package lime Jell-O
- 6 oz. cold pineapple juice
- 1 cup of Cool Whip
- 1/2 cup small curd cottage cheese
- 1/2 cup chopped pecans or walnuts
- 8 oz. crushed pineapple
- 6 maraschino cherries

Add 1 cup boiling water to gelatin in a bowl and stir until completely dissolved. Stir in the cold pineapple juice and refrigerate until half way set, about 1 to 2 hours.

Remove from refrigerator and add in the Cool Whip, cottage cheese, chopped nuts, and crushed pineapple. Fold until completely incorporated and chill 2 more hours before serving. Garnish with maraschino cherries.- Serves 4

STRAWBERRY JELL-O PARFAIT

- 3/4 cup boiling water
- 1 package strawberry Jell-O
- Ice cubes
- 1/2 cup cold water
- 1/2 cup Cool Whip
- Additional Cool Whip and strawberry slices

Add boiling water to powdered Jell-O in medium bowl; stir until completely dissolved. Pour into blender. Place 1/2 cup cold water in a large measuring cup and then add enough ice cubes so water level will measure 1-1/4 cups and pour that into blender. Blend on high until smooth. Add Cool Whip and blend for 30 seconds more. Pour mixture into 4 dessert glasses and refrigerate until firm. Top with additional Cool Whip and strawberry slices. - Serves 4

ITALIAN STUFFED MEATLOAF - And here's a few non-demanding recipes for all you bachelors.

- 2 lbs. lean ground beef
- 1/2 cup Italian bread crumbs
- 2 eggs, beaten
- 1/4 cup milk
- 1 Tbs. Worcestershire sauce
- 1 cup cubed mozzarella cheese
- 1 cup sliced pepperoni
- 1/2 cup onion, diced
- 1/2 cup green pepper, diced
- 1 Tbs. oregano
- 2 cups prepare spaghetti sauce
- 1 cup shredded mozzarella cheese

Preheat oven to 350° F.

Combine ground beef, breadcrumbs, eggs, milk and Worcestershire and mix well by hand. Scoop about 2/3 of the meat mixture into the bottom and up the sides of a loaf pan, about 1 inch thick.

Combine cheese, pepperoni, onion, green pepper and oregano in a mixing bowl and fold together. Dump pepperoni mixture into the well created in the meat. Top with remaining meat mixture and press to seal.

Bake for 1 hour. Drain off any excess fat; pour spaghetti sauce over the meatloaf, top with shredded mozzarella and bake 15 to 20 minutes longer. Remove from the oven and allow to rest 10 minutes. Carefully remove meatloaf from pan, using two spatulas and transfer to a platter. - Serves 8

B-B-Q

Sauce:

- 1 Tbs. smoked paprika
- 1 Tbs. chili powder
- 1 Tbs. salt
- 1 Tbs. yellow mustard
- 1/2 cup butter
- 1 cup brown sugar
- 1 cup Heinz ketchup
- 1 cup Worcestershire sauce
- 1/2 cup white vinegar
- 1 cup water

Combine mustard, paprika, chili powder and salt in a cool iron skillet and stir into a paste. Place skillet over medium heat and add butter. When butter has melted, add ketchup and brown sugar and stir until sugar has dissolved. Add the Worcestershire, vinegar and water. Increase heat to medium-high and cook 5 minutes, stirring consistently.

Ribs:

- 2 racks of pork spareribs

Dry Rub:

- 2 tsp. garlic salt
- 2 tsp. cumin
- 1 tsp. black pepper
- 2 tsp. smoked paprika
- 2 tsp. chili powder
- 1 tsp. oregano
- 1/2 cup dark brown sugar

Preheat oven to 250° F.

Combine all ingredients for the dry rub in a small bowl. Remove the membrane from the back side of the ribs by making a small incision just under the membrane, at the narrow sides of the rack. Work a finger under the membrane and pull membrane up and across the bones in one sheet.

Line a baking pan with tin foil. Place the racks in the pan, bone side up and rub a generous amount of the dry rub onto the racks. Flip the ribs and apply the remaining dry rub on the top meaty side. Roast uncovered for 2 hours.

After the 2 hours, remove the pan from the oven and pour about 1/3 of the sauce over the top of the ribs (reserve remaining sauce for dipping). Use a balled up paper towel to "mop" the sauce over the ribs. Cover pan tightly with tin foil and place the pan back into the oven for another 1 and 1/2 hours. - Serves 4 to 6

ROASTED CHICKEN

- 1 (5-6 lb.) large chicken, whole
- Salt and pepper
- 1/4 cup apple cider vinegar
- 1/2 cup vegetable oil
- 3 Tbs. light brown sugar
- 6 cloves garlic, minced

Remove any giblets or neck bone from the chicken. Rinse chicken and pat dry with paper towel, inside and out. Generously salt and pepper chicken, also inside and out. Place chicken in a plastic container just large enough to hold the bird.

In a small bowl, combine the cider vinegar, oil, brown sugar, garlic and mix well. Pour the marinade over the chicken, cover with plastic wrap and refrigerate. Let the chicken marinate for 3 hours, flip chicken over and continue marinating an additional 3 hours.

Preheat oven to 375° F.

Remove the chicken from the container and place it on a wire rack. Allow the chicken to air dry and come up to room temperature, about 20 minutes.

Place chicken, breast side up in a roasting pan and roast for 1 hour and 20 minutes or until the temperature inside the thickest part of the thigh has reached 160° F. - Serves 4 to 6

ITALIAN SPECIALTY - Just like Grandma's, from the old country.

- 1-1/2 lb. ground beef, lean
- 1 lb. ground pork, lean
- 1/2 lb. pancetta, diced
- 2 onion, finely chopped
- 2 carrots, diced

- 2 stalks celery, diced
- 1/2 cup dry red wine
- 4 Tbs. tomato paste
- 3 cups Swanson's beef broth
- 1 cup milk
- 3 bay leaves
- Salt and pepper to taste

Place the pancetta in an iron skillet over low heat and cook until the fat has melted. Add the onions and cook until they are translucent, about 5 minutes.

Add the carrots, celery and bay leaves and continue cooking until the vegetables just begin to soften, about 10 minutes.

Turn the heat up to medium-high and add the ground beef and ground pork.

Stir until the meat is well browned, then salt and pepper to taste.

Pour in the wine and simmer until the wine has reduced and cooked away.

Reduce heat to low and add the tomato paste and 2 cups of the beef broth. Continue cooking slowly over the lowest heat for 2 hours. If mixture becomes too dry add a bit more beef broth.

Add half the milk and a bit more of the stock, stir and adjust the heat just to a slow boiling.

Add the remaining milk and stock and simmer for 30 minutes. Re-adjust the seasoning with salt and pepper to taste, turn off the heat, cover and allow the sauce to rest 30 minutes.
Serve over your favorite pasta with fresh, finely grated Parmesan cheese. - Serves 6 to 8

THE 5 MOTHER SAUCES - These will be the foundation for countless variations in your repertoire.

Béchamel Sauce:

- 5 Tbs. butter
- 4 Tbs. all purpose flour
- 4 cups milk
- 2 tsp. salt
- 1/4 tsp. freshly grated nutmeg

In a medium saucepan, heat butter over medium-low heat until melted. Add flour and whisk until it forms a smooth paste or roux. Raise the heat to medium and continue cooking until the mixture turns a light, golden color.

Heat milk in a separate pan to scalding, but do not boil. Add the hot milk to the butter mixture a small amount at a time, whisking continuously, until very smooth. Bring to a simmer and cook 10 minutes, stirring constantly. Remove from heat and season with salt and nutmeg.

Use this sauce in lasagna, gratins and scalloped potatoes. This is also great to use as a base for mac' and cheese and casseroles.

Veloute Sauce:

- 5 Tbs. butter
- 4 Tbs. all purpose flour
- 4 cups Swanson's chicken broth, warmed
- Salt and black pepper to taste

Place a large saucepan over medium heat, melt the butter and whisk in the flour until it forms a smooth paste or roux. Continue whisking for about 2 minutes then gradually add the warm chicken broth. Continue whisking and cook until the sauce has completely thickened. Remove from the heat and season with the salt and pepper to taste.

The term velouté comes from the French "velour", meaning velvet. Substitute fish broth, mushrooms, oysters or shrimp and their cooking juice instead of the chicken broth to accompany the appropriate main dish.

Sauce Espagnole:

- 2 Tbs. diced bacon
- 1/2 cup carrot, sliced
- 1/4 cup onion, chopped

- 1 tsp. thyme
- 1 bay leaf
- 1/2 Tbs. salt
- 1 tsp. pepper
- 1-1/2 cups flour
- 1/3 cup butter
- 1-1/2 quarts beef broth
- 1 lb. fresh tomato, peeled and chopped
- 1 cup white wine

In a large stockpot brown carrots and onions slowly with the bacon and add thyme, bay leaf, salt and pepper.

Add flour and butter and cook 2 minutes, mixing well.

Add a quart of broth and cook at a low simmer for 3 hours. Pour sauce through a metal strainer into a large container and refrigerate overnight. Return sauce to the pot. Add remaining broth, tomatoes and wine and simmer slowly for 2 hours. Remove from heat and allow the pot to cool 1 hour then skim the fat and strain again. This is a true "Mother" sauce; Variations or "Children" are sauces such as Demi-glace, Bordelaise, Madeira, and Mushroom sauce to name a few.

Hollandaise Sauce:

- 3 egg yolks
- 1 Tbs. water
- 1 Tbs. fresh lemon juice
- 6 to 8 oz. unsalted butter, softened
- 1 dash cayenne pepper
- Salt and white pepper, to taste

Whisk the yolks, water, and lemon juice in the saucepan for 2 minutes or until thick and pale yellow.

Set the saucepan over low heat and continue to whisk, being sure to scrape the sides and bottom of the pan.

Frequently move the pan off of the heat for a few seconds, and then back again to slow the cooking process.

The eggs will increase in volume and start to get thick. When the eggs are thick and smooth, remove the pan from the heat.

Add in the softened butter a bit at a time, whisk to in each piece before adding the next. Continue adding the butter until the sauce has thickened to desired consistency.

Season the sauce with salt, pepper and cayenne. Taste and add a few drops of lemon juice if needed. Serve lukewarm.

Drizzle this sauce over eggs, asparagus, green beans or Brussels sprouts. To create a Béarnaise sauce add shallot, chervil, peppercorn and tarragon.

Tomato Sauce:

- 2 Tbs. butter
- 1 Tbs. onion, fine dice
- 2 Tbs. carrot, fine dice
- 1 Tbs. celery, fine dice
- 1 clove garlic, crushed

- 2 Tbs. flour
- 1 cup tomatoes (peeled, diced, seeded)
- 16 oz. tomato Puree (not paste)
- 1 each bay leaf
- 1/4 tsp. thyme, dried
- 1/4 tsp. salt
- 1/8 tsp. white pepper

Melt the butter in a large saucepan, over medium heat. Add in onions, carrots, celery and garlic and sauté until very tender. Whisk in the flour and add in the herbs and the tomatoes.

Reduce heat to very low, and allow the sauce to simmer for 30 minutes. Remove bay leaf and adjust seasoning with salt and white pepper to taste. For a smooth sauce just strain it after seasoning.

By varying the seasoning this sauce can be served with pasta, fish, vegetables, beef, veal, chicken, breads and gnocchi.

RACK OF LAMB WITH A BURGUNDY POMEGRANATE PERSILLADE - its perfection.

- 1 tsp. extra virgin olive oil
- 2 shallot, minced
- 1/2 cup dry Burgundy
- 2/3 cup Pom pomegranate juice
- 2 cups beef or veal stock
- 2 Tbs. water mixed with 1/2 tsp. cornstarch

In an iron skillet over medium heat, add the olive oil and shallots. Sauté the shallots for about 1 minute and add the wine and cook for about 2 minutes longer. Add the pomegranate juice and stock and allow the sauce to simmer until it reduces to about 1/2 cup. Add the water/cornstarch mixture and stir until thickened. Cover sauce, set aside and keep warm.

Lamb:

- 1 racks of lamb, Frenched
- Olive oil
- 1 tsp. sea salt
- 1/2 tsp. course black pepper
- 1 bundle parsley
- 2 cloves garlic, chopped
- 1/2 stick butter, melted
- 1/2 cup bread crumbs
- 1 tsp. lemon zest

Preheat the oven to 450° F.

Place the lamb in a roasting pan, fat side up. Rub the lamb liberally with olive oil and season well with salt and pepper. Place the roasting pan in the oven and roast for 10 minutes.

While lamb is roasting, place the parsley, garlic, and butter in a food processor and pulse into a paste. Add the bread crumbs and lemon zest and pulse to combine.

Remove the roasting pan from the oven and press the crumb mixture firmly on top of the meat. Quickly return the lamb to the oven and continue roasting for 15 minutes.

Take the pan out of the oven and cover the lamb with tin foil. Allow it to rest for 15 minutes. Slice into double chops and serve with the pomegranate Burgundy sauce on the side. - Serves 2 to 4

EPINARDS A LA CRÈME - You'll be truly amazed - that this dish is almost effortless.

- 3 lbs. fresh spinach (4 bags)
- 2 Tbs. flour
- 1 cup whipping cream (heated in microwave)
- 3 Tbs. butter
- Salt and pepper to taste
- 1/8 tsp. nutmeg

In a large pot, bring 2 quarts of water to boil. Add 3 tsp. of salt to the water and stir. Remove all stems from the spinach, add the spinach to the water and boil 3 minutes. Drain and place spinach in a large bowl of ice water. Drain again and dump spinach in the middle of a large, clean cotton towel. Gather the four corners of the towel together and twist, squeezing out as much water out of the spinach as possible.

Using a large pan, over medium-high heat, add the butter and heat until it starts to brown; add in the flour. Stir for 1 minute and create a paste or roux. Add the spinach and hot cream. Gently fold to combine. When sauce starts to thicken, lower heat to medium and simmer 10 minutes covered. Season the creamed spinach with salt, pepper and nutmeg to taste. - Serves 4

ROTISSERIE CHICKEN - This recipe is damn hot...........not.

- 1 whole chicken (about 4 pounds)
- 4 Tbs. white vinegar
- 3 Tbs. dry white wine
- 3 Tbs. extra virgin olive oil
- 2-1/2 Tbs. garlic powder
- 2 Tbs. paprika
- 1 Tbs. cumin
- 2 tsp. black pepper
- 1 tsp. salt
- Juice of 3 limes
- 1 quart cold water

In a small bowl, combine the vinegar, wine, oil, garlic powder, cumin, paprika, black pepper, and salt. Mix well to form a paste. Add the lime juice to the 1 quart cold water. Wash chicken thoroughly with the lime water and then place the chicken in an extra large Ziploc bag. Pour the spice paste over chicken. Coat chicken completely with mixture, rubbing it into every surface with your hands. Wash your hands, seal the bag and place chicken in refrigerator for at least 2 hours (over night is best).

Preheat grill and prepare rotisserie*. Place chicken on rotisserie for approximately 1 and 1/2 hours at around 300° F. To test chicken for doneness, a kitchen thermometer should read 165 in the thickest part of the thigh.

Serve chicken with a dipping sauce of 1/2 cup of Hellmann's mayonnaise, 2 Tbs. brown mustard and 2 Tbs. lime juice.

* If no rotisserie is available:
Preheat oven to 450° F and cook chicken for 15 minutes. Reduce temperature to 350° F and roast for 20 minutes per pound. - Serves 4 to 6

CUCUMBER SANDWICHES AND ROSE HIP TEA -
Transports you back to an earlier, more dignified time.

- 1/2 cucumber, peeled
- Salt
- 6 slices country white bread
- Unsalted butter, softened
- White pepper

Cut the peeled cucumber into thin slices and put them in a colander that has been set on a dish. Sprinkle lightly with salt and allow them to leach for 20 minutes.

Place several layers of paper towel on a work surface and place the cucumber slices on them and pat dry.

Lay out the bread slices and generously apply the softened butter to each. Arrange the cucumber on half the slices, overlapping each round. Lightly dust cucumbers with ground white pepper and top with the remaining slices of bread.

Pressing down firmly to adhere and trim off the crust with a sharp knife. Cut the sandwiches into 3 strips of equal sizes. Serve immediately a good cup of rose hip tea. - Serves 2 to 4

TWINKIES – Seems hard but for Mime it's a piece of cake.

Filling:

- 1 cup milk
- 1/2 cup sugar
- 3 Tbs. flour
- 1/8 tsp. salt
- 2 egg yolks, slightly beaten
- 2 bananas, mashed
- 2 Tsp. lemon juice

Heat the milk in a medium saucepan until very hot but not boiling.

Mix the sugar, flour, and salt together in a bowl, stir in the hot milk and beat until well blended. Pour back into the pan and continue stirring vigorously over low heat for 4 to 5 minutes, until very thick and smooth. Add the egg yolks and cook for a few minutes more. Allow filling to cool completely.

Mash the bananas and beat until smooth, add the lemon juice and stir the banana mixture into the cooled filling.

Cake:

- 1/2 cup cake flour
- 1/4 cup all purpose flour
- 1 tsp. baking powder
- 1/4 tsp. salt
- 2 Tbs. milk
- 4 Tbs. unsalted butter
- 1/2 tsp. pure vanilla extract
- 5 eggs, at room temperature
- 3/4 cup sugar
- 1/4 tsp. cream of tarter
- 1 crème snack cake pan*

- Nonstick cooking spray

Sift the cake and all purpose flours, baking powder, and salt together into a bowl.

Heat the milk and butter together in a microwave set at 50 % until the butter has completely melted. Stir in the vanilla. Cover with plastic wrap to keep warm and set aside.

Separate the eggs and place the whites in a medium mixing bowl and set the yolks aside.

Beat the whites on high speed until foamy with an electric mixer. Add the cream of tartar then start adding 6 Tbs. of sugar, a Tbs. at a time. Continue to beat until the egg whites form soft peaks.

Preheat of to 350° F.

Place the egg yolks with the remaining 6 Tbs. of sugar in a second mixing bowl and beat on medium speed until the yolks are very thick, about 5 minutes. Add the beaten egg whites to the beaten yolks.

Sift the flour mixture, one more time, over the egg mixture and then mix everything on low speed for just 10 seconds. Make a dimple in the batter, and pour the hot milk mixture into the dimple. Fold the batter gently with a wooden spoon until just combined, about 12 strokes.

Spoon the batter into the molds about 3/4 full. Bake until the cake tops are light brown, 13 to 15 minutes, then remove from the oven.

Remove each cake from the mold and allow them to cool. Use the handle of a wooden spoon to make three holes in the flat bottom of each cake. Gently wiggle the tip of the spoon handle back and forth to make some space for the filling.

Transfer the filling to a pastry bag fit with a small tip and squeeze into the holes in the bottom of the cakes. Take care not to over fill the cakes. - Serves 12

PASTRAMI SANDWICH - What do you mean you don't do Pastrami?

Horseradish Sauce:

- 4 Tbs. Hellmann's mayonnaise
- 1 Tbs. sour cream
- 2 Tbs. prepared horseradish
- 1/2 tsp. chopped fresh parsley
- 2 Tbs. Heinz ketchup
- 1/2 tsp. fresh thyme
- Salt and pepper, to taste

In a bowl, mix together all the ingredients and season with salt and pepper to taste.

Coleslaw:

- 8 Tbs. Hellmann's mayonnaise
- 4 Tbs. white vinegar
- 1 Tbs. sugar
- 2 Tbs. fresh parsley, chopped
- 1 tsp. fresh thyme, chopped
- 2 Tbs. celery seed
- 1 bag shredded cabbage chopped
- Salt and pepper, to taste

Prepare the coleslaw: In a bowl, mix together mayonnaise, vinegar, sugar, parsley, thyme and celery seed until blended. Add shredded cabbage and combine. Season with salt and pepper to taste.

Pastrami Sandwich:

- 4 slice Jewish rye bread
- 1 lb. pastrami, sliced
- 4 slices Swiss cheese

On a clean work surface, place 2 slices of rye bread and spread each with the horseradish sauce. Layer each bread slice with pastrami followed Swiss cheese. Spread more horseradish sauce on the remaining 2 slices of bread and top.

Press in a Panini press or grill on a buttered griddle, for 4 minutes. Serve with coleslaw and extra horseradish sauce for dipping. - Serves 2

NEW YORK CHEESECAKE - Can't make it to Carnegie's? No problem, make your own.

Crust:

- 8 whole graham crackers, broken into pieces
- 1 Tbs. sugar
- 5 Tbs. butter, melted

Cheesecake Filling:

- 5 (8 oz.) packages cream cheese, at room temperature and cut into 1 inch pieces
- 1-1/2 cups sugar, divided
- 1/8 tsp. salt
- 1/3 cup sour cream
- 2 tsp. lemon juice
- 2 tsp. pure vanilla extract
- 2 egg yolks
- 6 whole eggs

Fresh Strawberry Topping:

- 3 cups strawberries, cleaned and sliced
- 1/2 cup sugar
- Pinch of salt
- 1 cup Smucker's strawberry jam
- 2 Tbs. lemon juice

To make the crust, preheat oven to 300° F.

Using a food processor, grind the graham crackers into fine crumbs. In a medium bowl stir together the graham cracker crumbs and sugar. Pour the melted butter into the bowl and toss the mixture until it is evenly moistened. Transfer the crumbs to a 9 inch spring form pan and press evenly into the bottom of the pan. Bake the crust for about 10 minutes. Remove the pan from oven and allow it to cool.

Preheat oven to 500° F.

To make the filling, use an electric mixer at medium-low speed to beat the cream cheese for about 1 minute. Add 3/4 cup of the sugar and the salt and beat on medium-low speed for about another 1 minute or so. Add the remaining 3/4 cup of sugar and beat again on medium-low speed for 1 minute more.

Add the sour cream, lemon juice and vanilla, and beat on low speed for 1 minute.

Add the egg yolks and beat on medium-low speed for 1 minute. Add the whole eggs and beat at medium-low for 2 minutes more.

Spray the sides of the cooled spring form pan with cooking spray. Pour the filling into the pan and bake for 10 minutes at 500, then reduce the oven to 200° F and continue to bake for 1 and 1/2 hours. (Do not open the oven door and peek while baking!)

Remove the pan from the oven. Run a wet knife around the side to loosen the cake from the pan and allow the cake to cool for 3 hours at room temperature. Cover the cake in plastic wrap and refrigerate at least 3 more hours.

To make the topping, toss together the sliced strawberries and the sugar in a large bowl. Let them sit for 30 minutes, tossing occasionally to coat.

Place the jam in a small saucepan and bring to a simmer over medium heat, for about 3 minutes. Stir in the lemon juice, then pour the syrup over the strawberries and stir to combine.

Allow the topping to cool to room temperature, then cover with plastic wrap and refrigerate until for at least 3 hours. - Serves 10 to 12

TRUFFLE TORT CHEESECAKE

Crust:

- 30 Nabisco famous chocolate wafer cookies
- 2 Tbs. sugar
- 1/4 cup butter, melted

Filling:

- 1/4 cup semi-sweet chocolate chips
- 1/4 cup heavy whipping cream
- 3 packages (8 oz. each) cream cheese, softened
- 1 cup sugar
- 1/3 cup baking cocoa
- 3 eggs, lightly beaten
- 1 tsp. pure vanilla extract

Topping:

- 1-1/2 cups semisweet chocolate chips
- 1/4 cup heavy whipping cream
- 1 tsp. pure vanilla extract
- Whipped cream and miniature chocolate kisses for garnish

Preheat oven to 350° F.

In a food processor, pulse the chocolate wafers until crumbled. In a small bowl, combine the wafer crumbs and sugar; stir in melted butter. Press onto the bottom and 1 and 1/2 inches up the sides of a well greased 9 inch spring form pan. Place the pan in the oven and bake for 10 minutes. Remove the pan from and allow to it cool completely.

Reduce oven to 325° F.

To make the filling, melt chocolate chips in a microwave and stir until smooth; add cream, whisk together and set aside. In a large bowl, beat the cream cheese and sugar until smooth with an electric hand mixer. Add cocoa and eggs and beat on low just until combined. Stir in the vanilla and the reserved melted chocolate mixture. Pour the batter into the spring form pan and bake for 45 to 50 minutes, until center is just about set.

To make the topping, melt chocolate chips in a microwave and stir until smooth. Stir in cream and vanilla; mix well. Spread over cake and allow to cool for 10 minutes at room temperature. Carefully run a wet knife around edge of pan and cool 1 hour longer. Refrigerate the cake overnight.

Remove sides of pan just before serving. Garnish the cheesecake with whipped cream and miniature chocolate kisses. - Serves 10 to 12

UPTOWN NEW YORK B.L.T. - Put this together in a New York minute.

- 1 French baguette, split and buttered
- 5 Tbs. Hellmann's mayonnaise
- 3 Tbs. basil pesto
- 10 slices bacon, cooked until crisp
- 2 large tomatoes
- 1/4 head red leaf lettuce

House Dressing:

- 1/4 cup balsamic vinegar
- 3 Tbs. sugar
- 2 Tbs. Dijon mustard
- 1/2 tsp. light soy sauce
- 1/2 cup extra virgin olive oil

Combine all dressing ingredients in a food processor - except for the olive oil. With the blade turning, slowly pour in the olive oil and mix until it becomes thick.

On a griddle, lightly toast the inside of the baguette. Spread the mayonnaise on the bottom half and pesto on the top half of the baguette.

Layer the bacon on of the bottom half of the bread. Lay the tomato slices on top of the bacon then the lettuce. Drizzle with dressing over the lettuce. Close the sandwich and cut into 4 pieces on the diagonal. - Serves 1 to 4

DOVER SOLE WITH TRUFFLE BUTTER - This is just the thing to serve to "unexpected" guests.

- 4 Sole fillets
- 1/2 cup flour
- 1/2 tsp. Lawry's Seasoned Salt
- 1/4 tsp. black pepper
- 5 Tbs. unsalted butter
- 2 Tbs. truffle butter*
- 1/4 cup fresh lemon juice
- 2 Tbs. chopped fresh parsley

Mix the flour with season salt and pepper in a shallow dish. Dredge the fish fillets in the flour mixture.

Heat a large iron skillet over medium-high heat and add 3 Tbs. of the butter to the hot skillet.

Sauté the fillets in 2 batches, cooking on each side 2 minutes or until just cooked through. Transfer the fish to a plate and cover to keep warm.

Add in the remaining 2 Tbs. of the butter and melt until butter is a golden in color; add lemon juice and then add in the parsley. Add the truffle butter at the last moment and season the sauce with salt and pepper to taste. Pour the warm sauce over the fish and serve immediately. -Serves 2 to 4

*http://www.surlatable.com/product/PRO-197315/

MOUSSE OF ROASTED ROOT VEGETABLES

- Butter, softened
- 1 butternut squash, peeled and seeded
- 1 large parsnip, peeled
- 1 large carrot, peeled
- 1/2 red onion
- 6 garlic cloves, minced
- 3 Tbs. fresh thyme
- 3 Tbs. extra virgin olive oil
- 1 cup heavy cream
- Salt, black pepper, white pepper and nutmeg to taste
- 1/4 cup chopped parsley for garnish

Coat the inside of 6 ramekins well with butter and set aside.

Preheat oven to 425° F.

Line a roasting pan with tin foil. Cut all the vegetables into 1 inch chunks. Toss vegetables in a large bowl with garlic, thyme, and olive oil until. Spread vegetables out evenly in the pan. Sprinkle generously with salt and black pepper. Roast the vegetables for an hour (Flip the vegetables once halfway through with a spatula).

Separate and transfer the parsnips to a food processor. Add 1/3 cup heavy cream and 1 egg and purée until combined. Season with salt and white pepper to taste. Spoon a layer of parsnip purée into each prepared ramekin.

Separate and purée the carrots and onions; along with 1/3 cup heavy cream and 1 egg. Season with salt and black pepper to taste. Spoon a layer of carrot/onion purée on top of the parsnips.

Purée the butternut squash with 1 egg and the remaining heavy cream. Season with salt, black pepper and nutmeg. Spoon a layer of squash purée on top of the carrots.

Place the ramekins in a roasting pan and add enough hot water to come halfway up the sides of the ramekins. Cover the roasting pan with a piece of tin foil, and bake for 30 minutes or until set. Let the mousses cool for 10 minutes before removing from the water bath.

Run a thin knife around the edges of the ramekins to loosen each mousse, then carefully invert onto warm plates to serve. Garnish with chopped parsley. - Serves 6

BIALY WITH LOX SPREAD - Sit back and watch the world go by while noshing on this deli standard.

Lox Spread:

- 1 (8 oz.) package cream cheese, at room temperature
- Scallions, trimmed and coarsely chopped
- 6 oz. slices lox
- Salt and pepper, to taste

In a food processor, blend the cream cheese until it is smooth. Add the scallions, lox, salt and pepper. Continue pulsing the cream cheese mixture until it is well blended.

Remove cream cheese mixture and place in a small bowl, wrap in plastic wrap and refrigerate until ready to serve.

Bialy:

- 2 cups bread flour
- 1/2 tsp. instant yeast
- 1-1/2 tsp. salt
- 3/4 cup warm water

In the bowl, whisk together the flour, yeast and salt. Gradually add the warm water, mixing dough until soft and stretchy.

Place the dough in a large, lightly greased bowl. Lightly spray the top of the dough with cooking spray as well. Cover the bowl with plastic wrap and place in a warm spot until dough has doubled in size, about 2 hours.

Deflate the dough with your hands and transfer it to a lightly floured work surface. Cut dough into 6 equal pieces with a sharp knife. Gently round each piece by pulling the dough together, stretching to make a smooth skin and pinching it together where the edges meet underneath. Set them on a floured baking sheet. Dust the tops with flour and cover with plastic wrap. Allow the bialys to rise for another 2 hours.

Filling:

- 2 tsp. vegetable oil
- 1/4 cup white onion, chopped
- 1 tsp. poppy seeds
- 1/4 sea salt
- Black pepper, to taste

Heat the oil in a small nonstick pan, over medium heat. Add the onions and sauté for until tender. Add the poppy seeds, salt, and pepper to taste, remove from heat and allow filling to cool.

Place the oven rack at the lowest level and place a baking stone or baking sheet on it. Then place a rimmed sheet pan on the floor of the oven (resting under the heating element), before preheating. 30 minutes before baking, preheat the oven to 475° F.

Gently stretch the 6 dough balls into a 5 inches diameter disc, form a 1 inch wide divot in the center of each disc with your thumb .

Place them on a baking sheet lined with parchment paper and spoon 1 tsp. of poppy seed filling in the center of each bialy.

Slide the parchment with the bialys onto the stone or sheet. Dump 1 cup of ice cubes into the rimmed sheet pan on the oven floor for steam. Quickly close the oven door and bake for 6 to 10 minutes or until bialys are a pale golden color.

Allow the bialys to cool a bit and top with a schmear of the lox spread. - Makes 6

LASAGNA (veggie) - Share this dish and make a new friend.

- 2 lbs. eggplant, thinly sliced
- olive oil cooking spray
- 2 Tbs. olive oil
- 1/4 cup onion, chopped
- 12oz. button mushrooms, sliced
- 9 lasagna noodles
- 1 jar (16 ounces) spaghetti sauce
- 8 oz. cottage cheese
- 6 oz. shredded mozzarella cheese
- 1/2 cup grated Parmesan cheese

Preheat oven to 375° F.

Sprayed a large skillet with cooking spray, place the skillet over medium-high heat lightly brown eggplant slices and set aside. In the same skillet, heat olive oil and cook onion for about 3 minutes or until soft. Add the sliced mushrooms and cook until mushrooms are just tender.

Cook the lasagna noodles as directed on package. Into an 11x 7 inch baking dish, spoon about 1/4 of the prepared spaghetti sauce on the bottom. Arrange a layer of lasagna noodles, cottage cheese, onion/mushroom mixture, mozzarella cheese, eggplant slices, sauce and Parmesan cheese. Repeat layers two more times. Bake the lasagna for 30 to 40 minutes uncovered. - Serves 6

"The sound of a gunshot came from behind the bench and
Pendergast felt a terrible blow to his back."

TWO GRAVES

BEEF JERKY

COOKIES

POTTED MEAT

CREVETTES REMOULADE

POMPANO PONTCHARTRAIN

BIG MAC

CHALLA BREAD FRENCH TOAST

COFFEE CRUMB CAKE

MOZUKU

SHIOKARA

CARAMEL CREAM DOUGHNUTS

COFFEE DOUGHNUTS

EGGS SAUSAGE TOAST W/ O.J.

TOAST WITH BUTTER AND JAM

SAUSAGES & BACON

BLUEBERRY PANCAKES

GERMAN BREAD

BREAD AND JAM

SOFT BOILED EGGS

BEEF JERKY - Sometimes life is anything but a picnic or a walk in the park.

- 3 lb. sirloin or beef tenderloin
- 1/2 cup honey
- 5 Tbs. light soy sauce
- 2 Tbs. Red Boat fish sauce
- 2 Tbs. ground coriander

Wrap beef with plastic wrap and place in freezer for 1 hour or until firm.

Once meat is ready, place on a cutting board, unwrap, trim away any fat, and slice along the grain into 1/8 inch thick strips.

Place all remaining ingredients in a large Ziploc bag and shake until combined. Place beef strips in the marinade, shake and massage to coat. Place in the refrigerator overnight, turning and squeezing several times.

Place beef strips in a colander to drain, and allow them to come to room temperature.

Remove the racks from the oven and completely line the bottom of the oven with tin foil.

Preheat oven to 160° F.

Spray oven racks with cooking spray, blot away any excess marinade and arrange beef strips horizontally across the racks, making sure strips do not touch or overlap.

Place the racks back in the oven and dry out the meat for about 4 hours. Jerky should be pliable when bent, but not break or snap.

Blot off any excess oil from the jerky and cool completely on the racks before storing in a breathable container.

COOKIES

Quick Cookies:

- 2 sticks butter, softened
- 1 cup powdered sugar, divided
- 1 tsp. pure vanilla extract
- 2 cups all purpose flour
- 1 cup finely chopped nuts (pecans, almonds, peanuts etc.)

Preheat oven to 350° F.

Beat butter, 1/2 cup powdered sugar and the vanilla together in large bowl with an electric mixer until light and fluffy. Add flour and nuts, a bit at a time and mix at low speed after each addition, until well blended.

Form the dough into 1 inch balls by rolling them with the greased palms of your hands. Place 2 inches apart on ungreased cookie sheets.

Bake for 15 minutes or until bottoms of cookies are lightly browned. Cool completely while on the cookie sheets.

Place cookies and remaining powdered sugar in a Ziploc bag and gently shake until evenly coated and remove cookies to a serving plate.

Border Crossing Spice Cookies:

- 1-1/4 cups all purpose flour
- 1/4 cup unsweetened cocoa powder
- 1 tsp. baking soda
- 1/2 tsp. salt
- 1 stick butter, softened
- 1 cup white sugar
- 1 cup light brown sugar
- 2 eggs
- 1/4 cup white sugar
- 2 tsp. cinnamon
- 1/2 tsp. chili powder
- A pinch cayenne pepper

Preheat oven to 375° F.

In a medium mixing bowl, sift together flour, cocoa powder, baking soda and salt.

In a larger mixing bowl, using an electric mixer, beat butter, white and brown sugars for about 3 minutes. Add eggs and beat to incorporate. Using a wooden spoon, slowly add flour mixture and mix until well combined.

In a small bowl, combine 1/4 cup white sugar, cinnamon, chili powder and cayenne. Form dough into 2 inch balls by rolling with the greased palms of the hand and then roll in spiced sugar mixture. Place dough balls about 3 inches apart on a prepared cookie sheet. Place cookies in oven and bake about 10 minutes or until they start to crack. Remove from oven and let the cookies cool for 5 minutes before transferring to a serving plate.

POTTED MEAT

- 1 lb. beef stewing meat, cut into 1/2 inch pieces
- Water
- 1 stick butter
- Salt and black pepper to taste
- Paprika to taste
- Ground allspice to taste
- Cracked pepper corns

Place a Dutch oven over medium heat. Add the stewing beef and just enough water to cover the meat. Place the lid on the Dutch oven and stew for 3 hours. Check and replacing the water as necessary. After 3 hours drain the beef broth into a medium bowl and set aside.

Mince the stewed beef in a food processor in small batches, until it is all the consistency of a thick paste.

Melt the butter in a small saucepan. Line a metal strainer with a few layers of cheesecloth or clean gauze and set the strainer over a heatproof container. Pour the melted butter through the sieve to clarify it.

In a second medium bowl, mix the minced meat with 3/4 of the clarified melted butter. Season the mixture with salt, pepper, paprika and allspice to taste. Stir in just enough of reserved broth to moisten the mixture.

Transfer the potted beef to a large ramekin or terrine, pour the remaining clarified butter over the surface of the beef and sprinkle with cracked pepper corns. Cover with plastic wrap and chill in the refrigerator until serving. - Serves 6

CREVETTES REMOULADE - Sip a glass of iced lemonade and dream of the mist drifting through the formal gardens of your favorite plantation.

Shrimp Boil:

- 5 lb. 15 count shrimp, shell on
- Cajun seasoning, to taste
- 1 large onion, chopped
- 1 head garlic, sliced in half
- 2 celery stalks
- 3 bay leaves
- 2 lemons, halved
- 3 Tbs. fresh lemon juice
- Salted ice water
- Lettuce leaves, for garnish

Fill a large stockpot with salted water and season heavily with Cajun seasoning. Add onion, garlic, celery, bay leaves and lemons halves. Once water starts to boil, add shrimp and reduce to a simmer.

Cook for 5 to 10 minutes. Test for doneness and once shrimp have fully cooked, remove them from the water and transfer them into a salted ice water bath. Remove the chilled shrimp from the ice bath, peel and devein.
Remoulade Sauce:

- 1-1/2 cups Hellmann's mayonnaise
- 1/2 cup Creole mustard
- 2 shallots, minced
- 1 tsp. garlic, minced
- 1/4 cup prepared horseradish
- 1/4 cup white wine vinegar
- 1/2 tsp. celery salt
- 1 tsp. paprika
- 3 Tbs. Cajun seasoning

- 2 tsp. lemon juice
- 1 tsp. Tabasco sauce (or more)
- 1/2 tsp. salt

Place all of the remoulade ingredients in a food processor and blend. Pour remoulade into a large non-reactive bowl and fold the chilled shrimp in the sauce. Cover and let shrimp marinate for a least 1 hour in the refrigerator before serving. Serve the shrimp on beds of lettuce leaves. - Serves 6 to 8

POMPANO PONTCHARTRAIN

- 4 (8 oz.) pompano fillets, skin on
- Salt and white pepper
- 2 Tbs. vegetable oil
- 1 lb. lump crab meat
- 1 stick butter, melted
- Celery salt and white pepper to taste
- 2 Tbs. fresh chives, chopped
- Parsley sprigs, for garnish
- 2 lemons, cut in wedges

Season the pompano fillets with salt and white pepper. Heat the oil in a large iron skillet, over medium-high heat. In two batches, if necessary, add fish, skin side up to hot oil and cook for about 3 minutes or until browned. Flip fish and cook for an additional 3 minutes or until cooked through. Transfer fish to a platter and cover with tin foil to them keep warm.

While the fillets is cooking, heat the crab meat and melted butter in a sauté pan over medium heat and season with celery salt and white pepper to taste. Watch carefully and cook the crab only until the meat is heated through.

Place a pompano fillet in the center of a plate, and top with crab meat. Garnish with chopped chives, parsley sprigs, and lemon wedges. - Serves 4

BIG MAC - Hey, it beats Dumpster diving, right?

Special Sauce:

- 1/2 cup Hellmann's mayonnaise
- 2 Tbs. French dressing
- 4 tsp. sweet pickle relish
- 1 Tbs. white onion, minced
- 1 tsp. white vinegar
- 1 tsp. sugar
- 1/4 tsp. salt

Mix all special sauce ingredients together until well combined and chill in refrigerator.

Burger:

- 4 sesame seed hamburger buns + 4 extra bottom halves - all lightly toasted
- Special sauce
- 2 cups shredded lettuce
- 2 lbs. ground beef, made into 8 patties and grilled
- 16 pickle slices
- 1/8 cup white onion, thinly sliced
- 8 slices American cheese

To build your Big Mac, start with the bottom bun, add a spoonful of special sauce, then shredded lettuce, hamburger patty, two pickles and a slice of cheese. Next a bottom bun, special sauce, shredded lettuce, onions, another burger patty, two more pickles, and finally the top bun. - Serves 4

CHALLA BREAD FRENCH TOAST - This just might become your favorite breakfast, don't turn it down.

- 1 loaf challah bread
- 5 eggs
- 1-1/2 cup heavy cream
- 1 tsp. honey
- 1 tsp. pure vanilla extract
- 1 tsp. sugar
- 1/2 tsp. salt
- 2 Tbs. butter
- 1 tsp. vegetable oil
- 1/4 cup fresh raspberries
- 1/4 cup fresh blueberries
- Powdered sugar
- Honey

Combine the eggs, milk, and honey, sugar, vanilla and salt in a bowl a whisk until well blended.

Cut the challah bread into 1 inch thick slices. Pour egg mixture into a shallow pan.

Place the slices of the bread in pan and let the bread soak for 2 minutes. Flip bread and soak 3 minutes more.

Heat an iron skillet over medium heat and add the butter and oil.

Grill the bread 3 minutes per side or until golden brown. Plate the toast and top with the berries, powdered sugar and honey. - Serves 2 to 6

COFFEE CRUMB CAKE - Get something good going on in your stomach.

Crumb:

- 2-1/2 cups all purpose flour
- 1-1/4 cups sugar
- 1-1/2 tsp. ground cinnamon
- 2 sticks butter melted and set aside
- 1 tsp. pure vanilla extract
- 3/4 tsp. almond extract

Whisk together the flour, sugar and cinnamon in a medium mixing bowl. Stir the vanilla and almond extracts into melted butter. Slowly pour the melted butter mixture into the flour mixture while continuously and gently tossing with a fork to make the crumbs.

Cake:

- 1 stick butter, softened
- 1 cup sugar
- 2 eggs
- 1 tsp. pure vanilla extract
- 1 cup sour cream
- 2 cups all purpose flour
- 1/2 tsp. baking soda
- 1/2 tsp. salt
- 1 tsp. baking powder
- Powdered sugar, for garnish
- Fresh mint, for garnish

Preheat oven to 350° F.

Grease a 9 x 13 inch pan, dust the pan with flour, and knock out any excess flour into the sink.

Whip the butter and sugar together with an electric mixer about 3 minutes until fluffy. Add the eggs and then beat in the vanilla and the sour cream. In a separate bowl, whisk together the flour, baking soda, salt and baking powder. Add to the flour mixture to the egg mixture and beat on low, until smooth.

Pour the batter into the prepared pan and spread it out evenly. Evenly sprinkle the crumb mixture over the batter.

Bake for 30 to 35 minutes. Remove the coffee cake from the oven and let the cake cool completely. Cut the cake into squares and transfer to plates. Dust with powdered sugar and garnish with mint leaves. - Serves 12

MOZUKU (Stir-Fried) - Tempt your guests with these famous Okinawan delicacies.

- 1/2 cup Mozuku*
- 1/4 cup carrot, sliced into matchsticks
- 1/4 cup green pepper, diced
- 1/4 shiitake mushrooms, thinly sliced
- 2 bacon strips, cut into thin strips
- 1 Tbs. soy sauce
- Salt and pepper to taste
- 2 tsp. sesame oil
- 2 tsp. toasted white sesame seeds

Wash mozuku, drain and cut into bite sized pieces. Heat the sesame oil in a wok or in a medium size non-stick pan. Cook the bacon until crisp. Add and stir-fry carrot and green pepper until tender. Add and stir-fry the shiitakes and mozuku. Season stir-fry with salt and pepper to taste. Sprinkle toasted white sesame seeds before serving. - Serves 2

*Mozuku is usually sold frozen at most Asian grocery stores.

SHIOKARA (Ika no Shiokara -Fermented Squid)

- 5 fresh squid
- 2 Tbs. sea salt
- Sriracha pepper sauce
- 2 tsp. lemon zest

Separate the tentacles and remove the entrails from the bodies of the 5 squid by first gently pulling the tentacles away from the body, removing the head. Remove the cartilage spines of the squid by gently pulling it away from the flesh.

Scoop out the remaining entrails from the squid. Split the bodies and cut ears (the triangular portion of the squid) off of the main portion of the squids, using a sharp knife. Peel away the spotted brown outer membrane from the bodies. Find and gently remove the orange-ish brown gland sags (liver/digestive gland) from the guts and set them aside. Wash all the bodies, ears, tentacles and the outside of the gland sags thoroughly.

Cut up the flesh into short noodle-like sections, including the tentacles and ear. Place the sliced squid into the bottom of an airtight container. To this squeeze the contents of the orange-ish brown sacs. Add sea salt, a few drops of Sriracha sauce and the lemon zest. Stir to combine and seal tightly. Allow the Ika no Shiokara to ferment for 24 hours in the refrigerator. Eat within 1 day of fermenting. - Serves 2 to 4

CARAMEL CREAM CRUNCH DOUGHNUTS - These are just to die for.

Doughnuts:

- 1/2 cup butter, softened
- 1/2 cup dark brown sugar
- 1 egg
- 2/3 cup vanilla yogurt
- 1/2 cup half & half
- 1 tsp. pure vanilla extract
- 1/2 tsp. salt
- 1 tsp. cinnamon
- Dash nutmeg
- 2 tsp. baking powder
- 1 tsp. baking soda
- 2 cups all purpose flour

Crumble:

- 3 Tbs. cold butter, cut into chunks
- 1/2 cup dark brown sugar
- 1/3 cup flour
- 1 tsp. cinnamon

Grease 2 (6 cavity) doughnut pans with cooking spray and set aside.

Preheat oven to 375° F.

In a large bowl, blend together the butter and brown sugar with a wooden spoon. Add the egg, vanilla, half & half and yogurt and mix to combine.

Sift salt, cinnamon, nutmeg, baking powder, baking soda and flour into a separate bowl. Mix together the flour mixture to the butter mixture and stir it into a thick batter.

Spoon the batter into a quart size Ziploc bag. Remove any excess air from the bag and cut a 1/2 inch hole into one of the corners. Squeeze the batter into the doughnut pans molds about 2/3 full.

In a small bowl, cut the crumble ingredients together with a fork until small crumbs are formed. Sprinkle the crumble mixture on top of each raw doughnut.

Bake donuts for 10 to 12 minutes or until firm. Remove from oven and allow the doughnuts to cool completely before removing from the pan. - Makes 12 doughnuts

COFFEE DOUGHNUTS - Grab a few and get ready to cross-check some 1870 personnel files.

Glaze:

- 1/4 cup boiling water
- 6 tsp. instant coffee powder
- 1-1/2 cups powdered sugar
- 1 Tbs. light corn syrup
- 1/4 tsp. pure vanilla extract
- 1/4 tsp. salt
- 1/4 cup sugar

To make the glaze, stir together boiling water and coffee powder in a medium bowl, then stir in powdered sugar, corn syrup, vanilla, and salt until smooth.

Doughnuts:

- 1 package active dry yeast

- 2 Tbs. warm water
- 3-1/4 cups all purpose flour
- 1 cup milk, at room temperature
- 1/2 stick butter, softened
- 3 egg yolks
- 2 Tbs. sugar
- 1 tsp. salt
- 1/2 tsp. cinnamon
- Vegetable oil for deep frying

To make the dough, combine the yeast and warm water in a small bowl and stir until dissolved. Allow yeast to bloom for 5 minutes.

In a medium bowl, mix together flour, milk, butter, egg yolks, sugar, salt, cinnamon. Add the yeast mixture and mix until a soft, sticky dough is formed.

Sprinkle the surface of dough lightly with some flour. Cover the bowl with plastic wrap and allow the dough to double, about 1 to 2 hours.

Scoop the dough out onto a fairly well floured work surface. Sprinkle some flour of the top of the dough and coat a rolling pin as well. Roll the dough out to a 1/2 inch thickness. Cut out all the rounds you can using a 3 inch cutter, and then cut a hole in center of each round with a 1 inch cutter. Transfer the doughnuts to a large floured baking sheet. Cover the doughnuts with a sheet of plastic wrap and let them rise in a warm spot until slightly puffy, about 30 minutes.

Place 2 and 1/2 inches oil in a Dutch oven or an electric skillet; heat the oil to 350° F. Fry the doughnuts, a few at a time, until plump and golden brown, about 1 minute per side. Transfer them to paper towels to drain. (Don't forget the donut holes!).

Dip the doughnuts into the glaze, then place them on a wire rack set in a shallow baking pan. While the glaze is still wet, sprinkle the tops of the doughnuts with sugar. - Serves 6

EGGS, SAUSAGE, TOAST AND ORANGE JUICE - Ah, a full American breakfast.

- 3 Tbs. butter, melted
- 6 slices white bread, crust trimmed off
- 6 eggs
- Salt and pepper to taste
- 1 pack pre-cooked breakfast sausages, chopped
- 1/2 cup shredded cheese
- Chopped chives for garnish

Preheat oven to 350° F.

Brush the 6 muffin cups and both sides of the trimmed bread slices with melted butter. Press one slice into each muffin cup, creating bread cups. Bake 5 minutes, or until lightly toasted and remove from oven.

Crack one egg into each toast cup and season them with salt and pepper to taste. Sprinkle the eggs with chopped sausages and cheese. Bake 15 to 20 minutes, or until eggs are cooked to a desired firmness. Garnish with chives and serve with fresh squeezed orange juice. - Serves 6

Fresh Juice:

- 10 large oranges
- 2 to 3 ice cubes

Prepare the oranges for the food processor by peeling them, and then cut them into chunks. If the oranges have seeds, be sure to remove all of them.

Place orange chunks and ice cubes in processor and pulse a few times to break up the ice. Then process continuously until the oranges are liquefied. Pour the orange puree through a wire strainer, working the pulp back and forth, into a pitcher and serve. - Serves 2

TOAST WITH BUTTER AND JAM TERRINE - Never in your life have you tasted anything so wonderful.

- 1/2 stick butter, softened
- 8 slices country white bread
- 3/4 cup Smucker's strawberry jam
- 4 eggs, plus 1 yolk
- 1/3 cup sugar
- 1-3/4 cups milk
- 3/4 cup heavy cream
- 1 tsp. pure vanilla extract
- 1/4 tsp. salt

Preheat oven to 450° F.

Butter the bread on one side and arrange in a single layer, buttered side up, on baking sheets. Bake until the tops are golden, about 6 minutes and remove toast. Reduce oven to 350° F.

Butter a 4 x 8 inch loaf pan and spread all the jam in an even layer on the bottom. Fold the toast in half and arrange them in the pan, so the folded sides are pointing up.

In a medium bowl, whisk together the eggs, egg yolk, and sugar.

In a saucepan, over medium heat, combine milk, cream, vanilla, and salt and heat just until warm. Allow milk mixture to cool for 5 minutes and then whisk it into egg mixture. Carefully pour the milk/egg mixture over toast and let it soak into the bread for 30 minutes.

Bake the terrine for 1 hour or until the custard becomes set in middle. Remove the pan from oven and allow it to cool for 1 hour. Run a knife around edges of loaf pan before inverting onto a serving platter. - Serves 6

SAUSAGES (Bratwurst Kebabs) – It's okay, salivate over the aroma.

- 1/2 cup light soy sauce
- 1/4 cup frozen apple juice concentrate, thawed
- 3 Tbs. spicy brown mustard
- 1 package bratwursts, cut into 1 inch pieces
- 1 onion, cut into 2 inch pieces
- 2 apples cut into 2 inch pieces
- 1 red bell pepper, seeded and cut into 2-inch pieces
- 1 green bell pepper, cut into 2-inch pieces
- Metal or wooden kebab skewer

If using wooden skewers, soak them in water at least 30 minutes before placing on the grill or under the broiler.

Whisk together the soy sauce, apple juice and mustard in a small bowl. Place the soy sauce mixture in a large Ziploc bag. Add the onions, apples and peppers to the bag and refrigerate for two hours.

Empty the bag into a metal strainer held over a medium bowl and drain off the excess marinade.

Thread bratwurst, apples and vegetables alternately on skewers, until all ingredients are used. Brush the kebabs with the reserved marinade.

Grill or broil them over medium heat, turning and basting often, until the vegetables are soft and the sausage cooked, approximately 15 to 20 minutes. - Serves 6

BACON (Candied) - Nothing is better than bacon.

- Cooking spray
- 1 lb. thick sliced bacon
- 1/2 cup apple cider vinegar
- 2 cups apple cider
- 3/4 cup brown sugar
- 1 tsp. cinnamon
- Dash cayenne pepper

Preheat oven to 350° F.

Separate the bacon and place the strips in a medium bowl along with vinegar and apple cider.

Line a rimmed baking sheet with tin foil, and then place a wire rack on top of the pan. Spray the rack generously with cooking spray.

Combine the brown sugar, cinnamon, and cayenne pepper in a shallow dish. Take each strip of bacon and press it into the sugar mixture, then turn it over and coat the other side. Place the coated bacon on the wire rack. Sprinkle any remaining sugar over the top of the bacon. Bake the bacon for 20 to 25 minutes or until crisp and slightly dark along the edges. - Serves 6

BLUEBERRY PANCAKES - You're running this show, go large.

- 2 cups all purpose flour
- 3 Tbs. sugar
- 1 leveled tsp. baking powder
- 1/2 tsp. salt
- 1/2 tsp. baking soda
- 1 1/2 cup buttermilk
- 1/2 cup ricotta cheese
- 3 eggs
- 1/2 stick melted butter
- Vegetable oil
- 2 cups frozen blueberries

- 1/2 stick butter and 2 cups pure Highland County maple syrup, heated and mixed together

Preheat oven to 200° F.

In a wire strainer over a large bowl, combine flour, sugar, baking powder, salt, and baking soda and sift into a large bowl.

In separate bowl combine buttermilk, eggs, and melted butter and whisk until well blended.

Add the liquid to the dry ingredients and stir with a wooden spoon 30 strokes, just until all the ingredients are blended but still lumpy. Let batter rest 5 minutes.

Heat an iron skillet or a griddle over medium heat for 5 minutes. Coat the surface with a thin film of vegetable oil using a balled up paper towel.

Using a 1/2 measuring cup as a ladle, pour batter into the heated surface. Sprinkle each pancake with blueberries. Cook about 3 minutes, until small bubbles appear on the pancake's surface. Flip with a metal spatula and cook until golden brown, about 2 minutes.

Transfer the pancakes to a baking sheet and place in the warm oven. Repeat until all the batter is used. Serve with the maple butter syrup. - Serves 2 to 4

http://www.southernmostmaple.com/maplesyrup.html

GERMAN BREAD - Herzlich Willkommen or a hearty welcome.

- 2 packages active dry yeast
- 1/8 tsp. sugar
- 1/2 cup warm water
- 2 cups water
- 1/4 cup molasses
- 1/4 cup apple cider vinegar
- 4 Tbs. butter
- 1 oz. unsweetened chocolate
- 1/2 cup whole wheat flour
- 3 cups medium rye flour
- 3 cups bread flour
- 1 cup bran
- 2 Tbs. caraway seeds, crushed
- 1/2 tsp. fennel seeds, crushed
- 1 Tbs. salt
- 1 Tbs. instant coffee powder
- 1 Tbs. shallots, minced
- 1/4 cup cornmeal

- 1 Tbs. bread flour
- 1 Tbs. caraway seeds

Add the yeast and sugar to a small bowl containing 1/2 cup of warm water. Stir to dissolve and set aside.

Heat the two cups water, molasses, and vinegar to a simmer in a small saucepan. Add the butter and chocolate, stir until melted and set aside.

Sift together the whole wheat, rye and bread flour in a large bowl and set aside as well.

Transfer two cups of the flour mixture, the bran, the 2 Tbs. caraway seeds, fennel seeds, salt, coffee powder and shallots in a large bowl and stir to combine. To this add the yeast mixture and then the warm molasses mixtures. Mix with a wooden spoon until smooth, about 3 minutes.

Add the remaining flour mixture and mix to combine with your hands.

Scoop the dough out onto a lightly floured work surface and knead for 10 minutes.

Form the dough into a ball and place in a bowl sprayed with cooking spray. Turn the dough over once to coat. Cover with plastic wrap and let rise in a warm spot until doubled, about 2 hours.

Combine the cornmeal, 1 Tbs. flour and 1 Tbs. caraway seeds, and set aside.

Gently press the dough down in the bowl and scoop it out again on the floured work surface. Cut the dough into 2 equal portions and form into rounds.

Placed the dough rounds, seam down, on a greased baking sheet. Sprinkle rounds with the cornmeal mixture. Cover them loosely with plastic wrap and let rise until they have doubled in size again about 1 hour. With a very sharp knife, slice an X into the top of a round before baking.

Bake at 425° F for 45 to 50 minutes or until loaves are well browned. - Makes 2 loaves

BREAD AND JAM BITES

- 4 -1/2 cups all purpose flour
- 1 package dried yeast
- 1/2 cup butter
- 1/2 cup milk
- 3 Tbs. sugar
- 1/4 tsp. pure vanilla extract
- 1 tsp. salt
- 2 eggs, beaten
- Oil for frying
- 1-1/2 strawberry jam
- Powdered sugar for dusting

Sift the flour and then add yeast to a large mixing bowl and blend together.

Combine the butter and milk in a small saucepan over low heat and heat until the butter is melted and milk is warm.

Add the warm milk mixture, sugar, salt, eggs, and vanilla to the flour. With a wooden spoon, stir until well combined and then knead the dough for 5 minutes until the dough is very smooth. Cover the bowl with plastic wrap and let it rise in a warm spot until the dough has doubled.

Scoop out the dough onto a lightly floured work surface. Knead the dough gently for 1 minute and then cut into 18 equal pieces. Roll each piece into balls and place them on a floured baking sheet. Cover the dough balls with a clean kitchen towel and let them rise for 30 minutes.

In a Dutch oven or deep fat fryer, heat oil to 350° F.

Gently slide the balls into the hot oil in small batches and fry evenly on both sides until they are golden brown.

Remove with a slotted spoon and drain on paper towels.

Spoon the jam into a piping bag with a long tip and pipe the jam into the pastry and dust with powdered sugar. - Serves 2 to 6

SOFT BOILED EGGS WITH SOLDIERS

- 2 large eggs, room temperature
- 2 slices whole wheat bread
- 2 Tbs. butter, softened

Bring a saucepan of water to a boil over medium-high heat. Set the eggs in the water, cover the saucepan and turn the heat to low. Allow the eggs to simmer for 5 minutes exactly.

While the eggs are simmering, toast the bread and spread with softened butter. Slice the toast into one inch strips.

After 5 minutes, remove the eggs from the water with a slotted spoon and transfer them to a wire strainer. Run eggs under cold water for 30 seconds. Tap and peel the eggs carefully. Set the eggs in a shallow bowl and dice with a small spoon. Salt and pepper to taste and serve with toast "soldiers" for dipping. - Serves 1

"What are you, Forty-Seven, but a bag of blood and organs –
a genetic garbage dump?"

EXTRACTION

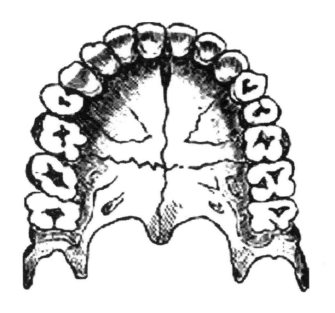

TAGLIATELLA AL TARTUFO BIANCO - A refined, yet simple dish. Remember to serve al dente.

- Salt
- Water (for boiling pasta)
- 1/2 cup heavy whipping cream
- 3 oz. white truffle butter *
- 1/2 tsp. salt
- 1/2 tsp. ground white pepper
- 1 (8 oz.) package tagliarelle pasta**
- 3 Tbs. fresh chives, chopped
- 1 small block Parmesan, shaved thin with a vegetable peeler
- Fresh white truffle (optional)***

Add 1 Tbs. salt to a large stock pot of water and bring it to a boil.

In a large sauté pan over medium heat, bring the heavy cream to a low simmer. Add the truffle butter, salt, and white pepper. Lower the heat to the lowest setting and stir until the truffle butter has melted completely. Cover the sauté pan and keep it warm over very low heat.

Add the pasta to the boiling water and cook for exactly 3 minutes (do not over cook). Drain the pasta but be sure to save back 1/4 cup of the pasta water to use later. Add the drained pasta to the cream sauce and gently toss to coat.

Because the sauce will be somewhat absorbed by the pasta, add a bit of the pasta water to keep the dish smooth and creamy. Adjust to taste with a bit of salt and white pepper.

Serve the pasta in shallow pasta bowls, garnished with chopped fresh chives, shaved Parmesan cheese and shaved truffle (if using), - Serves 2

*http://www.amazon.com/Savini-Tartufo-Bianco--Butter-Truffles/dp/B002ZZ8QFY/

**http://www.amazon.com/Cipriani-Food-Tagliarelle-Extra-Pasta/dp/B000VA0PU4/

***http://www.amazon.com/Fresh-White-Truffles-ounce-Truffle/dp/B004BIOE40/

"...you would sneak over to the Dufour mansion and leave the tooth in a particular place on the front porch."

WHITE FIRE

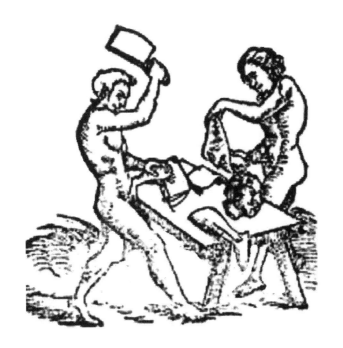

POTTED SHRIMP

GALANTINE OF CHICKEN

TRIPE FRIED IN BATTER

BISQUE DE HOMARD

COLORADO RACK OF LAMB

TEXAS BARBECUE

SHEPHERD'S PIE

MINESHAFT TAVERN BURGER

LINZER TORTE

HAZELNUT DACQUOISE

SALTED CARAMEL MOUSSE

FINANCIER BISCUIT

APRICOT MOUSSE

COFFEE AND ORANGE ÉCLAIR

APRICOT, QUINCE AND ROSEMARY TART

MANGO, VIOLETS AND CURRENT MACAROON

KIR ROYALE COCKTAIL

GINGER SCONES

PLOUGHMAN'S PICKLE AND CHEDDAR,

SMOKED SALMON AND WASABI SANDWICH

TERIYAKI CHICKEN AND GRILLED AUBERGINE

HARRISON & CORFIELD JASMINE TEA

MOCKEY JONES 80 DOLLAR STEAK

RARE PORTERHOUSE STEAK

SCALLOPED POTATOES

ROMAINE SALAD

CHOCOLATE BROWNIE SUNDAE

BEANS & RICE

CUCUMBER SANDWICHES

BACON AND EGGS

EGGS BENEDICT (SOUTHWESTERN)

BELGIAN WAFFLES

FRIED EGG

PRAWNS

SUCKLING PIG W/APPLE

CHERRIES JUBILEE

POTTED SHRIMP - The Langham, if you please. They set such a brilliant table.

- 5 Tbs. unsalted butter
- 1/2 lb. shrimp, peeled and de-veined
- 1/4 cup shallot, sliced
- 1/2 tsp. ground mace
- 1/2 tsp. powdered ginger
- Dash freshly grated nutmeg
- 3 Tbs. Amontillado sherry
- 2 to 4 dashes green Tabasco sauce
- Lemon juice, to taste
- Salt, to taste
- 8 slices thin white bread

In an iron skillet, melt 1 Tbs. butter over medium heat. Add the shrimp, shallots, mace, ginger and nutmeg. Stir to coat and cook 1 minute. Add the sherry and cook another 2 and 1/2 to 3 minutes.

Remove from heat; add the hot sauce and lemon juice. Place the shrimp mixture in a food processor and pulse until finely chopped, but not to a paste. Season the ground shrimp with salt to taste.

Melt remaining butter in the iron skillet over medium low heat. When foaming subsides, remove skillet from heat and stir two-thirds of the butter into the shrimp mixture.

Pack shrimp mixture into a ramekin and top with the remaining butter. Cover with plastic wrap and refrigerate for 4 hours or until completely firm.

Return to room temperature before serving with slices of thin toast with crusts trimmed off and cut into triangular pieces. - Serves 2

GALANTINE OF CHICKEN WITH A MOREL CREAM SAUCE

- Salt and pepper
- 1 (4 lb.) de-boned chicken*
- 2 cup ground pork, lean
- 4 chorizo sausages, chopped
- 4 oz. button mushrooms, cleaned and stemmed
- 3 Tbs. capers
- 1/4 cup parsley, coarsely chopped
- 1/4 cup basil, coarsely chopped
- 1 tsp. smoked paprika
- 2 clove garlic, coarsely chopped

Preheat oven to 350° F.

Season the de-boned chicken inside and out with salt and pepper and set aside.

In a large bowl, combine the pork, chorizo, mushrooms, capers, paprika, parsley, basil and garlic.

Lay the chicken out (skin side down) and arrange the stuffing length ways along the inside of the bird. Tuck some stuffing down in the leg and thigh cavity as well.

Wrap the chicken around the stuffing and fasten the seam closed with a skewer. Truss the chicken with kitchen twine. Generously re-season the outside of the chicken on all sides.

Roast the chicken for 1 hour and 15 minutes or until internal temperature of the galantine reaches 165 on a kitchen thermometer.

Allow galantine to rest for 15 minutes before carving. Carve into thin slices in the same manner as slicing a loaf of bread and serve with morel cream sauce. - Serves 6

*Ask the meat dept. to de-bone the chicken if unfamiliar with technique.

Sauce:

- 2 oz. dried morels
- 3 Tbs. unsalted butter
- 1/4 cup finely diced shallots
- 1 clove garlic, minced
- 1 cup Marsala wine
- 2 cups heavy cream
- Salt
- 1 Tbs. fresh lemon juice
- 1 Tbs. fresh chives, thinly sliced
- 1 Tbs. fresh tarragon, minced
- Salt and pepper to taste

In a small saucepan, bring 2 cups water to a boil over high heat. Take the pan off the heat and add the dried morels. Cover and soak until rehydrated, about 30 minutes. Lift them out with a slotted spoon and gently squeeze excess liquid back into the saucepan.

Cut any large ones in half, and set the mushrooms aside. Strain the mushroom broth through a wire strainer lined with cheesecloth. Return the broth to the saucepan and over medium-high heat; reduce the broth to about 1/4 cup.

Melt the butter in a medium saucepan over medium heat. Add the shallots and cook for 3 minutes. Add the garlic and cook for 1 minute more; then add the morels.

Reduce the heat to low and cook for 2 minutes. Add the Marsala and increase the heat to bring the mixture to a simmer. Reduce the wine sauce to a syrup and then add the reduced broth, cream, and 1/2 tsp. salt.

Simmer until the sauce thickens slightly, about 10 minutes. At this point add the lemon juice and herbs. Season the sauce to taste with salt and pepper.

Langham Hotel 1889

TRIPE FRIED IN BATTER

- 3 lbs. honeycomb tripe, cut in 1 x 3 inch pieces
- 2 cups buttermilk
- 1 cup onions, sliced
- 1 green pepper, chopped
- 2 bay leaves
- 4 whole cloves
- 2 tsp. salt
- 1 tsp. white pepper

- Oil for frying
- 2 cup flour
- 1 Tbs. salt
- 1 Tbs. pepper
- 1 egg, beaten
- A pinch cayenne pepper
- 1-1/2 cup water
- 1 Tbs. garlic powder
- Malt vinegar, for dipping

Place the tripe, buttermilk, onions, green pepper, bay leaves, clove, salt and pepper in Crock-pot. Cover with water. Cook the tripe for 6 to 8 hours on low. Drain the mixture through a colander, remove tripe and allow it to cool.

Preheat oil in a Dutch oven or deep fat fry to 325° F.

In a medium mixing bowl, combine the flour, salt, pepper, egg, cayenne and 1/2 cup water; stir until well blended.

In a second bowl mix 1 cup of water with garlic powder and stir to combine. Dip the tripe pieces in garlic mixture, dip in the batter and fry until golden brown.

Serve the fried tripe hot with vinegar for dipping - Serves 6

BISQUE DE HOMARD - Time consuming, but most excellent.

- 1-1/2 lb. fresh lobster, cut into pieces
- 6 Tbs. of butter
- 1 onion, chopped
- 1 carrot, diced
- 1 stalk of celery, diced
- 3 Tbs. brandy
- 1 cup of dry white wine
- 4 cups fish stock
- 1 Tbs. tomato paste
- 1/2 cup of long grain rice
- 1 fresh bouquet garni: (Mix together 1 Tbs. parsley, 1 tsp. thyme and 1 bay leaf. Wrap in a piece of cheesecloth and tie with kitchen twine.)
- 3/4 cup whipping cream plus 1/4 cup for garnish
- Salt and ground white pepper to taste
- Cayenne pepper to taste

Melt 3 Tbs. butter in a large saucepan over medium heat. Add the onions, carrot and celery and cook until soft. Add the lobster and stir until the shells turn bright red. Pour in the brandy and ignite it with a long grill lighter. When the flame dies down, add the wine, increase the heat to medium-high and bring to a simmer. Cook until the liquid is reduced by half. Pour in fish stock and simmer 3 minutes, then remove lobster segments.

Stir in the tomato paste and rice; add the bouquet garni. Cover and cook until the rice is tender, about 20 to 25 minutes.

Remove lobster meat from the shells and return the large sections of lobster shell to the saucepan. Slice the lobster meat and set to the side.

After the rice has cooked, remove the lobster shells and the bouquet garni.

Pour the mixture into a food processor and pulse to a fine puree. Press the puree through a metal strainer positioned over the cleaned pot. Place the pot over medium heat and bring the puree to a low simmer.

Season the puree with salt, white pepper and cayenne, to taste. Decrease heat to low and slowly stir in the whipping cream.

Add the remaining butter and whisk it into the bisque, 1 Tbs. at a time.

Add the lobster meat and serve immediately in bowls with a splash of cream (and sherry if desired) in the center. - Serves 4

*http://www.amazon.com/Btrthb-Fish-Base-8-OZ/dp/B007A4XY7A/ref=sr_1_1?s=grocery&ie=UTF8&qid=1399112201&sr=1-1&keywords=fish+stock

COLORADO RACK OF LAMB - A 2001 Château Pichon-Longueville would be a lovely accompaniment, as the 2000 seems "corked."

- 1 rack of lamb, trimmed
- Salt

- Black pepper
- 1 Tbs. olive oil
- 2 Tbs. Dijon mustard
- 2 tsp. garlic, minced
- 2/3 cup panko bread crumbs
- 2 tsp. fresh thyme, chopped
- 2 tsp. fresh rosemary, chopped
- 2 tsp. fresh Italian parsley, chopped

Season the lamb rack on all sides generously with salt and pepper. Heat a large iron skillet over medium-high heat and, once hot, add the oil. Wait 30 seconds; add the lamb rack and brown it on all sides. Transfer the lamb to a plate and set aside to cool 5 minutes.

Preheat the oven to 450° F.

Using your hands spread the mustard all over the lamb rack and then spread on the minced garlic. In a small bowl combine the panko crumbs and herbs. Again with your hands, press the Panko mixture evenly all over the lamb rack.

Place the prepared lamb on a rimmed baking sheet and roast for 12 to 15 minutes for rare. Allow the lamb to rest for 10 minutes before carving. - Serves 2 to 4

TEXAS BARBECUE - Imagine low lighting, stone walls and a sawdust covered floor, as you enjoy this "hole in the wall" recipe.

Sauce:

- 1/4 cup butter
- 1/4 cup onion, minced
- 3 celery stalks, finely chopped
- 1 cup water
- 1 beef bouillon cube
- 1 cup Heinz ketchup
- 1/2 cup apple cider vinegar
- 3 Tbs. Worcestershire sauce
- 2 Tbs. spicy brown mustard
- 2 Tbs. honey
- 2 cloves garlic, minced
- 1 Tbs. smoked paprika
- 2 tsp. chili powder

- Salt and pepper to taste

Melt butter in a medium sauce pan. Add the garlic, onion, and celery. Sauté until lightly browned. Add water and bullion cube and stir to dissolve. Add the remaining ingredients, stir and simmer for about 15 minutes.

Brisket:

- 2 Tbs. chili powder
- 2 Tbs. salt
- 1 Tbs. garlic powder
- 1 Tbs. onion powder
- 1 Tbs. ground black pepper
- 1 Tbs. sugar
- 2 tsp. dry mustard
- 1 bay leaf, crushed
- 1 (4 to 5 lb.) beef brisket, trimmed
- 1-1/2 cups Swanson's beef stock
- Boiling water

Preheat oven to 350° F.

Combine the chili powder, salt, garlic and onion powders, black pepper, sugar, dry mustard, and bay leaf. Sprinkle the seasoning generously on all sides of the brisket and rub the seasoning firmly into the meat. Place the brisket in a deep roasting pan and cook, uncovered, for 1 hour.

Remove pan from oven and add stock and enough boiling water to fill the pan to about 1/2 inches deep. Cover the roasting pan tightly with tin foil, lower the oven temperature to 300° F and continue cooking the brisket for 3 hours. - Serves 6 to 8

MINER'S SHEPHERD PIE (hand-held) - Cheap, low-down and wow...... quite good.

- 1 lb. ground lamb
- 3 Tbs. onion, finely chopped
- 1/2 tsp. garlic, minced
- 1/3 cup Heinz chili sauce
- 1 Tbs. apple cider vinegar
- 1/2 tsp. salt
- 1-1/4 cups water
- 5 Tbs. butter
- 1-1/4 cups instant mashed potato flakes
- 3 oz. cream cheese, cubed
- 1 package refrigerated biscuits
- Paprika
- 1 (8 cupped) muffin tin, spray with cooking spray

In a large skillet, cook the lamb and onion over medium heat until browned. Add garlic and cook for 1 minute and then drain the skillet of excess fat. Stir in the chili sauce, vinegar and salt; set aside.

In a small saucepan, bring water and butter to a boil. Remove from heat and whisk in potato flakes until blended. Whisk in cream cheese until smooth.

Preheat oven to 375° F.

Press 1 biscuit onto the bottom and up the sides of each of the muffin tin cups. Fill with the lamb mixture. Spread potato mixture over lamb and sprinkle with paprika. Bake for 20 to 25 minutes or until golden brown. - Serves 8

MINESHAFT TAVERN BURGER - The Holy Grail of hamburgers.

Grilled Chile Relish:

- 10 large mild chili peppers
- 1 large onion, cut into 1/2 inch thick slices
- Vegetable oil
- 1/4 cup dark brown sugar
- 1 Tbs. Dijon mustard
- 2 Tbs. apple cider vinegar
- Salt and freshly ground pepper

Heat up a grill to high. Rub the chilies and onion with oil and grill until charred, about 10 minutes. Peel and seed the chilies and cut into thin strips; medium dice the onion. Transfer the vegetables to a medium saucepan. Add the brown sugar, mustard, vinegar. Add salt and pepper to taste. Bring the relish to a simmer over medium heat, cook for 5 minutes. Remove from heat and allow it to cool completely.

Burger:

- 1-1/2 lb. ground chuck, 80 /20
- Basil infused olive oil
- Salt and freshly ground pepper
- 6 oz. shredded sharp Cheddar cheese
- 1/2 tsp. Colman's dry mustard
- 1/4 tsp. black pepper
- 1 Tbs. Hellmann's mayonnaise
- 2 Tbs. chopped pimentos
- 4 onion rolls, split, buttered and toasted
- Grilled Chile Relish

Preheat grill on high heat.

Form four 4 inch patties about 1 and 1/2 inches thick. Make a 1/2 inch deep divot in the center of each patty, and then rub lightly with the olive oil and season with salt and pepper.

In a food processor, combine cheese, dry mustard, pepper, mayonnaise and pimentos. Pulse until mixture is smooth and creamy.

Fill each divot in the beef patties with the cheese mixture and bring the edges of the burger up and over the cheese and pinch to seal, creating a large meatball. Gently press back into patties 1-1/2 inches thick.

Grill the burgers, turning once, about 3 minutes per side. Transfer the burgers on to buns, top with the chili relish and serve. - Serves 4

LINZER TORTE - A perfect Saturday supper dessert. You'll be counting the days.

- 1 cup butter, softened
- 1 cup sugar
- 1 large egg
- 2 hard boiled egg yolks, cooled
- 1 Tbs. DeKuyper (cherry liqueur)
- 2 tsp. lemon zest
- 1/4 tsp. cinnamon
- 1/4 tsp. ground cloves
- 2 cups all purpose flour
- 1 cup finely ground unsalted almonds
- 16 oz. Smucker's seedless red raspberry jam
- Powdered sugar

Preheat oven to 325° F.

In a large mixing bowl combine the butter, sugar, egg, egg yolks, cherry liqueur, lemon zest, cinnamon, and cloves. Whisk it all together until it's well incorporated. To this add the flour and ground almonds and blend into a smooth dough. Form 2/3 of the dough into a disk and place in a 1 gallon Ziploc bag. Form the other 1/3 of the dough into a ball and wrap in plastic wrap. Refrigerate 2 hours.

Position the larger disk of dough to the middle of the sealed Ziploc bag. Using a rolling pin, flatten the dough into a 12 inch circle. Using a pair of scissors, cut along both sides of the Ziploc bag, unzip the bag and fold the bag open.

Transfer dough to an un-greased 10 inch tart pan with a removable bottom by first inverting the pan on the dough. Slide one hand, palm up, under the cut Ziploc bag with the other hand, palm down, on the pan. Lift both hands and flip. Peel back the cut Ziploc bag and gently press the dough into the pan. Work the dough up sides of the pan.

Spread the jam evenly over the crust.

Preheat oven to 325° F.

Roll out the remaining 1/3 dough to about 1/2 an inch thick. Cut dough into 12 strips. Weave the dough strips over the top of the jam in a lattice pattern. Press the ends of the strips into the rim and trim off any excess dough.

Bake for 40 minutes or until golden brown. Cool to room temperate in the pan and then remove the ring.

Sift powdered sugar over top just before serving. - Serves 8

HAZELNUT DACQUOISE - Delightfully, this "Chic and Shock."

- 1 cup roasted hazelnuts
- 2 Tbs. cornstarch
- 1-1/2 cups powdered sugar
- 6 egg whites
- 1/2 tsp. cream of tartar
- 3 cups heavy cream
- 1 tsp. pure vanilla extract
- 3 oz. semi-sweet chocolate, melted
- 4 Tbs. powdered sugar
- 1 Tbs. instant coffee powder
- Chocolate curls, garnish
- Sliced strawberries, garnish

Preheat oven to 300° F.

Prepare 2 large cookie sheets by lining them with parchment paper. Use a pencil to trace 2 circles on each sheet, using an 8 inch round cake pan or plate as a guide. Place hazelnuts, cornstarch, and 3/4 cup powdered sugar into a food processor and blend until everything is finely ground.

Beat egg whites and cream of tartar in a large mixing bowl with an electric mixer, at high speed until they form soft peaks. Sprinkle 3/4 cup powdered sugar, 2 Tbs. at a time, into egg whites, beating well after each addition. Beat until all the sugar dissolves and whites stand in stiff peaks.

Using a rubber spatula, fold hazelnut mixture into egg whites. Spread 1/4 of the meringue mixture inside each of the circles on the parchment paper. Bake the meringues 45 minutes. Turn the oven off and leave meringues in oven for 1 hour to dry. Do not open oven door and peek.

Transfer the meringues with the parchment paper, to wire racks and cool completely. Carefully loosen and remove meringues from the paper.

Preparing the chocolate cream:

In a medium bowl, heat chocolate in microwave at 30 second intervals, until just beginning to melt. Stir the chocolate until smooth.

In a small mixing bowl, with an electric mixer at medium speed, beat 1 and 1/2 cups heavy cream, 1 Tbs. powdered sugar and vanilla to soft peaks. With rubber spatula, fold half of whipped cream into the melted chocolate until just combined and then fold in rest of the whipped cream. Set 1/4 cup of the chocolate cream aside for a garnish.

Preparing the coffee cream:

In a cup, dissolve the instant coffee in 2 Tbs. heavy cream. In small bowl, beat remaining heavy cream and 3 Tbs. powdered sugar until soft peaks form. Add the coffee mixture; beat until stiff peaks form.

Place first meringue layer on a serving plate and spread with half of the chocolate cream. Top with another meringue and then half of the coffee cream. Continue building your dacquoise, ending with a layer of coffee cream. Spoon the reserved 1/4 cup chocolate cream in a 4 inch circle on top as a garnish. Refrigerate the dacquoise, uncovered, overnight. Garnish with chocolate curls and strawberry slices. - Serves 6 to 8

SALTED CARAMEL MOUSSE WITH CHOCOLATE GANACHE

Ganache:

- 6 oz. chocolate chips
- 1/2 cup whipping cream

Place chocolate chips in a medium bowl.

In a small saucepan heat the whipping cream over medium-high heat until it just starts to a boil.

Remove from heat and pour the hot cream over chocolate and stir until completely mixed together and glossy.

Divide the ganache between 6 parfait glasses. Tilt the glasses in 4 directions to coat the interior of the glasses with the ganache into a tulip pattern.

Mousse:

- 1-1/4 tsp. unflavored powdered gelatin
- 8 Tbs. cold water, divided

- 1 cup sugar
- 2-3/4 cups heavy cream, warmed
- 1 Tbs. pure vanilla extract
- 1 Tbs. coarse sea salt for the garnish

Sprinkle powdered gelatin into 2 Tbs. of cold water. Allow it to sit for about 5 minutes.

Dissolve the sugar and 6 Tbs. of water in a medium saucepan while the saucepan is off the stove. Place pan over medium heat until it begins to turn from pale amber to a rich, caramel color, approximately 8 minutes (watch closely). Do not stir the mixture once it's on the heat; just let it heat to the proper color.

Immediately remove pan from heat as the sugar will continue to darken as it cools. If there are any sugar crystals that have formed on the sides of the pan, gently swirl the pan to remove them. Allow sugar mixture to cool slightly, but remember, do not stir.

Very slowly, whisk 3/4 cup whipping cream into the saucepan of caramel and set aside to cool.

In a large mixing bowl, whip together 2 cups of the warm whipping cream and vanilla with an electric mixer, until soft peaks form. Whisk the gelatin water into the warm caramel cream and then gently fold caramel into the bowl of whipped cream.

Transfer mousse to a piping bag with a large star tip; pipe mousse equally into the 6 prepared parfait glasses and refrigerate until ready to serve. Garnish with sea salt just before to serving. - Serves 6

FINANCIER BISCUITS

- Butter flavored cooking spray
- 1 stick butter, cut into small pieces
- 1/3 cup orange blossom honey
- 2 cups toasted almonds, finely ground
- 1/2 cup sugar
- 1/4 cup powdered sugar
- 3/4 cup cake flour, sifted
- 1/2 tsp. salt
- 5 egg whites
- 1 cup Smucker's seedless raspberry jam

Preheat oven to 350° F.

Generously coat a 12 cup mini muffin pan with cooking spray.

Place butter in a small saucepan over medium-low heat, whisking frequently, for 5 minutes until in reaches a golden brown. Add the honey; whisk until well combined and remove from heat.

Using a whisk, blend together the ground almonds, sugar, powdered sugar and flour in a large bowl. Switch to an electric hand mixer set on low speed and start adding the egg whites a bit at a time. Once all the egg whites have been added turn mixer up to medium and beat for about 1 minute.

Reduce the speed back to low, and slowly pour in the honey/butter mixture. Increase speed to high, and beat for 1 minute longer.

Fill muffin cups about half way with the batter. Place a dot of raspberry jam just off center on top of each cookie. Draw the tip of a toothpick across each cookie and it will form a little raspberry heart (How cute!).

Bake for about 15 minutes until the edges are a light golden color. Remove pan from the oven and let the cookies cool slightly before gently removing them from the muffin pan. - Makes 12 biscuits

APRICOT MOUSSE

- 6 Tbs. sugar
- 1/2 cup dry white wine
- 20 fresh apricots, peeled and pitted (canned may also be used)
- 1 egg white
- 2 Tbs. unflavored gelatin
- 2 cups heavy cream whipped with 4 Tbs. powdered sugar

Whip together the heavy cream and powdered sugar. Cover and place in the refrigerator.

Place the sugar in a large saucepan, Add 1/2 of the white wine and bring it to a boil. Add apricots and cook for 20 minutes until fruit has broken down. Remove from heat, pour into a medium mixing bowl and allow to cool completely.

Add the egg white to the apricot mixture and beat into a thick foam.

In a second pan, heat the remaining wine with the gelatin, stirring until it has completely dissolved. Add gelatin mixture to the apricots and mix together thoroughly. Allow the apricot/gelatin mixture to cool completely and then fold it into the whipped cream.

Pour the mousse into 6 small decorative desert molds that have been chilled in the freezer for 15 minutes. Transfer and refrigerate the mousse until they set, about 3 hours.

To serve, dip the bottom of molds into very warm water for a few seconds and invert onto chilled serving dishes. - Serves 6

COFFEE AND ORANGE ÉCLAIR

Pastry:

- 1 cup flour
- 1/4 tsp. sugar
- 1/2 cup milk
- 1 stick butter
- 4 eggs

Sift the flour, sugar and salt in a medium mixing bowl. Place the milk, butter and 1/2 cup water in a large saucepan over medium, and heat until is completely melted. Raise heat to medium-high and bring milk mixture to a slight boil. Take saucepan off the heat and add the flour mixture to the saucepan. Stir with a wooden spoon until the dough is smooth. Transfer dough back to the medium mixing bowl and allow dough to cool for about 1 hour. Stir in the eggs and mix until well incorporated.

Orange Filling:

- 1-1/4 cups milk

- 1/4 cup sugar
- 2 egg yolks
- 2 tsp. pure vanilla extract
- 4 tsp. all purpose flour
- 4 tsp. corn starch
- 2-1/2 cup heavy whipping cream
- 2 cups fresh squeezed orange juice

Add the milk to a medium saucepan and slowly bring it to a simmer (do not boil) and then remove it from heat.

Whisk egg yolks, vanilla and sugar in a small bowl until smooth, then stir in the flour and cornstarch. Whisk the mixture together until very smooth, about 5 minutes.

Whisking constantly, add egg mixture to the hot milk. Return saucepan to heat and cook for about 5 minutes, whisking constantly, until it becomes thick.

Transfer the filling to a bowl, cover with plastic wrap and place in refrigerator for 3 hours.

In a small saucepan, over medium heat, reduce the orange juice to 1/4 cup. In a large bowl, whip the heavy cream until they make very firm peaks. Remove the bowl of filling from the refrigerator and whisk in the orange syrup. Fold the filling into the whipped cream and return the finished filling to refrigerator.

Coffee Topping:

- 8 oz. dark chocolate chips
- 2 tsp. instants coffee powder
- 4 oz. heavy cream, warmed
- 3 Tbs. butter, melted
- 2 oz. light corn syrup
- 1 pinch of salt

Melt chocolate in a medium bowl set over a pot of boiling water. Warm cream, coffee powder, butter, and salt in microwave until the butter has completely melted. Pour cream mixture over chocolate and stir until chocolate is smooth. Add the corn syrup to chocolate and blend.

Adjust the oven racks so they are both set at the 2 middle positions and preheat oven to 425° F.

Line 2 baking sheets with parchment paper. Fold each sheet of paper into thirds the long way. Unfold paper and place them back in the 2 baking sheets.

Fill a piping bag that has been fitted with a medium round tip with the dough. Using the creases as a guide, pipe the dough into 3 inch lengths, leaving 2 inches between each.

Bake for 20 minutes, then rotate the pans (top to bottom, bottom to top) and drop the oven to 350° F and bake 20 minutes longer. Remove the pans from oven and allow the shells to cool completely.

Put the orange filling into the cleaned piping bag fitted with a smaller round tip, and stick the tip into one end of the éclair. Pipe the filling into the éclair.

Hold each éclair face down and dip the top directly into the glaze to coat the top. Place back on bake sheet and allow the chocolate glaze to set. - Makes 16 éclairs

APRICOT, QUINCE AND ROSEMARY TART

- 1 frozen pie crust sheet, thawed
- 1 egg yolk, beaten
- 12 oz. Penguen quince jam*
- 1/4 cup water
- 2 Tbs. brandy
- 2 Tbs. fresh rosemary, coarsely chopped
- 10 to 12 apricots, peeled, pitted and halved
- 1/4 cup sugar
- 1 tsp. fresh ground cinnamon
- 1/2 tsp. fresh ground nutmeg
- 4 Tbs. butter, cut into small chunks

Preheat oven to 425° F.

Lightly butter a 10 inch tart pan (one with a removable bottom). Roll out the pie dough and press it into the pan; brush dough lightly with the beaten egg yolk.

Spread 1 cup of the quince jam over the bottom of dough. Place remaining jam into a small saucepan with water, rosemary and brandy and warm over a low heat.

Arrange the apricots, cut side down, in a circular pattern over the jam covered dough and sprinkle with the sugar, cinnamon and nutmeg. Drizzle the warm jam mixture over top of apricots and scatter the butter chucks on top.

Bake tart for 30 minutes or until the apricot have caramelized and the pastry is a light golden color.

Allow the tart to cool completely before removing the rim. - Serves 8

MANGO, VIOLETS AND BLACKCURRANT MACAROON

Cookie:

- 1 cup powdered sugar
- 1 cup almonds, very finely ground
- 1/4 cup plus 2 Tbs. water
- 1 cup sugar
- 2 egg whites, in a small bowl
- 4 egg whites, in a small bowl
- 3/4 tsp. mango flavoring*
- 1/4 tsp. orange food coloring

Line two baking sheets with parchment paper.

Mix together the powdered sugar and almonds in a large bowl. Pour the 2 egg whites into the almond mixture and stir into a thick paste. Add 1 tsp. of orange food coloring and mix until the color is blended.

In a saucepan, bring the water and sugar to the boil. Use a kitchen thermometer to make sure the temperature of the syrup just reaches 230° F and no higher.

Using an electric mixer beat the remaining egg whites into soft peaks. Decrease the speed of the mixer to medium and slowly pour in the sugar syrup. Add the mango extract and continue beating until the mixture has cooled, about 5 minutes.

Fold the mango egg whites into the almond paste mixture with a rubber spatula. Once blended, transfer macaroon batter to a piping bag fitted with a medium round tip.

Pipe the macaroons into 2 inch rounds, about 2 inches apart, onto the prepared baking sheets. Lightly tap the bottom of the tray on the counter top to remove air bubbles. Put the trays aside for 1 hour to allow the macaroons to dry.

Preheat oven to 125° F.

Bake the macaroons for about 15 minutes. Remove the macaroons from the oven and slide parchment paper onto a clean work surface. Let macaroons cool completely carefully before peeling from the parchment sheets.

Filling:

- 1 cup of white chocolate chips
- 2/3 cups whipping cream
- 4 drops violet essence**
- 3 drops purple coloring
- 1 jar of blackcurrant jam***

Heat half of the cream in a small saucepan over medium-high heat until almost boiling. Remove from heat, add the white chocolate chips and stir until smooth. Transfer the white chocolate cream to a medium mixing bowl, add the remaining cream and the violet essence and whip it together with an electric mixer. Place a sheet of plastic wrap in contact with the surface of the filling and place in a cool place for 3 hours.

Place the filling into the cleaned piping bag and apply a generous amount of filling to half of the macaroons. Place 1 tsp. of black currant jam in the center of the filling and cover with another macaroon. Cover and store the macaroons in a cool place for 24 hours before serving. Makes 12 to 14 macaroons

*http://bakingpleasures.com.au/p495/lorann-mango-oil-flavour

**http://bakingpleasures.com.au/p9033/violet-essence
***http://www.amazon.com/Bende-Black-Currant-Jam-12oz/dp/B000LRFYE4

KIR ROYALE COCKTAIL - One word – Espelette

- 2 Tbs. Crème De Cassis (currant liqueur)
- 6 oz. champagne or sparkling wine
- 2 fresh raspberries

Pour Crème De Cassis into a champagne flute. Top with chilled champagne or sparkling wine. Drop raspberries into glass. - Serves 1

GINGER SCONES WITH CLOTTED CREAM - Serve this with a flute of Laurent-Perrier if you're feeling a bit of jet lag.

- Cooking spray
- 4 cups all purpose flour
- 1/2 cup sugar
- 4 tsp. baking powder
- 1/2 tsp. salt
- 1-1/2 sticks chilled butter, diced
- 1 cup golden raisins
- 1/3 cup candied ginger, minced
- 1 cup heavy whipping cream
- 2 eggs
- 1 Tbs. pure vanilla extract
- 1 Tbs. lemon zest
- 1 egg beaten with 2 tsp. water (for an egg wash)

Preheat oven to 400° F.

Generously coat 2 baking sheets with cooking spray.

Sift the flour, sugar, baking powder and salt into a large bowl using a wire colander. Add the chilled butter and cut it into the flour with a fork until mixture looks like a coarse corn meal. Add the raisins and candied ginger and fold everything together.

In a separate medium bowl, beat the cream, the 2 eggs, vanilla and lemon zest together. Add the egg mixture to flour mixture and stir until just combined (do not over mix).

Scoop the dough onto a lightly floured work surface. Form the dough into a ball and knead lightly. Roll the dough out into a 3/4 inch thickness with a floured rolling pin.

Using a small juice glass cut the dough out into rounds.

Place the scones on the prepared baking sheets about 2 inches apart. Brush the tops of the scones with the egg wash.

Bake the scones about 20 minutes or until golden brown. Remove the scones and serve warm with clotted cream.

Clotted Cream:

- 6 oz. cream cheese, room temperature
- 1 pint sour cream
- 2 cups whipping cream
- 4 Tbs. powdered sugar

In a bowl, combine all ingredients and whip 2 minutes, or until thick and fluffy, using an electric mixer.

- orange marmalade

Serve warm scones with orange marmalade and clotted cream on the side. - Makes 16 to 18 scones

PLOUGHMAN'S PICKLE AND MONTGOMERY CHEDDAR SANDWICH - Nothing "Irregular" here, let alone down on Baker Street.

- 2 slices whole grain bread
- 4 slices Montgomery's Cheddar cheese *
- 2 Tbs. Branston sweet pickle**
- Hellmann's mayonnaise
- 2 tomato slices
- Salt and pepper
- Chopped parsley

Spread a generous portion of Branston sweet pickle over the entire bottom layer of bread (all the way to the edges). Spread mayonnaise across the top piece of bread in the same manner.

Slice 4 thin pieces cheese and place on top of the sweet pickle. Place tomato slices on top of cheese. Salt and pepper to taste. Add the top piece of bread, trim the crusts and cut into 3 pieces. Lightly spread mayonnaise around the edges of the trimmed sandwiches and then press the edges in chopped parsley. – Serves 1

*http://www.murrayscheese.com/cheddar-montgomery-s.html

**http://www.amazon.com/Branston-Pickle-520g-18oz-Gold/dp/B0001LVX4K/ref=pd_sim_sbs_gro_1

SMOKED SALMON AND WASABI CREAM CHEESE TEA SANDWICH

- 3 tsp. wasabi paste
- 8 oz. package cream cheese, softened
- 12 slices whole wheat bread
- 10 oz. thinly sliced smoked salmon
- 2 tsp. lemon zest
- 3 Tbs. fresh cilantro, chopped

Place wasabi paste and cream cheese in a medium bowl. Using an electric hand mixer, beat until fluffy and well combined, about 3 minutes.

Spread each slice generously with wasabi cream cheese all the way to the edges. Top half the bread slices with slices with smoked salmon and sprinkle on lemon zest and cilantro. Top with remaining bread slices.

Carefully trim the crusts and cut each sandwich into 4 triangles. Place sandwiches on a platter pointed side up. - Makes 24 tea sandwiches

TERIYAKI CHICKEN AND GRILLED AUBERGINE TEA SANDWICH - Take a bite, then another, close your eyes and chew. Scrumptious.

Chicken:

- 3/4 cup dark soy sauce
- 1/4 cup honey
- 1-1/4 tsp. fresh ginger, peeled and finely grated
- 1 lb. boneless, skinless chicken breasts
- Freshly ground black pepper
- 4 tsp. vegetable oil

In a small saucepan over medium heat, bring the dark soy sauce and honey to a light simmer. Remove from the heat, whisk in the grated ginger and set aside.

Place chicken breasts on a clean work surface and cover with a sheet of plastic wrap. Using a meat mallet, gently pound the chicken to a 1/2 inch thickness and cut each breast in half.

Heat oil in an iron skillet, over medium-high heat and then add chicken in a single layer. Cook the chicken for about 2 minutes. Flip and cook the second side, about 2 minutes more.

Lower heat to medium; pour in the teriyaki sauce and cook (flip the chicken to coat) until thoroughly cooked, about 5 minutes.

Transfer meat to a clean cutting board, allow chicken to rest 10 minutes and then slice or shred in small pieces.

Aubergine:

- 1 large aubergine/eggplant
- Olive oil
- 1/3 cup shallots, minced
- 1 tsp. fresh tarragon, minced
- Salt and pepper to taste

Preheat a griddle or large skillet on stove top over high heat.

Slice aubergine/eggplant into 1/4 thick slices. Brush both sides of the slices with oil, and cook them for about 2 minutes per side until golden and tender.

Sprinkle eggplant with shallot and tarragon, and season with salt and pepper to taste.

Sandwich:

- Sliced teriyaki chicken
- Grilled aubergine/eggplant
- 24 slices white bread
- 1/4 cup Hellmann's mayonnaise
- 1/2 cup finely chopped smoked almonds

Lay out 12 slices of bread on a work surface and divide the chicken evenly. Top chicken with grilled aubergine/eggplant and top with the reserved 12 slices of bread and press together gently. Using a 2 inch round cutter, cut 2 rounds from each sandwich.

Place chopped almonds on a small plate and lightly spread edges of rounds with mayonnaise to coat well. Roll edges in almonds. - Makes 12 tea sandwiches

HARRISON & CROSFIELD JASMINE TEA WITH A WHEATMEAL BISCUIT, DIPPED TWICE - Always be serious about your "Elevense's," always.

Use bottled water that is nearly boiling. Water should be at least 170 F. Water that is too hot may cause bitterness.

Add 1 heaping Tbs. of loose Harrison & Crosfield* tea leaves per teapot (roughly 3 to 5 cups of tea). Steep the tea for 1 to 5 minutes.

Strain the tea, pouring into warmed teacups and sip gently while the tea is still hot.

Serve with wheat meal digestive biscuits***, dunked twice.

*The Harrison & Crosfield brand is no longer available, as the company has gone out of business, but tea that is just as good is **Taylors of Harrogate.

**http://www.amazon.com/Taylors-Harrogate-Green-Jasmine-6x50/dp/B000MN69CS/ref=sr_1_3?s=grocery&ie=UTF8&qid=1379797888&sr=1-3&keywords=Taylors+of+Harrogate+JASMINE+tea

***http://www.amazon.com/Mcvities-Digestive-Bicuits-14-1-Pack/dp/B00CO24MTM/ref=sr_1_5?s=grocery&ie=UTF8&qid=1379797457&sr=1-5&keywords=WHEATMEAL+biscuit

MOCKEY JONES' 80 DOLLAR STEAK (MARTINI) -

"Smash"ingly simple and no one can accuse you of "dinning too well."

- 2 (1 lb.) sirloin steaks, thick cut
- 1-1/2 tsp. sea salt
- 1/4 tsp. coarse ground black pepper

Martini Marinade:

- 1/3 cup Grey Goose vodka
- 3 Tbs. dry vermouth
- 1/2 cup olive oil
- 1/4 cup fresh lemon juice
- 2 Tbs. honey
- 1 1/2 tsp. lemon zest
- 2 Tbs. juice from green olives
- 3 Tbs. mustard seed
- 1 tsp. minced garlic

In a medium mixing bowl, combine all the marinade ingredients and whisk until well incorporated.

Rub the steaks with salt and pepper and place them in a large Ziploc bag. Pour the marinade into the bag and refrigerate for 30 minutes.

Remove steaks from the marinade and grill the steaks, covered, for 3 minutes per side for rare. Place steaks on a platter, tent with tin foil and allow to rest 10 minutes.

Side:

- 3 Tbs. olive oil
- 3 Tbs. butter
- 16 small cippolini or pearl onions
- 16 large pimiento-stuffed green olives

- 1 bag (10 oz.) baby spinach

In a large sauté pan, heat the olive oil and butter over medium-high heat. Add onions and olives and cook for 2 minutes or until lightly browned. Add spinach and toss to lightly coat all of the spinach leaves and cook about 4 minutes.

Serve each steak with the sautéed spinach on the side. - Serves 2

RARE PORTERHOUSE STEAK WITH MAITRE D'
BUTTER - Set this up right, cozy and romantic, with candles and low lighting.

- 2 Tbs. butter
- 8 Tbs. butter, softened
- 1 cup minced shallots
- Coarse sea salt
- 2 tsp. green peppercorns
- 3 tsp. Dijon mustard
- 1/2 tsp. lemon juice
- 1/2 tsp. lemon zest
- 3 Tbs. Worcestershire sauce
- 1 Tbs. freshly chopped thyme
- 2 Tbs. freshly chopped parsley leaves
- Freshly ground black pepper
- Salt
- 1 Porterhouse steak, about 2-1/2 lbs. and about 2-1/2 inches thick

To make the maître d' butter, heat the 2 Tbs. of the butter in a medium sauté pan over medium heat. Add shallots and season with salt to taste. Cook shallots for about 5 minutes.

Place the shallots in a bowl with the green peppercorns, mustard, lemon juice, lemon zest and the Worcestershire sauce; stir until well blended. Add the remaining butter to the bowl and blend. Stir in the thyme, parsley and re-adjust the seasoning with salt and pepper to taste.

Place the compound butter on the front edge of a large sheet of plastic wrap, roll the butter into a 2 inch cylinder; twist the ends to seal and place in the freezer until firm.

Place a large iron skillet over medium-high heat until it begins to smoke. Dry any moisture from the steak and season well with salt and pepper. Turn the burner off and put the steak in the skillet. Raise the heat to high and brown on the first side for 5 minutes, being sure not to disturb the meat so it gets a good sear.

Lower the heat to medium and cook for an additional 6 minutes. Turn the steak over, using tongs, raise the burner temperature to high again and brown for 5 minutes. Once again, lower heat to medium and cook for an additional 6 to 8 minutes. (At this point turn the oven broiler on). Turn the steak onto an edge and sear for 5 minutes. Finish the steak by cooking for an additional 3 to 5 minutes per side.

Transfer the steak from the skillet to a cutting board and allow it rest for 10 minutes covered in tin foil. Cut the steak along the bone and the meat into slices. Transfer to a serving platter. Arrange the sliced meat back around each side of the bone. Top the steak with the maître d' butter, cut into1/2 inch thick rounds.

Place the heat-proof platter under the broiler for about 20 seconds or until the butter softens. - Serves 2 to 4

"...a dark figure appeared in the doorway.....The clown mask leered down at her."

SCALLOPED POTATOES

- 1/4 cup butter
- 1/4 cup all purpose flour
- 3 cups milk, warmed
- 12 oz. extra sharp Cheddar cheese, shredded

- 1/4 tsp. onion powder
- 1/2 tsp. salt
- 1/2 tsp. pepper
- 4 lbs. potatoes, washed and thinly sliced

Topping:

- 1-1/2 cups bread, torn into small pieces
- 1/4 cup unsalted butter, melted
- 1/4 cup grated Parmesan cheese

Preheat oven to 350° F.

Melt butter in a medium saucepan over medium heat. Whisk in flour, and cook, whisking constantly for 3 minutes to form a roux. Whisk the warm milk into the roux and bring to a boil. Reduce heat, and simmer for about 2 minutes or until thickened. Stir in the Cheddar cheese, onion powder, salt and pepper. Continue stirring until all the cheese has melted.

Spread about 1/2 cup of cheese sauce into the bottom of a greased casserole dish or Dutch oven. Layer 1/3 of potatoes over sauce; top with some more cheese sauce. Repeat twice with remaining potatoes and the last bit of the cheese sauce. Cover with a lid or with tin foil. Place potatoes in the oven and bake them for 1 and 1/2 hours.

In the cleaned saucepan used for the cheese sauce, melt the butter. Turn off the burner and stir in the torn bread and Parmesan cheese. After 1 and 1/2 hour cooking time, remove potatoes from oven and spread bread/cheese mixture evenly over potatoes. Return to the oven and bake, uncovered, for about 30 minutes or until potatoes are tender and topping is golden brown and bubbling. - Serves 6 to 8

ROMAINE SALAD (grilled)

- 2 heads romaine lettuce
- Extra-virgin olive oil
- Parmigiano-Reggiano

Heat up a gas grill to medium-high.

Rinse and shake the lettuce dry over the sink. Cut the heads in lengthwise. Brush the cut surface of the lettuce lightly with olive oil and grill about 5 minutes. Place each wedge on a salad plate and drizzle with vinaigrette. Using a micro-plane, shave some cheese generously over each salad before serving. - Serves 4

Vinaigrette:

- 1 clove garlic, minced
- 1 Tbs. grated lemon zest
- 3 Tbs. fresh lemon juice
- 1 tin anchovies, drained and diced
- 1 Tbs. white wine vinegar
- 2/3 cup extra-virgin olive oil

Place all ingredients in a clean jelly jar with a lid. Secure the lid, and then shake for 2 minutes to blend.

MINESHAFT CHOCOLATE BROWNIE SUNDAE

Brownie:

- 1 cup unsalted butter
- 8 oz. semi-sweet chocolate chips

- 6 eggs
- 1/2 cup sugar
- 1/4 cup unsweetened cocoa
- 2 tsp. pure vanilla extract
- 1 cup pecans, finely chopped

Preheat oven to 300° F.

Grease a 9 inch square bake pan. Line the pan with greased parchment paper. Combine butter and chocolate in a microwavable bowl and microwave at 30 second intervals until butter is just melted. Stir until smooth. Stir in cocoa powder and set aside.

Beat the eggs and the sugar together with an electric mixer for 5 minutes. Add in the vanilla. Gently fold the chocolate mixture into the egg mixture and then fold in nuts. Pour the batter into the prepared pan and bake for 35 to 40 minutes or until risen in center. Let the brownies cool completely in pan. Cover and refrigerate for 4 hours.

Sauce:

- 2/3 cup unsweetened cocoa
- 1-2/3 cups sugar
- 1-1/4 cups water
- 1 tsp. pure vanilla extract

To make the sauce, combine cocoa, sugar and water in a medium saucepan over medium heat, Bring sauce to a boil and continue boiling for 1 minute. Remove from heat and stir in vanilla. Cover and keep warm.

Whipped Topping:

- 1 cup chilled whipping cream
- 1/4 cup powdered sugar
- 1 tsp. pure vanilla extract

To make whipped cream, beat the cold cream for 2 minutes. Add in the sugar and beat until very thick. Add vanilla and refrigerate, covered, until ready to use.

Garnish:

- French vanilla ice cream
- Hershey chocolate bars
- Chocolate shavings

To assemble the sundae, break the chocolate bar in half. Cut the brownies to the same size as the chocolate bar sections. Place each brownie on a serving plate and microwave 20 seconds. Place the chocolate bar section on top of the brownie and return to the microwave for 10 seconds or until it just begins to melt. Top with a scoop of French vanilla ice cream, warm chocolate sauce, whipped cream and the chocolate shavings.   - Serves 6

BEANS & RICE - Pick the thermostat lock and warm up with this effortless yet comforting meal.

- 2 cups Swanson's chicken broth
- 1 cup water
- 1 cup lentils, rinsed
- 1/2 cup whole grain brown rice, uncooked
- 1 small onion, chopped
- 2 tsp. dry Italian seasonings
- 2 cloves garlic, minced
- 1/2 cup carrots, shredded
- 1/2 cup celery, diced
- 1 cup pepper jack cheese, grated

Preheat oven to 300° F.

In a 13 × 9 baking dish, combine all of the ingredients, except the cheese. Stir to combine.

Cover with foil and bake for 1 hour and 15 minutes.

Remove the bake dish from oven, remove foil and spread the cheese over the beans mixture. Return to oven and bake, uncovered, for another 20 minutes. - Serves 6

CUCUMBER TEA SANDWICHES WITH MINT CREAM CHEESE - Just like an invitation to the Ritz.

- 1 seedless cucumber, peeled, thinly sliced
- 1/4 cup fresh mint leaves, rinsed, dried and finely chopped
- 1/4 cup unsalted butter, room temperature
- 1/4 cup cream cheese, room temperature
- 16 slices white bread
- Salt and pepper, to taste

Lightly sprinkle cucumber slices with salt and place them between layers of paper towels to absorb excess moisture.

In a small bowl, combine the mint, butter, cream cheese and mix well. Spread cream cheese mixture on one side of each slice of bread. Lay the cucumber slices onto 8 slices of bread. Sprinkle with salt and pepper. Top with the remaining slices of bread.

Trim the crusts from each sandwich with a serrated knife. Cut the sandwiches in half diagonally and then cut them in half again. - Makes 32 tea sandwiches

BACON AND EGG FRITTATA – Plow on ahead, it's only bacon and eggs after all.

- 8 strips bacon
- 2 Tbs. olive oil
- 1 onion, finely chopped
- 8 eggs
- 1/2 cup Fontina cheese, grated
- 2/3 cup goat cheese, crumbled
- 1/4 tsp. salt
- 1/8 tsp. pepper

Preheat the oven to 325° F.

In a large skillet, fry the bacon over medium heat until it's cooked but not crispy. Drain on a paper towel and then chop into bite-size pieces.

Pour off the bacon fat and add 1 Tbs. of olive oil to the skillet. Adjust heat to medium-low and add the onions. Cook until softened, about 5 minutes and let them cool.

In a large mixing bowl, beat the eggs until fully combined. Add the onion, bacon, Fontina and goat cheeses, salt and pepper and stir gently.

In a 10 inch ovenproof sauté pan, heat the remaining Tbs. of olive oil over medium-low heat. Be sure the whole bottom is coated. Add the egg mixture and cook, without stirring, until the sides start to set, about 3 to 4 minutes. Place the sauté pan in the oven and bake until the frittata is firm, about 20 to 25 minutes.

Remove the hot pan from the oven with a mitt and gently run a rubber spatula around the sides of the pan to loosen. Place a serving plate over the sauté pan and carefully invert the pan to release the frittata onto the plate. - Serves 4 to 6

EGGS BENEDICT - (southwestern) - A deal at twice the price.

- 1 cup prepared black beans, rinsed & drained
- 1 Tbs. olive oil
- 1/2 tsp. ground cumin
- Salt
- Pepper
- 2 Tbs. minced cilantro
- 4 Thomas' Corn English Muffins
- Butter, softened
- 2 avocados, pitted, sliced and peeled
- 8 large eggs
- 1 tsp. white vinegar
- 1 cup chunky salsa
- 1/4 cup cilantro leaves, for garnish

In a medium bowl, combine black beans and olive oil. Crush the beans with a fork and blend, creating a chunky paste. Add ground cumin, salt, pepper and cilantro to the black bean paste and stir to combine.

Split Corn English muffins in half, toast to a golden brown and spread them with butter. Place two halves on each plate.

Divide the black bean mixture evenly between the muffins and spread. Top the black beans with avocado slices.

Fill a saucepan with water to 3/4 full, over medium-high heat. Bring to the water to a simmer (not boiling). Add the vinegar to water. Carefully crack the eggs directly into the water.

Cook the eggs for 3 minutes and then remove them from water using a slotted spoon. Press the back of the spoon on a thick layer of paper towel to remove any excess water.

Set one poached egg on top of each prepared muffin and top with 2 Tbs. of salsa. Garnish with chopped cilantro and serve immediately. - Serves 4

BELGIAN WAFFLES - More than smitten, you might just love these.

- 2 cups all purpose flour
- 3/4 cup sugar
- 3-1/2 tsp. baking powder
- 2 eggs, separate whites from yolks
- 1-1/2 cups milk
- 1 cup butter, melted
- 1 tsp. pure vanilla extract
- Sliced fresh strawberries
- Favorite syrup

In a large mixing bowl, combine flour, sugar and baking powder.

In separate bowl, lightly beat egg yolks. Add milk, butter and vanilla to egg yolks and mix well.

Stir yolk mixture into dry ingredients until just combined. With an electric mixer, beat the egg whites until they form stiff peaks. Gently fold eggs whites into the batter. Cook in a preheated waffle iron, sprayed with cooking spray, until golden brown. Serve with strawberries and syrup. - Serves 2 to 4

THE PERFECT FRIED EGG - Learning the tricks of the trade, yes?

- 1/2 tsp. unsalted butter
- 1 egg
- 2 tsp. water
- Salt and freshly ground pepper

Heat a small nonstick skillet over medium-high heat. Add butter and swirl to coat the skillet. Firmly crack an egg on a flat surface, open the shell and gently place the egg into the skillet.

Add the water to the pan and reduce the heat to medium-low. Cover skillet with a lid or a sheet of tin foil and cook for 1 minute 30 seconds or until a white film just appears on the yoke.

Remove the egg from the pan immediately. Season the egg to taste with salt and pepper to taste and serve. - Serves 1

PRAWNS

- 1/3 cup unsalted butter
- 2 Tbs. olive oil
- 4 cloves garlic, minced
- 2 fresh red chilies, finely chopped
- 2 lbs. green prawns with tails intact, peeled
- Salt and pepper
- 2 Tbs. fresh lime juice
- 3 tsp. lime zest
- 1/4 cup fresh cilantro, chopped
- Baby spinach, garnish
- French bread, sliced, brushed with olive oil and toasted

Heat the butter and oil in a large iron skillet, over medium-high heat. Add the garlic and chilies and sauté for 1 minute.

Add the prawns and season with salt and pepper. Sauté for 3 to 4 minutes or until the prawns are cooked through.

Add the lime juice, lime zest and cilantro to the prawns and fold to combine.

Serve prawns on beds of spinach with toasted bread. - Serves 2 to 4

SUCKLING PIG WITH APPLE - Ah, the requisite baked apple – your guests will reduce this Christmas classic to its rib cage.

- 1 whole suckling pig, (12 to 15 lbs.)
- 4 gallons water
- 6 cups salt
- 6 cups brown sugar
- 1 small to medium red apple
- Butter
- 1/2 cup vegetable oil, for basting

Rinse the pig with cold water and place to the side. Add water, salt and brown sugar to a large stockpot and stir to dissolve, but do not heat.

Line a heavy duty garbage bag with 2 more garbage bags and place in a sturdy 15 quart plastic container. Pour the water/salt/sugar mixture into the tripled layered garbage bags.

Place pig in the bags, be careful not to poke any holes in the bags, press out any extra air, and tie tightly with a twist-tie.

Place the container in the fridge and marinade for 24 hours, turning the bag several times during the brining process.

Position oven rack on a low position and preheat to 250° F.

Remove the pig from the marinade and pat it dry with paper towels.

On a clean work surface, lay the pig on its side and stuff the interior with large, lightly crumpled pieces of tin foil until the cavity has filled out and the pig has a natural look to him.

Transfer the pig to a large disposable roasting pan (place a large metal roasting pan under this for stability), fitted with a roasting rack.

Arrange the pig, stomach side down, with the legs tucked underneath and to its sides. Prop the head up with a tin foil ball and place the apple in the pig's mouth.

Cover the pan tightly with buttered tin foil and using the metal pan for support, place in the oven.

Roast the pig about 3 hours or until it reaches 130° F on a meat thermometer.

Remove the foil, brush on the oil with a basting brush, and increase the oven temp to 400° F.

Roast (basting every 15 minutes with oil) about 45 minutes to 1 hour or until the internal temperature reaches 160° F.

Remove from the oven and let the pig rest 20 minutes before transferring to a platter and carving. (If the apple looks over-cooked, replace it with a fresh one the same size). - Serves 12 to 18

CHERRIES JUBILEE - How marvelous, but that flame could be quite hazardous!

- 1/2 cup sugar
- 2 Tbs. cornstarch
- 1/4 cup water
- 1/4 cup orange juice
- 1 lb. dark cherries, washed, pitted and cut in half
- 1/2 tsp. orange zest
- 1/4 tsp. almond extract
- 1/4 cup Kirsch brandy (cherry brandy)
- 4 bowls of vanilla bean ice cream

Whisk the sugar and cornstarch in a cold medium saucepan. Whisk in the water and orange juice and bring to a boil over medium-high heat. Continue whisking until sauce has thickened. Whisk in cherries and orange zest.

Once sauce has returned to boil, immediately reduce heat to medium-low and simmer for 10 minutes.

Remove saucepan from the heat and stir in the almond extract.

Dim the light and pour brandy onto the surface of the cherry sauce and ignite with a long-headed lighter.

Carefully shake the pan until the blue flame has extinguished.

Spoon the cherries over the bowls of ice cream and serve immediately. - Serves 4

"...the body had dropped to the floor; a carbonized hand remained in the cuffs..."

BLUE LABYRINTH

POI

KALUA PORK

OPIHI STYLE OYSTERS

HAUPIA

ITALIAN FRIED SAUSAGE ROLLS

FISH LIP SOUP

TRIPES A LA MODE CAEN

SCALLION PANCAKES

LICORICE TOFFEE CANDY

QUIBE (BRAZILIAN FRIED MEAT)

PANQUECA DE BATATA

CURED MEAT AND BROWN BREAD

SALT ENCRUSTED SALTON SEA BASS

POI – Ah, a honeymoon feast. Mahalo.

- 2 large taro roots, scrubbed and rinsed
- cold bottled water (15 bottles)

In a medium stockpot, cover taro with the cold bottled water and bring to a boil over high heat. Reduce heat to low and simmer until the taro is fork tender, about 25 minutes. Drain into a colander and rinse with more cold bottled water.

Peel the cooked taro roots, like a potato and cut into small chunks. Place the taro root chunks into a food processor. Add about 1 Tbs. of bottled water and pulse the processor until a smooth paste appears. The poi will be really thick and sticky.

Transfer the poi to a stainless steel bowl and trickle a thin layer of the bottled water on top of the poi and cover the bowl tightly with plastic wrap.

Allow the poi to stand at room temperature for 2 to 4 days or until it ferments and takes on a somewhat tangy taste. – Serves 4

KALUA PORK

- 1 pork shoulder (about 3lbs.), trimmed
- 2 Tbs. liquid smoke

- 3 Tbs. Hawaiian sea salt*

Place the trimmed pork shoulder in the crock pot. Puncture the meat on all sides with a meat fork. Rub the pork all over with the Hawaiian salt. Pour in the liquid smoke and place the lid on the crock pot. Set the dial on the crock pot to low; cook about 7 hours.

Transfer the pork to a serving platter and shred with two forks. Serve with rice and some of the reserve juice from the crock pot. - Serves 6 to 8

*http://www.worldmarket.com/product/alaea-red-hawaiian-sea-salt.do

OPIHI STYLE OYSTERS

- 3 Tbs. Hawaiian sea salt
- 1 cup Hawaiian Kine Chili Pepper Vinegar Sauce*
- 1 cup water
- 3 tsp. garlic, minced
- 12 opihi or oysters, shucked (save 12 shells)
- Butter
- Shoyu sauce
- 2 Thai or Hawaiian bird peppers, diced with seeds removed
- 1 tsp. Hawaiian sea salt

Combine the pepper vinegar, water and garlic in a small stainless steel bowl. Marinate the opihi or oyster meat for about 20 minutes. Place 12 shells on the grill and allow them to become hot. Using a spoon, place the meat and a bit of the liquid into each shell.

Add a small pat of butter, shoyu sauce and diced pepper on top while the opihi or oysters are cooking.

Grill until the meat is just firm and the butter begins the brown, about 4 to 6 minutes. Season the grilled opihi or oysters with Hawaiian sea salt to taste. – Serves 2 to 6

http://www.hawaiiankineflavors.com/Gourmet_Chili_Pepper_V inegar_s/1825.htm

HAUPIA

- 2 cups unsweetened coconut milk
- 1 cup milk, warmed
- 6 Tbs. sugar
- 5 Tbs. cornstarch

Whisk together the coconut milk, sugar and cornstarch in a medium saucepan. Place the saucepan over low heat and, stirring consistently, cook until mixture thickened.

Add the warm milk and continue to cook until the mixture begins to bubble. Pour into 8 inch round cake pan lightly prepped with cooking spray and refrigerate until firm.

FRIED ITALIAN SAUSAGE ROLLS

- 4 cups bread flour
- 1/4 cup instant potato flakes
- 1/4 cup nonfat dry milk
- 3 tsp. salt
- 4 tsp. sugar
- 1 packet dry yeast
- 1-1/3 cups lukewarm water
- 3 Tbs. olive oil

Combine everything into a large mixing bowl and blend until smooth dough is formed. Turn the dough out on a floured work surface and knead for 10 minutes.

Place the dough in a large bowl sprayed with cooking spray, cover with plastic wrap and allow it to rise for 1 hour.

- Bread dough
- 12 hot Italian sausage links, pan fried and cut in half for a total of 24 links
- 1 cup red pepper relish

Roll the dough out into a large rectangle about 1/4 inches thick. Using a pizza cutter slice the dough into 4 x 4 squares.

Spread each square of dough with 1 Tbs. red pepper relish; place a link of sausage on the relish. Roll the dough around the sausage. Place the rolls, seam down, on a baking sheet sprayed with cooking spray. Drape a clean kitchen towel over the rolls and allow them to raise 30 minutes.

Preheat the oven to 375° F.

Bake for about 20 minutes or until nice and golden brown. Serve hot with more relish for dipping. – Serves 6 to 12

FISH LIP SOUP

- 2 large fish heads, split
- 1 large onion, sliced
- 1 large leek, washed and sliced

- 1 bay leaf
- 3 sprig parsley
- 2 sprig thyme
- 6 whole peppercorns

Rinse the fish heads in cold water. Place the heads in a large stockpot over medium high heat. Add all the remaining ingredients along with 12 cups cold water. Bring the liquid to a slow simmer but do not allow it to boil. Reduce heat to low and cook for 30 minutes. Skim off any foam and strain the stock through a colander lined with cheesecloth into another pot (throw away all the stuff in the cheesecloth).

- 8 cups fish head stock

- 1 cup dried fish maw, soaked in hot water until softened, then cut to small strips*

- 4 slices of fresh ginger, about 1/8 of an inch thick

- 8 dried cloud ear mushrooms, rehydrated and thinly sliced

- 8 fresh shiitake mushrooms caps, thinly sliced
- Up to 4 tsp. soy sauce
- 4 Tbs. cornstarch mixed with 8 Tbs. water
- Sea salt
- 1 lb. cooked crab meat (canned lump works well)
- Coriander
- Chinkiang vinegar
- White pepper

Bring the broth to a boil in a stockpot over medium heat. Add the fish maw and sliced ginger. Reduce heat to low and simmer, uncovered for about 20 minutes.

Add both types of mushrooms and simmer for 5 minutes. Slowly add the soy sauce, a bit at a time, until the soup reaches your desired taste.

Increase the heat and bring the soup to a boil, then add in the cornstarch mixture slowly, a bit at a time and stir. For a thin soup, add a little. For a thicker, richer soup add more. Add more broth if the soup seems too thick. Season the finished soup with some salt if needed.

Ladle the soup into 4 serving bowls and top with the crab meat and some coriander. Serve Chinkiang vinegar and white pepper on the side as condiments. – Serves 4

*http://www.amazon.com/Dried-Fish-Premium-Grade-50g/dp/B00B1CAR8G/ref=sr_1_5?s=grocery&ie=UTF8&qid=1416367750&sr=1-5&keywords=fish+maw

TRIPES A LA MODE CAEN

- 1 cup white onions, coarsely chopped
- 1/2 cup bacon, diced
- Salt and pepper
- 2 lbs. tripe, trimmed and cut into 2 inch squares
- 1 calf's or pig's foot, split
- 2 cups carrots, cut in 2 inch chunks
- 1 cup leeks, chopped
- 1/3 cup Cognac
- 2 cups dry white wine
- 2 whole cloves
- 1 bouquet garni, (2 sprigs fresh thyme - 2 dried bay leaves - 2 celery leaves stalks - 6 sprigs fresh parsley)
- 2 cloves garlic, crushed
- 6 cups Swanson's chicken broth

Preheat oven to 375°F.

Layer half of chopped onions in the bottom of a 3 quart stoneware casserole, and then layer In half of the bacon. Season generously with salt and pepper.

Now layer 1/3 of the tripe, press one split foot on top and season again with salt and pepper. Spread half of the carrots over top, another 1/3 of the tripe and the other split foot and then the rest of the carrots.

Finish off with the last of the tripe, the rest of the bacon, chopped onions and finally the leeks.

Pour the Cognac and the white wine over everything. Add the clove, garlic and the bouquet gari and cover with chicken stock.

Cover with the lid and cook in oven for 10 hours.

Stir to combine and readjust seasoning. Serve in bowls along with buttered French bread.

SCALLION PANCAKES WITH GINGER SAUCE – Mrs. Ishimura would be pleased.

Ginger Dipping Sauce:

- 1/4 cup soy sauce
- 1/4 cup Chinkiang vinegar
- 1/4 cup sliced scallions
- 1 tsp. minced ginger
- 1/4 tsp. garlic, minced
- 1 tsp. Thai chili pepper, minced
- 1 Tbs. brown sugar

Whisk everything together in a small stainless steel bowl until sugar dissolves and set aside.

- 1/4 tsp. garlic, minced
- 1 tsp. Thai chili pepper, minced
- 1 Tbs. brown sugar
- 2 cups all purpose flour
- 1 cup boiling water
- 1/2 cup scallions, diced
- 1 Tbs. sesame oil mixed with 1/2 cup vegetable oil

- Salt
- Black pepper

Place flour in the bowl of a food processor fitted with a metal blade and secure the lid. Turn the processor to the on position and wait 10 seconds, allowing the flour to sift. Now slowly add the boiling water while the blade continues to spin. Continue mixing until a firm dough ball forms. Remove the dough ball and wrap it in plastic wrap. Allow the dough ball the rest for 1 hour.

Unwrap the dough ball and roll it out into a rectangle about 1/16 of an inch thick with a rolling pin. Brush the surface of the dough with the sesame/vegetable oil mixture. Spread out the diced scallions and season generously with salt and pepper. Roll the dough up like a jelly roll and cut it into 4 segments. Roll each segment out into a rope and coil the rope into a coil, just like a cinnamon roll. Use the rolling pin to flatten each coil into a 6 inch disc.

Coat a hot non-stick pan with vegetable oil and grill both sides of the pancakes until golden brown.

Use a pizza cutter to slice the pancakes into wedges and serve them hot with the dipping sauce. Serves 4

LICORICE TOFFEE CANDY – Leaves a better taste in your mouth than the name "Slade" that's for damn sure.

- 2-1/2 cup sugar
- 3/4 cup water
- 1/2 cup Karo syrup (light)
- 1 cup margarine
- 1/4 cup honey
- 1/2 tsp. salt
- 1/2 tsp. real anise extract
- 3 drops black food coloring

Line a 13 x 9 pan with tin foil and spray with cooking spray.

Place sugar, water and Karo syrup in a medium saucepan and stir to combine. Place the saucepan over medium heat and cook until the mixture reaches 270°F on a candy thermometer.

Fold in the margarine, honey and salt and continue cooking until the thermometer reaches exactly 300°F. Remove the saucepan from the heat and stir in the anise extract and food coloring.

Carefully pour the hot mixture into the tin foil lined pan and allow the candy to spread out on its own. After about 5 minutes score the sheet of toffee, in 1 inch squares, with a greased knife and allow the sheet to cool overnight.

Flip the pan onto a clean work surface and peel the foil from the back. Break the toffee into piece along the scores and place in an airtight container.

QUIBE (BRAZILIAN FRIED MEAT) – Served in the Favela, the city of angels –Heavenly.

- 1 cup bulgur wheat, medium ground
- 1 lb. lean ground beef
- 2 Tbs. vegetable oil
- 1/2 yellow onion, finely chopped
- 2 cloves garlic, minced (divided)
- 2 Tbs. parsley, chopped   (divided)
- 1/4 cup mint leaves, chopped
- 2 tsp. sea salt
- 1 tsp. black pepper

- 1 tsp. dried oregano
- A dash of Tabasco sauce (optional)
- Vegetable oil, for fryer

Heat 4 cups of water to a boil in a small saucepan. Place the bulgur wheat in a medium heat-proof bowl and pour in the boiling water. Stir for 30 seconds then cover the bowl with plastic wrap. Set aside and allow the bulgur to soak for 1 hour.

Heat the 2 Tbs. of oil in an iron skillet over medium high heat. Add 2/3 of ground meat, onion and half the chopped garlic. Brown the meat completely and drain off any excess fat. Remove the skillet from heat and add half of the parsley. Set the skillet aside to cool.

Add the remaining ground beef to the rehydrated bulgur wheat along with the remaining garlic and parsley. Add in the mint, salt, pepper and oregano. At this point add the Tabasco if desired. Using your hands, fold the beef/bulgur mixture together for 5 minutes or until everything is well incorporated.

Scoop out about 2 Tbs. worth of the beef/bulgur mixture and roll it into a meatball. Flatten the meatball out and form a pocket in the center. Fill the pocket with some of the cooked beef/onion mixture and seal the pocket shut. Form the meatball into the shape of a small football. Continue the process until all of the mixture is used up.

Heat the vegetable oil in a deep fat fryer to 350°F.

Fry the quibes in small batches, spinning them occasionally in the oil so they will cook evenly. Fry the quibe until they turn a deep brown about 3 to 5 minutes. Drain the quibes on a platter lined with paper towel.

Serve the quibe with Tahini sauce and lemon slices. – Makes 16 portions

PANQUECA DE BATATA

- 3 cups prepared mashed potatoes
- 1/4 cup white onion, finely diced
- 1/4 green pepper, finely diced
- 4 Tbs. fresh cilantro, chopped
- 2 tsp. salt
- 1/4 tsp. ground pepper
- A pinch of cumin
- 1 clove garlic, minced
- 2 Tbs. grated parmesan cheese
- 4 Tbs. all-purpose flour
- 8 Tbs. bacon drippings or vegetable oil
- 2 cups extra flour for dredging

In a large mixing bowl combine all the ingredients except the bacon drippings and the extra flour. Stir until everything is well incorporated.

Coat your hands with flour and, using the palms, roll the mash potato mixture into balls about the sizes of golf balls. Press the balls into patties about 1/4 of an inch thick.

 Once all the patties are formed dredge them in the extra flour and place them on a cookie sheet. Cover the patties with plastic wrap and refrigerate for 30 minutes.

Preheat oven to 350°F.

Heat 2 Tbs. of bacon fat in a large non-stick pan over medium heat. Fry the patties 3 at a time, cooking undisturbed for about 2 minutes per side or until golden brown. Place the patties on a cookie lined with several layers of paper towels. Add 2 Tbs. of bacon drippings to the hot pan and continue frying the patties in batches of 3 until all have been cooked. Keep the patties warm by placing the cookie sheet in the preheated oven while the next batch is cooked. Serve with a garlic mayonnaise and orange slices. - Serves 6

CURED MEAT WITH BROWN BREAD

- 2 cups Warm water
- 3 Tbs. Molasses
- 2 Tbs. Fennel seed
- 2 tsp. Anise seed
- 2 tsp. Caraway seed
- 1 package dry yeast
- 2 cups Rye flour
- 2 cups Bread flour
- 2 tsp. Salt
- 3 tsp. Orange zest

Combine the water, molasses, seeds and orange zest in a large mixing bowl.

In a separate bowl, combine the yeast, rye and bread flour and salt.

Slowly add the dry ingredients into the bowl of wet ingredients and stir with a wooden spoon until a smooth dough is formed. Cover the bowl with plastic wrap and let the dough rest for about 20 minutes. After the 20 minutes, turn the dough out on a floured surface and knead for 5 minutes.

Clean and spray the mixing bowl with cooking spray; return the dough to the bowl. Again cover the bowl with plastic wrap and let the dough rise at room temperature over night.

Turn the risen dough out on a floured surface and shape into a oblong loaf. Gently place the loaf on a baking sheet and cover loosely with a large sheet of plastic wrap. Place the loaf in a warm spot and allow it to rise for 1 hour.

Preheat oven to 475°F about 30 minutes before baking.

Slit along the length of the loaf's surface with a sharp knife and bake for about 30 minutes or until crust is a rich brown color. Allow bread to cool for 30 minutes before slicing. – Makes 1 loaf

Serve bread with Swiss butter, thinly sliced Coppa* cured pork shoulder and Etter Kleines Pflümli**.

*http://fabriquedelices.com/product/dry-cured-whole-pork-shoulder-coppa/

**Etter Kleines Pflümli : Switzerland : Fruit brandy : Weinquelle Lühmann - specialty shop

SALT ENCRUSTED SALTON SEA BASS

- 5 cups coarse sea salt
- 1/3 cup Table salt
- 3 cups Flour
- 1 Tbs. Thyme, finely chopped
- 1/4 cup dill weed, finely chopped
- 6 egg whites
- 6 pats of butter
- 1 cup mushrooms, sliced
- 3 lb. whole sea bass

Preheat oven to 400°F.

Combine the salts, flour, thyme and dill weed. Add egg whites and mix together by hand creating a clay-like dough.

Roll the dough out to 1/2 inch thick on floured muslin towel. Place the butter, mushrooms and dill sprigs vegetables inside the fish.

Position the fish in the center of the dough and using the top and bottom edges of the towel, lift the dough over the fish. Use the towel for support and transfer the fish to a decorative baking dish. Roll the fish, seam side down into the baking dish (removing the towel as you go). Square up the dough, insuring it is completely sealed before placing it in the oven.

Bake the fish for 45 minutes. At tableside, crack and remove the salt crust from fish and serve with a béchamel sauce.

"...Constance moved out onto the limb until she was positioned above one of the two – Shaved Head..."

CRIMSON SHORE

FAKE SHAKE SHACK BURGER

LOBSTER ROLL

MIREPOIX

FRIED CLAMS

LEMON OYSTERS

CHART ROOM BAKED SCROD

PEMBROKE CASTLE SLIDERS

FRIED CLAM FRITTERS

JAMAICAN SHEPHERD'S PIE

FILET DE SOLE PENDERGAST

WHITE WITCH BREAD

MRS. TRASK'S MADELEINES

FAKE-SHAKE SHACK BURGER – Take on the case.

- 1/3 cup Hellmann's extra heavy mayonnaise
- 2 tsp. juice from McClure's Spicy Pickle Spears
- 2 tsp. Heinz ketchup
- 1 -1/2 tsp. French's yellow mustard
- 1/2 tsp. smoked paprika
- 1 small clove garlic, peeled
- 1/2 small shallot, minced

- 1/2 lb. ground beef brisket
- 1/4 lb. ground beef short rib
- 1/4 lb. ground beef chuck
- 8 slices American cheese
- 4 Martin's potato sandwich buns
- 4 pieces of leaf lettuce
- 8 slices plum tomato
- Black pepper

Place all sauce ingredients in a food processor and blend until smooth and completely combined. Transfer sauce into a squeeze bottle and set aside.

Preheat an iron skillet or griddle for 20 minutes over medium high heat (cooking surface should be extremely hot).
Blend the ground brisket, short rib and chuck together in a large mixing bowl and season well with salt and pepper.
Divide the ground beef into four equal meatballs and flatten them slightly.
Place the meatballs on that hot pan or griddle and squish them out into patties about 3/4 of an inch thick with the back of a spatula. Cook for about 3 minutes then scrape and flip. Top each burger with 2 slices of cheese and cook 2 minutes more.

Layer the bottom buns with lettuce, tomatoes. Season tomato slices with black pepper then add the burgers. Squirt 3 lines of sauce across the top buns and place them over the burgers. Wrap each burger in a sheet of parchment paper or paper towel for at least 30 seconds to allow the heat of the burger to steam the bun.

LOBSTER ROLL – How does one eat it?

- 12 quarts water
- 1/3 cups salt
- 3 live lobster (about 1.5 lbs. each)
- 1/2 cup celery, finely diced
- 1 tsp. fresh lemon juice
- 1/2 tsp. fresh tarragon
- 2 to 3 Tbs. Hellmann's mayonnaise
- 4 fresh bolillo rolls (with both sides trimmed flat)
- 1/4 cup melted butter
- 4 lemon wedges

Fill a 16 quart pot about 3/4 of the way full with tap water. Add 1/3 cup of salt to the water. Bring the water to a rapid boil.

Carefully lower each of the lobsters head first into the boiling water and cover the pot. Once the water returns to a boil, set kitchen timer for 20 minutes. When the timer goes off, turn the stovetop off, remove the lid and take the lobsters out of the pot with a pair of tongs. The lobsters should be bright red and steaming when done. Place the lobsters on a plate to drain and cool.

Once cooled, crack lobster shells and pick out the meat from tail and claws. Cut the meat into bite-sized pieces. In a medium bowl, fold the lobster meat, diced celery, lemon juice, tarragon, and mayonnaise together; season with salt and pepper to taste. Cover the bowl with plastic wrap and refrigerate for at least 30 minutes.

Heat a large iron skillet over medium heat. Brush the trimmed sides of bolillo rolls with melted butter. Grill the butter sides of the rolls until golden brown and crispy. Split the top of the rolls almost all the way through and remove some of the bread from the inside to make some room, forming a "boat".

Scoop a generous amount of lobster salad into each grill roll, drizzle with any of the extra melted butter and serve with a lemon wedge. Serves 4

MIREPOIX

Slice all the vegetables in half and lay them flat on the cutting board, so they will be easier and safer to dice. Cut the vegetables in even strips about the width of your ring fingernail. Now cut each strip into cubes about the width of your ring fingernail.

A true mirepoix should be 2 parts onion to 1 part celery and 1 part carrots.

Place the diced vegetables in a pan preheated over medium heat, with a little butter or oil and sauté for about 15 minutes.

FRIED CLAMS

- 2 lbs. shucked clams
- 1 can evaporated milk
- 1 cup Maseca corn flour
- 1 cup all purpose flour
- 1/2 cup Gold Medal Wondra flour
- 1 tsp. salt
- 1 tsp. black pepper
- Vegetable oil for frying

Place clams in a large sealable container and pour in the evaporated milk.
Seal the container and place the clams in the refrigerator overnight.
Sift all the dry ingredients into a large mixing bowl.

Set a deep fryer to 360° F.

Drain the clams in a colander and then dredge them in the flour mixture. Allow the dredged clams to rest in a single layer, while the fryer gets up to temperature.

Carefully drop a handful of clams in basket and fry for about 2 minutes or until clams are crispy and golden brown. Drain the fried clams on some paper towels. Serve hot with lemon wedges and tartar sauce. Serves 4 to 6.

LEMON OYSTERS ON THE HALF SHELL

- 24 fresh oysters
- Crushed ice
- 1/2 cup olive oil
- 1/3 cup fresh lemon juice
- 1/2 tsp. dried basil
- 1/2 tsp. dried oregano
- 1/4 tsp. garlic powder
- Smoked sea salt and cracked black pepper
- 2 Tbs. lemon zest

Whisk together the olive oil, lemon juice, basil, oregano and garlic powder in a small bowl and set it aside.
Set 24 shucked oysters on a bed of crushed ice, in a large rimmed serving tray. Spoon the lemon sauce on top of each oyster. Season the oysters lightly with sea salt and black pepper. Garnish each oyster with a pinch of lemon zest.

CHART ROOM BAKED SCROD

- 4 scrod fillets (7 oz. each)
- 2 Tbs. vegetable oil
- 1 onion, sliced
- 1 red bell pepper, sliced
- 1 cup pizza goldfish cracker, crushed
- 1/4 cup grated Parmesan cheese
- 1 Tbs. fresh basil, chopped
- 4 Tbs. butter, melted
- 1/2 tsp. crushed red pepper flakes
- salt and pepper
- olive oil

Preheat oven to 400° F.
 Heat the vegetable oil in a iron skillet over medium heat. Sauté the onions and peppers for about 3 minutes or until soft. Combine the crushed goldfish crackers, Parmesan, basil and the melted butter in a medium mixing bowl. Once the onions and peppers have finished cooking, add the red pepper flakes and some salt and pepper to taste. Spread the onion and peppers in the bottom of a prepared baking dish just large enough to hold the fillets. Next, place the fillets on top of the onions and peppers in a single layer. Divide the goldfish crumb topping evenly over the fillets and lightly drizzle some olive oil over the top. Bake for about 15 minutes, then cover the baking dish loosely with tin foil and continue baking for an additional 10 minutes or until the fish is cooked through.
Serves 4

PEMBROKE CASTLE SLIDERS – Tastes just like a different "Castle" burger, only better.

- 1 medium white onion, finely diced
- Salt and pepper
- 1-1/2 lbs. fresh ground chuck 80/20
- 12 dinner rolls, split
- 6 slices American cheese, cut in half
- French's mustard
- Sweet pickle relish

Preheat oven to 400° F.
Spread the diced onions out over the bottom of a 13 x 9 baking dish. Generously season the onions with salt and pepper. Crumble the ground chuck over the onions and then press it out to create a thin, solid slab of beef. Using the handle of a wooden spoon, poke holes about every 4 inches through the beef.

Bake the beef/onion slab for 25 minutes. The beef will shrink a bit when it's cooked, but don't worry.

Remove the baking dish from the oven and slice the beef into 12 equal squares with a pizza cutter.

Using a spatula, place a square patty on each bottom bun and top with a half slice of American cheese. Add the mustard, relish and then the top of the bun.

FRIED CLAM FRITTERS – Just short of cannibalism?

- 2 cups Bisquick baking mix
- 2 cans minced clams + juice
- 2 eggs, beaten
- 1/2 cup half & half
- 1 jalapeno, diced with seeds removed
- 1 Tbs. Old Bay seasoning

Set deep fryer to 360° F.

Gently blend ingredients together in a medium mixing bowl (do not over mix) and let the batter rest for 30 minutes.

Use a small ice cream scooper or 2 small spoons to make the fritters. It works best to dip the utensil in the oil, then into the batter. If using the two spoons, use one to scoop and the other to push the batter carefully into the hot oil. Roll the fritters around in the oil while frying until all sides are golden brown (about 2 minutes). Serve with tartar sauce and lemon wedges.

JAMAICAN SHEPHERD'S PIE – The perfect thing for an Exmouth Islander.

- 2 Tbs. olive oil
- 1/2 cup leeks or onion, finely chopped
- 1 Tbs. flour
- 1 clove garlic, crushed
- Salt and fresh cracked pepper
- 1 Tbs. tomato paste
- 1/2 tsp. ground cumin
- 1/2 tsp. ground ginger
- 1/4 tsp. Allspice
- 1/4 tsp. ground cinnamon
- A pinch cayenne pepper

- 1 lb. ground lamb
- 1 cup canned crushed tomatoes, drained
- 1/2 cup frozen corn
- 2 Tbs. chopped fresh parsley

Place a large iron skillet over medium-high and add olive oil. Once the oil is hot, add the leeks or onions and sauté until soft, about 4 minutes. Add in the flour and garlic; stir and cook 1 minute more. Now add the tomato paste, cumin, ginger, allspice, cinnamon and cayenne pepper; stir to combine. Add the ground lamb and cook until browned. Stir in tomatoes, corn and season to taste with salt and pepper. Reduce heat to low and simmer uncovered, for 15 minutes. Add the parsley, remove from heat and allow the filling to cool while preparing the potato shell.

- 2 lbs Yukon Gold potatoes, peeled and cut into chunks
- 1/4 cup sour cream
- 1 sheet puff pastry, cut into a 10" round
- 1 egg, beaten
- Pickapeppa Spicy Mango Hot Sauce

To make the potato shell simply boil the potato chunks in salted water until very tender, about 20 minutes. Drain and mash the potatoes a bit then add the sour cream and continue to mash until smooth. Salt and pepper to taste and allow to cool.

Preheat oven to 450° F.

Spray a 9 inch deep dish pie pan with cooking spray. Empty the mashed potatoes into the pan. Press the mashed potatoes out and away from the center, and then build up the sides to just above the top of the pan. Place the pan on a cookie sheet and bake until the shell turns a light brown, about 15 minutes. Remove from oven and turn temperature down to 350° F.

Add the lamb filling to the shell with a slotted spoon, leaving most of the liquid behind in the skillet. Place puff pastry over the top, tucking the edge down into the sides of the pan. Brush the puff pastry with the beaten egg. Make some slits in the top of the puff pastry to vent steam. Bake the lamb pie for 30-35 minutes or until the puff pastry is golden brown. Serve with Pickapeppa sauce. Serves 8

FILET DE SOLE PENDERGAST – You're not preparing fish sticks for 300 anymore.

- 1/4 cup clarified butter, divided
- 2 sole fillets
- Sea salt & black pepper
- 1/2 cup white wine
- 8 oz. button mushrooms, stemmed and quartered
- 1 clove garlic, minced
- 1 Tbs. flour
- 3/4 cup heavy cream, warmed
- 2 Tbs. parsley, chopped
- Half a lemon

Place a large, well-seasoned cast-iron pan over medium - high heat. Once the pan is hot, carefully pour in just enough clarified butter to coat the bottom of the pan. Season the sole on both sides with salt and pepper. Place the fillets in the pan and cook undisturbed, for 2 to 3 minutes depending on thickness. Gently flip the fish over using a long spatula. The first seared side is called the "presentation" side which means the side that will be up on the plate. Cook for another 2 to 3 minutes or until the flesh is firm and opaque. Remove fish to a warmed tray and cover with tin foil.

Pour in the wine to deglaze the pan. Once the wine has mostly evaporated, reduce heat to medium and add the remaining clarified butter. Now add the mushrooms and garlic; sauté until mushrooms have softened, about 2 minutes. Sprinkle in the flour and stir to combine. Pour in the warm cream and stir until thickened to the proper "nappe". Adjust seasoning with a bit more salt and pepper.

Place fillets (presentation side up, remember!!) on warmed plates and spoon the sauce over the top. Garnish with the parsley and a squeeze of lemon. Serves 2

WHITE WITCH BREAD – Hold the chai, please.

- 2 cups warm water
- 2/3 cup white sugar
- 1-1/2 Tbs. active dry yeast
- 1-1/2 tsp. salt
- 1/4 cup vegetable oil
- 6 cups bread flour

Pour warm water into a large bowl. Dissolve the sugar and yeast in the water. Let the yeast proof for 10 minutes. If the water doesn't get foamy, try some fresher yeast.

Add the oil and salt to the liquid. Add the flour and mix with a wooden spoon, one cup at a time. Once all the flour is blended. Turn the dough out onto a lightly floured surface and knead until smooth. Spray the bowl generously with cooking spray. Return the dough to the bowl and spray the top of the dough with the cooking spray. Cover the bowl with plastic wrap. Place the bowl in a warm spot and allow dough to rise for 1 hour or until it doubles in size.

Push the dough down and turn it back out on the floured surface. Knead the dough for a couple minutes. Slice the bread dough in half and shape the halves into loaves. Now place the loaves into two 9 X 5 loaf pans sprayed with cooking spray. Cover the pans loosely with plastic wrap and allow them to rise for 45 minutes.

Preheat oven to 350° F.
Bake the loaves for 30 minutes or until the tops are golden brown.

Serve hot with soft butter and Tiptree Tawny Orange Thick Marmalade.

MRS. TRASK'S MADELEINES – A treat before heading below.

- 4 eggs
- 1/4 tsp. salt
- 2/3 cup sugar
- 1 tsp. pure vanilla extract
- 1 cup all purpose flour
- 1/2 cup butter, melted
- 1 tsp. lemon zest

.Preheat oven to 400° F.

Prepare a 24 cup mini-muffin tin (a special pan is normally used but a muffin tin works just as well) with cooking spray.

In a large mixing bowl, combine eggs and salt. Mix with an electric hand mixer until eggs are light and foaming.

Add the sugar and vanilla extract. Continue to mix for 5 minutes or until the egg/sugar mixture becomes a pale yellow color.

Use a wooden spoon to fold the flour into the egg mixture a bit at a time. Once the flour is completely incorporated, slowly fold in the melted butter and lemon zest.

Pour the batter into each cup of the mini-muffin tin (fill each about 3/4 of the way full).

Place the tin on a cookie sheet and bake for about 10 minutes or until cakes are golden brown.

Remove muffin tin from the oven and invert onto a cooling rack. Allow the madeleines to cool completely, and then dust with powdered sugar.

"SUN!"

AUTHOR'S NOTE

Douglas Preston and Lincoln Child started collaborating on a book called Relic in 1995. It was an immediate success and in 1997 a film, loosely based on the novel, was released. As of early 2016 the two authors have written 25 best sellers together. Independently, Mr. Child has 6 books and Mr. Preston 15 (if my math is correct). All are amazing reads and come highly recommend.

Out of the 25 co-written, 16 stand out, in my opinion. These are known as "The Pendergast Novels." Starting with Relic, Mr. Preston and Mr. Child introduced the reader to an enigmatic New Orleans F.B.I. Agent, who seems to show up whenever and wherever any decidedly bizarre murders are perpetrated. Along the way, through all 15 tales, the reader is introduced and re-introduced to a large number of recurring characters. Each book has been crafted to stand alone, but when read as a whole, the series transports the reader into the thoughts and lives of this fictional community so convincing; you become emotionally invested and cannot seem to put the books down.

Preston and Child, true masters of the cliffhanger, will have you wanting more and more, whetting your appetite, with the turning of each page. Millions of fans can't be wrong.

http://www.prestonchild.com

The Pendergast Novels

Relic

Reliquary

Cabinet of Curiosities

Still Life with Crows

Brimstone

Dance of Death

Book of the Dead

Wheel of Darkness

Cemetery Dance

Fever Dream

Cold Vengeance

Extraction

Two Graves

White Fire

Blue Labyrinth

Crimson Shore

ABOUT THE AUTHOR

Chris Royal was born in Camp Lejeune, NC and grew up in the DC suburb of Kensington, MD. He developed a love of food from his Mom and started working in the restaurant industry at the age of 16. He opened and ran the successful restaurant Royal's for 10 years in beautiful Monterey, VA. He has also worked as an Assistant Park Ranger in North Carolina, volunteered in Disaster Services for the American Red Cross during Hurricanes Katrina and Rita, and currently deploys to combat areas for The American Red Cross – Service to the Armed Forces. He has completed six tours of duty in Iraq and Kuwait thus far. In his spare time, Chris enjoys writing, painting and cooking on the family farm in Blue Grass, VA. Chris can be contacted through Beyond Riverside Drive on Facebook and invites you to check out all the cool stuff at Beyondriversidedrive.com.

Please take this note immediately to Dr. Felder, care of Mount Mercy Hospital, Little Governor's Island.

PLEASE – <u>IT'S A MATTER OF LIFE OR DEATH.</u>

Felder will give you a monetary reward.

Mourning Meals – Breakfast

HAM AND CHEESE SCRAMBLED EGGS   6

CORNED BEEF HASH   10

RED FLANNEL HASH   42

REALTOR BREAKFAST   63

ALMOND CROISSANTS   64

DOUGHNUTS   91

BOILED EGG, TOAST O.J. AND TEA   118

EGGS AND BACON   135

BUTTER SCONES W/ ORANGE/HONEY BUTTER   180

EGGS BENEDICT FLORENTINE   181

BREAKFAST SANDWICH   196

CREAM CHEESE BLUEBERRY PANCAKES   201

EGGS BENEDICT W/ TARRAGON HOLLANDAISE SAUCE   211

QUICK HOMEMADE DOUGHNUTS   228

EGG WHITE OMELET   262

OVER WELL EGGS & RYE TOAST   263

GREEN TEA AND BUTTERED TOAST   331

POACHED EGGS   333

Mid-Day Madness — Lunch

CATFISH SANDWICH   14

TUNA SANDWICH   46

PEMMICAN   48

LUNCHBOX CHICKEN   52

HAM AND BRIE BAGUETTE   67

B.L.T. CLASSIC   70

DOUBLE CORNED BEEF WITH SWISS ON RYE W/ MAYO   89

MAISIE'S MEATLOAF   99

MAISIE'S CHICKEN FRIED STEAK   107

ROAST BEEF SANDWICH   121

BACCELLI E PECORINO ANTIPASTI PLATE   132

KANSAS STYLE PIZZA   133

PASTRAMI ON RYE W/ WARM RUSSIAN DRESSING   198

DECONSTRUCTED B L T   199

NEW YORK STYLE CHEESEBURGER   216

FUSSY SOUTHAMPTON SANDWICH   218

COUNT FOSCO'S PICNIC   219

VINNIE'S CHEESEBURGER AND FRIES   238

BIG MAC   468

SAUSAGES   481

MINESHAFT TAVERN BURGER   509

PLOUGHMAN'S PICKLE AND MONTGOMERY CHEDDAR
SANDWICH   528

SMOKED SALMON AND WASABI CREAM CHEESE TEA
SANDWICH   529

TERIYAKI CHICKEN AND GRILLED AUBERGINE TEA
SANDWICH   530

HARRISON & CROSFIELD TEA W/ A WHEATMEAL BISCUIT
533

CUCUMBER TEA SANDWICHES WITH MINT CREAM CHEESE
544

FAKE-SHAKE SHACK BURGER   583

LOBSTER ROLL   584

PEMBROKE CASTLE SLIDERS   589

JAMAICAN SHEPHERD'S PIE   592

Macabre Morsels – Appetizers

WHITTLESEY'S DRIED BEEF   3

HARE (RABBIT) PATE   7

GULF PRAWNS   17

TUNA & STURGEON CAVIAR BILINI   19

SCOTTISH COD ROE CEVICHE W/ CAPERS AND LEMON   20

ASSORTED HORS D'OEUVRE   22

SLICED KOBE BEEF   26

AHI TUNA WITH HONEY-ORANGE GLAZE   27

AHI TUNA SASHIMI   28

BAKED CAMEMBERT AND HOMEMADE CRACKERS   28

HOUSE PÂTÉ   30

HERB SCONES W/ MARMALADE AND CLOTTED CREAM   38

ASSORTED QUICHES   39

SPICED FILBERT NUTS   41

MOREL AND BLACK TRUFFLE MOUSSE   60

PIGS IN A BLANKET   67

NEW YORK STEAMED "BRAVE" OYSTERS   85

ALLIGATOR BITES   125

OYSTERS ROCKEFELLER   156

SHIPBOARD HORS D'OEVURES   163

ANTIPASTO PLATE   167

BLINI WITH CAVIAR   173

TRUFFLE PÂTÉ   175

CHARCUTERIE PLATE   186

GREEN CHILI BEEF JERKY   223

BRAISED PIGS FEET AND CHEEKS   227

BLINI WITH CAVIAR   233

BROILED OYSTERS ON THE HALF SHELL   276

BROILED LOBSTER TAILS WITH ORANGE BUTTER   276

SMOKED STURGEON SPREAD   277

CRUDITÉS   278

JUMBO COCKTAIL SHRIMP   281

HORS D'OEUVRES VARIES   299

FETA TURNOVERS   300

PÂTÉ DE FOIE GRAS EN CROUTE   308

SMOKED SALMON WITH CAVIAR   323

SEVRUGA CAVIAR WITH TRUFFLE CRAB CUSTARD   325

CAVIAR & CRÈME FRAICHE CREPES   327

OYSTERS ROCKEFELLER   328

FRENCH CHEESE BOARD   329

PAPER THIN PROSCIUTTO WITH MELON   330

RAW OYSTERS ON THE HALF SHELL   338

COARSE BREAD W/ WILD BOAR SALAMI AND OLIVES   344

LOBSTER CLAW COCKTAIL   361

SARDINES TOAST   376

PICKLED EGGS   393

PIG'S TROTTERS   394

BEER PICKLES   396

JALAPEÑO HUSH PUPPIES   410

BEEF JERKY   460

POTTED MEAT   463

POTTED SHRIMP   498

TRIPE FRIED IN BATTER   502

MINER'S SHEPHERD'S PIE   508

PRAWNS   550

OPIHI STYLE OYSTERS   560

ITALIAN SAUSAGE ROLLS   563

SCALLION PANCAKES   568

QUIBE (BRAZILIAN FRIED MEAT)   571

CURED MEAT W/ BROWN BREAD   575

FRIED CLAMS   586

LEMON OYSTERS ON THE HALF SHELL   587

FRIED CLAM FRITTERS   591

Sinister Sides – Side Dishes

CROISSANTS ROLLS   49

ROASTED VEGETABLES   83

BUTTERED RAG CORN ON THE COB   86

BREADCRUMBS   87

POTATOES & CABBAGE   88

MAISIE'S PORK & BEANS   100

MAISIE'S SWEET POTATOES FRIES   103

MAISIE'S GREEN GODDESS DRESSING   104

MAISIE'S VELVEETA FRIES   113

STEWED TOMATOES WITH GRILLED CHEESE CROUTONS
136

STEWED TOMATOES   137

EARS OF CORN   139

TIBETAN BUTTER TEA (PO CHA)   150

TSAMPA – (PA)   150

TIBETAN FLAT BREAD   152

WATERCRESS SALAD   178

POMMES FRITES   188

CREAMED SPINACH   189

JULIENNE CARROTS   214

CAESAR SALAD   215

MADONNA'S FRENCH FRIES WITH HOUSE KETCHUP   230

GREEN BEANS & CARROTS   244

LUMPY MASHED POTATOES   244

LARGE FRUIT SALAD   254

EGGS IN ASPIC   265

GRILLED ASPARAGUS   376

FRENCH BAGUETTE   280

AESH BALADI (EGYPTIAN BREAD)   288

SALATAT FWAKI (FRESH FRUIT SALAD)   291

DUKKAH   296

CONSOMMÉ' OLGA   301

VEGETABLE MARROW FARCIE   305

SCALLOPED POTATOES   538

GRILLED ROMAINE SALAD   540

BEANS & RICE   543

POI   558

FISH LIP SOUP   564

PANQUECA DE BATATA (POTATO PANCAKES)   574

MIREPOIX   586

WHITE WITCH BREAD   595

Desperate Measures – Entrees

CAFETERIA LASAGNA   5

THE BONES GUINNESS MEATLOAF   9

OVEN SMOKED PORK ROAST   12

ANTONIO'S PIZZA PEPPERONI & GREEN CHILIES   15

CRAYFISH GUMBO   33

POP EYE'S FRIED CHICKEN   37

TRACK RABBIT   43

COLD WATER SCALLOPS IN LEMON PHYLLO W/ CAVIAR   45

2 LB SWORDFISH STEAK   54

FRUTTI DI MARE SALAD   55

STEAK AU POIVRE   61

CHINESE PRESSED DUCK   71

CHINESE COOKED SQUID   73

COLD WATER LOBSTER TAILS W/ DRAWN BUTTER   75

BROILED LAMB W/ CAPERS   76

ROAST BEEF   78

ROAST GOOSE   78

ROAST MUTTON & POTATOES   80

BOILED HAM & CABBAGE   81

GRILLED CHEESE AND TOMATO BUTTER FLIED PORK CHOPS
98

MAISIE'S DOUBLE-DIPPED FRIED CHICKEN IN CORN BATTER
102

MAISIE'S FRIED STEAK   105

MAISIE'S CHICKEN FRIED STEAK   107

MAISIE'S BROILED STEAK   108

MAISIE'S GRILLED STEAK   109

MAISIE'S BROASTED STEAK   110

MAISIE'S POT ROASTED STEAK   112

RACK OF LAMB WITH BURGUNDY POMEGRANATE
PERSILLADE   434

ROTISSERIE CHICKEN   436

DOVER SOLE WITH TRUFFLE BUTTER   449

VEGGIE LASAGNA   454

CREVETTES REMOULADE   465

POMPANO PONTCHARTRAIN   466

SHIOKARA   473

TAGLIATELLA AL TARTUFO BIANCO   492

GALANTINE OF CHICKEN WITH A MOREL CREAM SAUCE   499

COLORADO RACK OF LAMB   504

TEXAS BARBECUE   506

MOCKEY JONES' 80 DOLLAR STEAK (MARTINI)   534

RARE PORTERHOUSE STEAK WITH MAITRE D' BUTTER   535

SUCKLING PIG W/APPLE   551

KALUA PORK   560

TRIPE A LA MODE CAEN   566

SALT ENCRUSTED SEA BASS   577

BAKED SCROD PARMESAN   588

FILET DE SOLE PENDERGAST   594

Deadly Delights – Desserts

GOING AWAY WHITE CAKE   31

LAP SANG SOUCHONG TEA BISCUITS   51

FRENCH CHOCOLATE TRUFFLES   88

FRESH PEACH COBBLER   116

COBBLER WITH CANNED PEACHES   116

SHOOFLY PIE   117

CHOCOLATE ÉCLAIRS   119

SWEET & SALTY PRALINES   131

CAP'N CRUNCH CHEESECAKE   138

GINGER SNAPS   143

TEA CAKES   145

YELLOW SHEET CAKE   161

CRÈME' BRULEE   177

CHOCOLATE FONDUE   191

MALODOROUS FRENCH CHEESE PLATE   192

PRALINE GENOISE W/ CALVADOS BUTTER CREAM   192

CARAMEL CREAM CRUNCH DONUTS   475

COFFEE DONUTS   476

TOAST WITH BUTTER AND JAM TERRINE   480

BREAD AND JAM BITES   487

LINZER TORTE   511

HAZELNUT DACQUOISE   512

SALTED CARAMEL MOUSSE WITH CHOCOLATE GANACHE
514

FINANCIER BISCUITS   516

APRICOT MOUSSE   517

COFFEE AND ORANGE ÉCLAIR   519

MANGO, VIOLETS AND BLACKCURRANT MACAROON   523

KIR ROYALE COCKTAIL   525

MINESHAFT CHOCOLATE BROWNIE SUNDAE   540

CHERRIES JUBILEE   553

HAUPIA   562

LICORICE TOFFEE CANDIES   570

MRS. TRASK'S MADELEINES   596

Made in the USA
Middletown, DE
09 July 2019